GOOD HOUSEKEEPING
ROUND THE YEAR MENUS

GOOD HOUSEKEEPING
ROUND THE YEAR MENUS

by

Margaret Coombes

GOOD HOUSEKEEPING INSTITUTE

EBURY PRESS
LONDON

First published 1975
by Ebury Press
Chestergate House, Vauxhall Bridge Road
London SW1V 1HF

ISBN 0 85223 066 4

Edited by Gill Edden

Cover picture: Stephen Baker

Other pictures: Stephen Baker, Anthony Blake,
Michael Boys, John Cook, Frank Coppins,
Melvin Grey, Gina Harris, Michael Leale

Filmset in Great Britain by
BAS Printers Limited, Wallop, Hampshire
and printed and bound in Italy by
Interlitho S.p.a., Milan

CONTENTS

Recipes marked with a star freeze well. See notes
on pages 171-180.

FOREWORD

Thousands of you are already enthusiastic followers of Good Housekeeping's famous creative cookery and know all about cookery editor Margaret Coombes' magic touch with even the most ordinary meals. For *Round the Year Menus* Margaret has sorted her recipes into seasonal chapters and drawn up mouthwatering, practical menus for all occasions—from summer evening dinner parties to cut-the-cost family meals.

What I think will appeal most to us about this cookery book is the delicious blend of flavours in the recipes—things we've never thought of like Pork and Orange Pie and Cheese Soup, the excellent shopping notes at the beginning of each section and the indispensable cookery hints which all reflect Margaret Coombes' instinctive knowledge of what the cook of the household wants.

Of course all the recipes have been tested by home economists in the Good Housekeeping Institute and tasted by us too. If you have any queries about the recipes in this book write to us at Good Housekeeping Institute, Chestergate House, Vauxhall Bridge Road, London SW1V 1HF.

Carol Macarthur

Director

CHAPTER ONE

SPRING

One of Spring's economy buys from the green-grocer is pink young rhubarb, there are plenty of grapes for the fruit bowl and pineapples should be good, too. For sweets, fresh soured cream with a little sugar added makes a good topping – cheaper than double cream. For a change in the vegetable dish that won't stretch the purse, try blue broccoli or Spring greens. April heralds the first English hot house cucumbers, lettuces and tomatoes; now that salad lines are becoming plentiful, introduce a dressed side salad as a change from winter greens. English asparagus and new potatoes make their first appearance, also baby carrots, tender young broad beans and garden spinach.

Easter means holiday time and children at home. For bigger budget meals think of serving turkey – this is a worthwhile buy that will stretch to cold salad meals, réchauffé dishes and titbits for sandwiches. Bacon is still a good standby; serve a collar joint hot with parsley sauce and butter beans or try it with creamy macaroni and cheese. Pasta on the shopping list always brings variety – one suggestion is bacon chops, slowly fried with onion rings and tomato halves and served with butter-tossed spaghetti. Well flavoured English cheese is a delicious change for a family pie if combined with crisply cooked cauliflower sprigs and sliced tomato and flavoured with herbs.

Herrings, mackerel, whitebait and kippers remain good value, their 'on the slab' prices depending on the weather; unfortunately, when it comes to white fish, cod and haddock are no longer an economy choice. For a dinner party river, sea and salmon trout are at their best in Spring. For family meals look to the fish and chip shop standby, huss (rock salmon) to fry or serve with a robust flavouring like curry or sweet-sour sauce. Moderately priced whiting is delicate and bland – to add flavour to sautéed fillets, add lemon juice, cheese sauce and breadcrumbs, then put under the grill until lightly browned. For continental-style saith (coley, coal fish) use oil, tomatoes and onions.

One of the biggest items on the food bill is meat. Look out for succulent English and Welsh spring lamb which, although more pricey than its imported counterpart, is very sweet. Roasts and grills are simple but, to economise a little, get the family eating sweet-tasting breast of lamb with herby forcemeat, or oxtail simmered long and slowly with a rich gravy. Revive old-fashioned potted beef – leg or shin – to rival the trendier pâtés and serve Irish stew for your next dinner party. Use lean belly rashers of bacon for oven baking and have home-boiled bacon instead of buying the more expensive cooked sliced ham.

For the freezer
If stocks are run down, early Spring is quite a good time to check, defrost and clean the freezer. Dabs and salmon could be good freezer investments if there is a family fisherman. Eggs could be down in price – choose cold sweet soufflés for the Easter break. Look ahead to half-term and outdoor eating and prepare sandwiches in bulk; these are great time savers, but avoid fillings like tomatoes and boiled eggs as these do not freeze well. Small pies and quiches are good for children on holiday outings. If you have a large Easter turkey or joint, base quantities of vegetables, stuffing and gravy on a few extra servings; then, when carving the hot bird, make up some extra servings on foil plates to be appreciated in a few weeks' time. Young rhubarb keeps its colour, flavour and texture better if it is cooked before freezing and now is the time to buy.

Spring fruit
The first apricots, cherries, gooseberries and early home-grown strawberries start to arrive. There are also Cape gooseberries, cumquats, limes, lychees, mangoes, ortaniques, passion fruit, rhubarb and fresh dates.

Spring vegetables
Aubergines, artichokes, avocados, broccoli, Brussels sprouts (just finishing), new carrots (arriving), celeriac (just finishing), celery (imported green), chicory (just finishing), courgettes, endives, fennel, French beans, Jerusalem artichokes, kohlrabi, leeks, salsify (towards the end of Spring), savoys, spinach, spring greens, sweet potatoes, chillis, garlic, swedes, watercress.

Spring poultry and game
Rabbit (season ends April 30th), wood pigeon, duck (March to September).

Spring menus

*(Dishes marked * are included in the recipes on pages 10 to 47)*

Week-end lunch for 6
Grilled grapefruit

*Poulet en cocotte bonne femme
Spring greens

*Jamaican crunch pie

Sunday lunch for 4
Consommé with sherry

*Beef olives with creamed
potatoes
*Casseroled sweet-sour onions
*Carrots Vichy

*Lemon fluff

Lunch foursome for Good Friday
Cream of asparagus soup

*Haddock à la bistro
Creamed potatoes
Buttered spinach

*Bakewell tart

Family lunch for 4
*Country soup

*Bacon in cider
Sprouts
Jacket potatoes

*Orange buttered apples

Informal dinner for 4
*Melon wedges with mint freeze

*Shish kebabs
Rice
Sliced tomato salad

*Oranges in caramel syrup

Dinner party for 6
*Tomato appetisers
Bread sticks

*Lamb maître d'hôtel
*Risotto
*Buttered cucumber
*Whole beans with pimiento

*Pineapple meringue Torte

Lunch from a fork for 16
*Tunafish creams
*Dressed leeks

Warm French bread
Rolled butter

*Fried salami chicken
*Battalian beef bake
*Dressed macaroni and
mushrooms
*Red cabbage and sweetcorn salad
Tossed green salad

*Peach and apple soufflé
*Shortcake gâteau

Fondue party
Melon wedges with lemon

*Fondue bourguignonne
Sauces: horseradish, curry,
paprika, tomato, mustard

*Jellied lemon syllabub

High tea for 4
*Latticed tuna flan
Dressed celery

*Pineapple pudding

Supper for 4
*Bacon steaks
Golden fries
Whole tomatoes

*Lemon frosted apricot pies

Easy dinner for 4
*Cheese puffs
*Pimiento beef balls
Buttered broccoli

*Raspberry whip

Lunch for 4
Chilled tomato juice
*Baked lemon chicken
Parslied or roast potatoes
Leaf spinach
*Rhubarb meringue

Cut the cost menus

*Aberdeen sausage
Broccoli
Potatoes lyonnaise

*Apricot crisp

*Fish pie Manitoba
Carrots Vichy

*Lemon freeze

*Cheese and onion soufflé
*Peanut slaw

*Banana en croûte

*Ragout of oxtail
Cabbage wedges
Boiled potatoes

*Rhubarb flake bake

Spring starters

Asparagus soup

1 oz. butter
6 oz. onion, skinned and very finely chopped
2 10-oz. cans green asparagus, drained
1 level tsp. curry powder
1 oz. flour
1½ pt. chicken stock or 1½ pt. water and 2
    chicken stock cubes
½ pt. milk
salt and pepper
fried croûtons

SERVES 6–8

In a saucepan, melt the butter, add the onion
and fry without colouring for 10 minutes. Add
the asparagus, curry powder and flour, stirring.
Cook for 5 minutes then slowly stir in the stock
or water and crumbled stock cubes. Cover,
reduce heat and simmer for 30 minutes. Put
the soup through a sieve and add the milk;
adjust the seasoning and reheat without boiling.
Serve hot with fried croûtons.

Cream of carrot soup

10-oz. can sliced carrots, drained
2 level tbsps. flour
1½ oz. butter
1 chicken stock cube
¾ pt. milk
¼ pt. water
1 bayleaf
1 level tsp. diced onion
salt and freshly ground black pepper
fried croûtons
chopped parsley

SERVES 4–5

Reserve a few wafer-thin slices cut from a
carrot for garnish, then tip the carrots, flour,
butter, stock cube, milk and water into a large
electric blender goblet. Switch on and blend
until smooth and pour into a saucepan. When
using a small goblet add only just as much liquid
as is practical then tip the contents into a saucepan; pour the remainder of the liquid into the
goblet and switch on again for a few minutes;
add to the pan. Add the bayleaf and diced onion.
Bring to the boil, stirring, and simmer for about
10 minutes. Adjust seasoning with pepper and

more salt if necessary. Serve in individual soup
dishes with thinly sliced rings of carrot and
croûtons tossed in chopped parsley.

✳ Crème vichyssoise

3 medium sized leeks
1 small onion, skinned
1 oz. butter
1 lb. potatoes, peeled
1½ pt. white stock
salt and pepper
1 egg yolk
¼ pt. single cream
chives

SERVES 4–6

Prepare the leeks by cutting off most of the
green tops and washing the white part thoroughly.
Slice the leeks and onion thinly. Melt the butter
in a saucepan, add the leeks and onion and sauté
without browning for 5 minutes. Add the roughly
chopped potatoes, stock and seasoning. Bring to
the boil, cover and simmer for about 30 minutes.
Sieve the soup, or purée it in an electric blender.
Return to the pan, add the egg yolk blended
with cream and reheat without boiling. Adjust
seasoning if necessary. Serve well chilled, with
a garnish of snipped chives.

✳ Country soup

Home-made stock gives this soup the best
flavour but a cube is an instant alternative.
Choose bread sticks for an accompaniment.

4 oz. carrots, pared
8 oz. potatoes, peeled
2 oz. onions, skinned
4 oz. green cabbage heart
1 oz. butter or margarine
2 pt. stock
salt and freshly ground black pepper
2 level tbsps. cornflour
chopped parsley

SERVES 4–6

Finely dice the carrot and potatoes and roughly
chop the onion. Finely shred the cabbage
heart. Melt the butter or margarine in a pan,
add the carrot, onion and potato, cover and

Dinner party for six (*see page 9*)

sweat them for about 10 minutes, shaking often. Add the cabbage and stock and adjust seasoning. Simmer for about 20 minutes. Blend the corn-flour to a cream with a little water, stir it into the soup and bring to the boil. Serve garnished with chopped parsley.

Cheese puffs

A quick soufflé appetiser to be eaten straight from the oven.

$1\frac{1}{2}$ oz. butter or margarine
2 slices bread from a small loaf
2 eggs, separated
1 level tsp. dry mustard
salt and freshly ground black pepper
red Leicester cheese

SERVES 4

Melt the butter and use a little to grease 4 $\frac{1}{4}$-pt. soufflé dishes. Cut the crust from the bread and cut each slice into triangles. Coat one side in the rest of the butter. Whisk the egg whites until firm, fold in the beaten yolks, mustard, seasoning and 1 oz. grated cheese. Divide be-tween the prepared dishes. Insert the bread triangles between egg and dish, two to each dish. Grate more cheese over and bake in the oven at 375°F, 190°C (mark 5) for about 15 minutes. Serve at once.

Melon wedges with mint freeze

Delightfully fresh-tasting as an appetiser to precede a roast; makes a pleasant dessert too.

8 fl. oz. water
$1\frac{1}{2}$ oz. granulated sugar
pared rind and juice 1 lemon
small handful mint leaves, picked from the
    stalks
sap green colouring
1 honeydew melon
6 sprigs fresh mint, on the stalks

SERVES 4–6

Boil the water, sugar and lemon rind together for 5 minutes. Off the heat, add the mint leaves and infuse for 10 minutes. Strain the syrup into a basin, stir in the lemon juice and add a little colouring. Pour into a freezer tray and freeze until firm. Cut the melon into 4–6 wedges and remove the seeds. Loosen the flesh from the skin and cut into bite-size pieces, but leave on the rind. Crush the mint freeze and spoon it over the melon. Garnish with sprigs of fresh mint. Serve at once.

Tomato appetisers

12 firm red tomatoes
3 oz. freshly grated Parmesan cheese
salt and freshly ground black pepper
dried basil
$\frac{1}{4}$ pt. single or double cream

SERVES 6

Peel the tomatoes and cut them in half. Arrange 4 halves in each of 6 individual soufflé dishes and sprinkle with Parmesan, salt and pepper. Sprinkle with more cheese and a dusting of basil, then spoon cream over the top. Place on a baking sheet towards the top of the oven and cook at 375°F, 190°C (mark 5) for about 15 minutes. Serve the appetisers hot.

Eggs en cocotte

Makes a delightful starter to an evening meal, served straight from the dishes with fingers of warm crisp toast on the side.

1 tbsp. double cream
salt and freshly ground black pepper
1 large egg
butter

SERVES 1

Put the warm cream, seasoned with salt and pepper, into a tiny soufflé or cocotte dish. Break an egg into the dish, add a few shavings of butter and place the dish in a roasting tin with water to come half-way up the sides. Cover and cook in the oven at 375°F, 190°C (mark 5) for about 10 minutes. Serve at once.

✳ Kipper pâté

A full flavoured garlicky starter, this does double duty as a spread between slices of thinly cut brown bread, or as a topping on plain crackers.

7-oz. bag frozen kipper fillets
5 oz. butter, softened
juice of $\frac{1}{2}$ lemon
$\frac{1}{2}$ clove garlic, skinned and crushed
yolk of 1 hard-boiled egg

SERVES 6

Immerse the bag of kippers in boiling water for 1 minute. Remove the fish from the bag and trim off any skin. Pound the flesh with the butter, lemon juice, garlic and egg yolk. Turn it into a small soufflé dish or 6 individual ramekin dishes and chill. Serve with toast triangles and sprigs of watercress.

* Chicken liver pâté

Pâté, served with fresh Melba toast or crusty bread, is far more in vogue today than soup. Pâté freezes well for up to 1–2 months; here is a simple recipe that can be made in bulk to serve 10.

$1\frac{1}{2}$ lb. chicken livers
3 oz. butter or margarine
1 medium sized onion, skinned and finely
   chopped
1 large or 2 small cloves garlic, skinned and
   crushed
1 tbsp. double cream
2 level tbsps. tomato paste
3 tbsps. sherry or brandy

SERVES 10

Rinse the livers in a colander and dry on absorbent paper. Fry them in butter until they change colour. Reduce heat then add the onion and garlic. Cover and cook for 5 minutes. Remove from the heat and cool. Add the cream, tomato paste and sherry or brandy and purée the mixture in an electric blender or pass through a sieve. Turn it into individual dishes, level the surface and garnish with parsley, or flood the tops with more melted butter and chill. For freezing omit the butter and add it when thawing.

HANDY HINT

Spaghetti and macaroni double in bulk when cooked, but noodles only swell about a quarter.

* Tunafish creams

$\frac{3}{4}$ pt. soured cream
4 tbsps. mayonnaise
salt and pepper
good dash of Worcestershire sauce
1 rounded tbsp. chopped chives
4 tsps. capers, chopped
1 level tbsp. finely grated onion
$\frac{1}{2}$ oz. powdered gelatine
4 tbsps. water
2 7-oz. cans tuna steak, drained and flaked
4 hard-boiled eggs, chopped
3 firm tomatoes for garnish
parsley sprigs

SERVES 16

Combine the first eight ingredients. Dissolve the gelatine in 4 tbsps. water in a basin over a pan of hot water. Cool it slightly and stir into the cream mixture, followed by the tuna steak and eggs. Mix thoroughly. Spoon into 16 individual soufflé or cocotte dishes and chill until set. Garnish with sliced tomatoes and parsley. If necessary, make the evening before, cover with plastic film and refrigerate. Remove from refrigerator 2 hours before serving, garnish the creams and cover again with plastic film.

* Taramasalata

(*see picture page 14*)

This is on nearly every menu these days so why not try it at home, served with fingers of hot crisp toast, gherkins and stuffed olives?

8 oz. fresh smoked cods' roes
12 tbsps. olive oil
2 tbsps. lemon juice
grated rind of $\frac{1}{2}$ lemon
1 level tsp. grated onion
1 level tbsp. chopped parsley
freshly ground black pepper
parsley to garnish

SERVES 8

Place the skinned cods' roe in a bowl with 6 tbsps. oil and leave for 15 minutes. Pass it through a fine sieve or blend in an electric blender until smooth, gradually adding 2 tbsps. lemon juice and a further 6 tbsps. oil. Turn into a bowl if the blender has been used and then stir in the finely grated rind, onion, parsley and pepper. Chill for a short time in a serving dish; add a garnish of parsley.

Note: Canned cods' roe is not suitable for this recipe. A little fresh breadcrumb can be added to the recipe for a less rich spread.

✳ Potted smoked salmon

3 oz. pkt. full fat soft cheese
finely grated rind of ½ lemon
1 egg yolk
¼ pt. double cream
salt and pepper
¼ level tsp. cayenne pepper
small clove garlic, skinned and crushed
3 oz. smoked salmon
2 tbsps. chopped parsley
1 oz. fresh white breadcrumbs
1 oz. butter

SERVES 4

Taramasalata (*see page 13*)

Place a small bowl over a pan of hot water. Add the cheese, lemon rind, egg yolk and cream; stir gently and cook until smooth and thick, then remove from the heat. Season with salt, peppers and garlic. Finely chop the smoked salmon and add it to the cheese mixture with the parsley and breadcrumbs. Spoon into small soufflé dishes or ramekins. Melt the butter, pour over the mixture and chill until firm.

Haddock mousse
(*see picture opposite*)

Dinner parties get off to a commendable start with chilled, creamy mousse; if you prefer use smoked salmon or minced ham in the same way. Add Melba toast for texture contrast.

Haddock mousse (*see opposite*)

½ pt. milk
1 small carrot, pared and halved
1 small onion, skinned and halved
1 bayleaf
3 parsley stalks
6 peppercorns
1½ oz. butter
1 oz. flour
½ lb. smoked haddock
1½ level tbsps. aspic jelly crystals
3 large eggs, freshly hard-boiled
1 tbsp. chopped parsley
¼ pt. double cream, stiffly whipped
salt and freshly ground black pepper
juice and grated rind of 1 small lemon
parsley sprigs and watercress to garnish

SERVES 6

Pour the milk into a saucepan, add the carrot and onion, bayleaf, parsley stalks and peppercorns. Bring to the boil, remove from the heat and allow to infuse for 10 minutes. Melt the butter in a saucepan, stir in the flour and cook for 1–2 minutes without colouring. Off the heat, strain the milk all at once on to the roux and stir with a wooden spoon to distribute the butter and flour. Return to the heat, bring to the boil and bubble, stirring, for ½ minute. Cut an 8-in. diameter round of greaseproof paper, cut 1-in. snips into the centre and brush it with melted butter. Pour the sauce into a basin and fit the greaseproof paper so that the buttered side of the paper is in contact with the whole of the surface of the sauce.

Bring half a frying pan of water to the boil and add the fish. Cover with a lid and poach gently for 10 minutes. Pour 8 fl. oz. boiling water into a measuring jug. Sprinkle over the aspic jelly crystals and stir to dissolve. Make the aspic up to ½ pt. with ice cubes or cold water. Fold all but 3 tbsps. of the aspic slowly into the white sauce, stirring. Drain the fish, discard the bones and skin and flake the flesh. Shell the 3 eggs. Using a sharp kitchen knife, chop 2 eggs with the parsley; add to the flaked fish. Fold the aspic sauce into the cream when on the point of setting. Season well with salt and freshly ground

HANDY HINT

A bottle of spirits serves approx.
15 double straight drinks and 25
mixes.

black pepper. Finally fold in the lemon rind, juice, flaked fish, chopped eggs and parsley. Turn into a 2½-pt. dish and leave to set in a cool place. Dilute the remaining aspic with a further

3 tbsps. water. Slice the remaining egg and arrange the slices over the surface of the mousse with parsley sprigs. Spoon the aspic over them when it is on the point of setting. Decorate with watercress.

Spring main course dishes

Salmon trout in aspic

Salmon trout is one of the most delicious fish to come from the sea. It gives value for money, too, since there is virtually no waste and the flesh is rich and sustaining. Little hot new potatoes with dill butter would make a perfect accompaniment.

4 oz. onion, skinned
3 lemon slices
2 bayleaves
8 peppercorns
2½–3 lb. salmon trout
1 pt. dry white wine
1 pt. water
½ oz. butter
1 pt. aspic jelly (made from crystals)

For fish decoration
cucumber and radish slices

For garnish
4 tomatoes
½ pt. thick mayonnaise
lemon
parsley

SERVES 6–8

Thinly slice the onion and put in a roasting tin with the lemon slices, bayleaves and pepper-corns. Slightly curve the fish to fit snugly into the tin. Pour over the wine and water – the liquid should come half-way up the fish – and cover the roasting tin with buttered foil. Cook at 325°F, 170°C (mark 3) for 10 minutes per lb. plus 10 minutes extra. Baste once during cooking. To ensure the fish is cooked, penetrate the thickest part of flesh with a skewer; if it is cooked, the flesh will offer no resistance to the skewer. Cool in the liquor, basting occasionally. Place a large wire rack over a plastic or metal tray. When the fish is completely cold, slip large palette knives under the length of the body of the fish and lift it on to the wire rack over the tray. Ease the skin of the fish away from the

body. Lay a piece of wet greaseproof paper over the skinned fish. Lightly lay a baking sheet on top and turn the wire rack, fish and baking sheet over so that it is possible to remove the skin of the underside. Reverse again. To remove the backbone, run a sharp knife down the flesh on the line of the backbone and gently ease the fillets apart. Slip two long palette knives along the length of the fish between the fillet flesh and backbone and lift the fillet on to another flat surface. Lift the remaining top fillet away. Snip the backbone close to the head and tail and ease the bone away, working from head to tail. Replace the fillets in their original position. Chill the fish in the refrigerator, still on the rack.

Make up 1 pt. aspic jelly using jelly crystals. To hasten setting, dissolve the jelly crystals in ¾ pt. boiling water and make up to 1 pt. with ice cubes. Ladle the aspic, at coating consistency, over the fish, working from head to tail. Reserve the surplus aspic and keep it in a liquid state for later use. Replace the fish in the refrigerator to set the glaze. Cut a 1-in. length of cucumber. Make about 10 small notches down the cucumber skin using a small sharp knife, then slice it thinly. First wash the radishes and then, to facilitate the cutting, hold them firmly at the root or stalk and slice them thinly. To decorate the fish, dip the cucumber and radish slices into the reserved aspic jelly and position along the length of the fish. Chill. Finally glaze the salmon trout with the remaining aspic, ladling it along the length of the fish. It is important at this stage that the aspic is on the point of setting, to avoid displacing the decoration.

Insert the point of a sharp knife ¼ in. into the stalk of each tomato and give it a twist. Put the tomatoes in a bowl and cover with boiling water for ½ minute to blanch them. Test one for easy peeling, then drain and skin the rest. Halve the tomatoes and remove the seeds with a teaspoon. Pipe stiff mayonnaise into each. Transfer the fish to a serving plate and garnish with tomato nests, lemon wedges and parsley sprigs.

Haddock creole

For oven-to-table ease – to satisfy the family appetite serve it with crisp oven-fried potatoes and spinach.

2 oz. long grain rice
1 oz. butter
½ lb. onions, skinned and sliced
2 tbsps. chopped parsley
1 lb. tomatoes, skinned, seeded and chopped
salt and pepper
1 lb. fresh haddock fillet, skinned
1 level tbsp. cornflour
1 level tsp. dried dill
¼ pt. soured cream
buttered crumbs

SERVES 4–5

Cook the rice in boiling salted water for 10 minutes and drain. Melt the butter and fry the onion slowly until lightly browned. Mix the parsley and tomatoes and season with salt and pepper. Cut the haddock fillet into pieces, dredge with cornflour, toss lightly and season. Lightly butter a 2½-pt. casserole, put the onion in the bottom, then the rice, then the tomatoes and lastly the fish sprinkled with 1 level tsp. dried dill; spread with the cream. Cover and cook in the oven at 375°F, 190°C (mark 5) for about 30 minutes. Remove the lid, lightly fork the fish and cover with a layer of buttered crumbs.

Smoked haddock and cheese flan

½ lb. smoked haddock
¼ pt. water
juice of ½ lemon
1 oz. butter
1 small onion, skinned and chopped
2 oz. mushrooms, diced
8-in. baked shortcrust flan case
2 eggs
3 tbsps. single cream
4 oz. plain cottage cheese
salt and pepper
chopped parsley

SERVES 4–6

Poach the haddock in a pan with water and half the lemon juice for about 10 minutes. Drain the fish, discard any bones or skin and flake the flesh. Melt the butter in a pan, cook the onion for a few minutes, add the mushrooms and cook for a further few minutes. Combine the fish and vegetables and spread the mixture over the flan base. Beat the eggs and add the cream, cheese and remaining lemon juice. Adjust the seasoning and pour over the fish mixture. Bake in the oven at 375°F, 190°C (mark 5) for about 35 minutes until set and golden. Garnish with chopped parsley and serve hot or cold.

Haddock à la bistro

This also makes a tasty hot appetiser, in which case halve the recipe for 4 servings.

2 tbsps. olive oil
4 portions fresh haddock fillet, skinned (about 1 lb.)
4 tbsps. dry white wine
2 tbsps. tomato ketchup
1 clove garlic, skinned and crushed with salt or a little finely chopped onion
freshly ground black pepper
1 bayleaf
2 tbsps. fresh white breadcrumbs
1 tbsp. chopped parsley

SERVES 4

Pour the olive oil into a shallow ovenproof dish. Arrange pieces of haddock in the dish and sprinkle with white wine. Add the ketchup, sprinkling it over the fish. Add the garlic or onion then black pepper and the bayleaf. Finally cover with breadcrumbs and chopped parsley. Bake at 350°F, 180°C (mark 4) for 25 to 30 minutes. Serve straight from the dish.

Thatched cod

1½ oz. margarine or butter
4 fillets cod or haddock, 4–6 oz. each
4 oz. onion, skinned and chopped
2 oz. fresh white breadcrumbs
2 oz. mature Cheddar cheese, grated
3 firm tomatoes, skinned and roughly chopped
¼ level tsp. salt
freshly ground black pepper
1 tbsp. chopped parsley
juice and grated rind of 1 lemon
parsley sprigs

SERVES 4

Melt ½ oz. fat in a small saucepan. Use a little to grease the inside of a shallow ovenproof serving dish. Arrange the fish fillets in a single layer in the dish and brush with the rest of the melted fat. Fry the onion in the remaining 1 oz. fat without colouring. Combine it with the breadcrumbs, cheese, tomatoes, salt, pepper, parsley, lemon juice and rind. Spoon the mixture evenly over the fillets and cook in the oven at 375°F, 190°C (mark 5) for about 30 minutes. Garnish with parsley.

Scallops mornay

Scallops are now at their best – serve mornay style as a light lunch or supper dish, or as a dinner party starter.

4 scallops
1 tbsp. lemon juice
½ pt. mornay sauce (1 oz. butter, 1 oz. plain
    flour, ½ pt. milk, 2–3 oz. cheese, grated)
2 oz. buttered crumbs
1 oz. grated cheese
butter

SERVES 4

Choose scallops with firmly closed shells. To open the shell, place the scallop in a warm oven 325°F, 170°C (mark 3). Discard the black part and gristly fibre and take out the scallop, leaving the red coral intact. Poach in salted water with lemon juice for 10 minutes and clean the rounded shells. Prepare the mornay sauce. Place 1 tbsp. sauce in each shell and sprinkle with a few buttered crumbs. Place the scallop on top and cover with the remainder of the sauce. Top with buttered crumbs and cheese and dot with butter. Bake for 20 minutes at 375°F, 190°C (mark 5), until the cheese has melted and browned.

✳ Latticed tuna flan

6 oz. shortcrust pastry (6 oz. flour, etc.)
4 oz. mushrooms, wiped
1 oz. butter or margarine
7-oz. can tuna steak, drained
1 egg
salt and freshly ground black pepper
good ¼ pt. milk
2 oz. anchovy fillets
2 tomatoes
1½ oz. cheese, grated

SERVES 4

Roll out the pastry and use it to line a 9½-in. French fluted flan tin. Finely chop the mushrooms and sauté in butter or margarine for 1–2

minutes. Off the heat, combine with the flaked tuna. Spread this over the flan base. Beat together the egg, salt, pepper and milk and strain it over the fish. Bake in the oven at 425°F, 220°C (mark 7) for 15 minutes, reduce heat to 350°F, 180°C (mark 4) and cook for a further 15 minutes. Meanwhile soak the anchovy fillets in a little milk to remove the excess salt and skin the tomatoes (blanch them first in boiling water). When the flan filling is set, sprinkle the cheese over and arrange tomato slices across, with a lattice of the drained anchovy strips. Return the flan to the oven for a further 10–15 minutes. Serve warm with dressed celery.

For dressed celery: Wash 5–6 large sticks of celery. Chop across into neat pieces. In a screw-topped jar shake together 4 tbsps. salad oil, 2 tbsps. wine winegar, pinch salt, mustard and ground black pepper. Pour the dressing over the celery and garnish the salad with parsley.

Buttery lamb grill

1 oz. butter
1 tbsp. corn oil
1 level tsp. each fresh chopped mint and
    rosemary
1 clove garlic, optional
fresh ground black pepper
1 tbsp. lemon juice
8 lamb cutlets, trimmed
salt

SERVES 4

In a small pan, melt the butter and add the oil, mint, rosemary, clove of garlic cut in half, a few turns of pepper and the lemon juice. Turn the cutlets in this marinade and leave for about 1 hour. Discard the garlic. Preheat the grill on maximum heat, reduce heat a little and place the drained chops on the rack. Cook for about 5 minutes on each side, brushing with the excess marinade as needed. Towards the end of cooking, season with salt. Serve barbecue-style

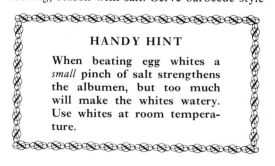

HANDY HINT

When beating egg whites a *small* pinch of salt strengthens the albumen, but too much will make the whites watery. Use whites at room temperature.

with paper napkins for easy handling, or as a main meal with buttered new potatoes, grilled tomato halves and sliced beans.

Roast stuffed breast of lamb

This inexpensive joint can be very meaty, especially when backed with a good stuffing. Try adding a sprig of rosemary under the breast of lamb whilst roasting or sprinkle chopped rosemary over it.

1 breast of lamb, boned (about 2 lb.)
salt and pepper
lemon juice
1 level tbsp. flour
1 oz. dripping

For stuffing
½ oz. dripping, melted
1 small onion, skinned and chopped
8 oz. sausage meat
1 tsp. chopped parsley
2 rounded tbsps. fresh white breadcrumbs

SERVES 4

Wipe the breast of lamb, sprinkle the inside with salt, pepper and lemon juice. Work together the ingredients for the stuffing and spread it over the lamb. Roll up loosely and tie with string in several places. Weigh. Season the flour and rub this into the surface of the lamb. Place in a roasting tin with the dripping. Roast at 350°F, 180°C (mark 4) for 30–35 minutes per lb. and 35 minutes over. Baste once or twice. Slice and arrange on a serving dish; serve redcurrant jelly separately.

Shish kebabs

Skewer food is quick and easy, a lemon marinade gives just the right piquancy.

1 thick slice of lamb cut from leg – about 1 lb.
3 tbsps. oil
1 tbsp. lemon juice
1 medium onion, skinned and sliced
1 clove garlic, skinned and crushed
pinch dried marjoram
1 tbsp. chopped parsley
salt and freshly ground black pepper
bayleaves
melted butter

SERVES 4

Cut the lamb into 1-in. cubes. In a bowl, combine the oil, lemon juice, onion, garlic, marjoram, parsley and seasoning. Add the lamb and leave in a cool place (not the refrigerator) for several hours.

To cook, drain off the marinade and thread the meat cubes with a few bayleaves on to 4 skewers. Brush with melted butter and cook on a rack under a moderate grill for 15–20 minutes turning about 3 times. To keep warm reduce grill heat. Serve on a bed of fluffy rice.

Lamb maître d'hôtel

6 lamb chump chops, about ¾ in. thick
2 oz. butter
1 small clove garlic, skinned and crushed
chopped parsley
lemon juice
salt and pepper

SERVES 6

Choose chops that are not excessively fatty and trim away most of the remaining fat. Using a small sharp knife, make a pocket in the side of the chops away from the bone. Beat the butter to soften it, then add the garlic with the parsley and lemon juice. Divide the butter between the pockets and press well in. Seal with cocktail sticks. Place the chops in a roasting tin, lightly cover with foil and cook in the oven at 375°F, 190°C (mark 5) for about 45 minutes; turn halfway through cooking time and if necessary raise the oven heat or pop under the grill to brown before serving on a bed of risotto.

Lemon-stuffed roast veal

3 lb. breast of veal, boned weight
salt and freshly ground black pepper
3 tbsps. lemon juice
1 oz. fresh white breadcrumbs, toasted
1 level tsp. dried rosemary
1 tbsp. chopped parsley
1 clove garlic, skinned and crushed
1 oz. butter
1 egg, beaten
4 thin slices lemon
4 rashers streaky bacon, rinded
1 tbsp. cooking oil

SERVES 6–7

Flatten out the meat and season with salt, pepper and 1 tbsp. lemon juice. In a bowl, combine the breadcrumbs, rosemary, parsley, garlic, melted butter, $\frac{1}{4}$ level tsp. salt, black pepper and egg. Using a palette knife, fill the pocket in the meat with stuffing and spread any remaining stuffing over the meat. With scissors remove the rind from the lemon slices, and arrange the fruit down the centre. Roll up and secure at intervals with string. Lay the bacon across the meat. Place the oil and remaining lemon juice in the base of a casserole just large enough to take the joint. Place the meat on top, cover and roast in the oven at 350°F, 180°C (mark 4) for about 3$\frac{1}{2}$ hours – until tender. Baste occasionally. Carve and serve hot or leave to go cold before slicing.

✳ Filet de porc chasseur

2 lb. pork fillet
2 tbsps. cooking oil
2$\frac{1}{2}$ oz. butter
8 oz. onions, skinned and chopped
8 oz. button mushrooms
3 level tbsps. flour
$\frac{1}{4}$ pt. beef stock
$\frac{1}{4}$ pt. dry white wine
salt and freshly ground black pepper
chopped parsley
croûtons

SERVES 6

Cut the pork into 1–1$\frac{1}{2}$ in. pieces. Heat the oil in a frying pan, add the pork and cook quickly to brown and seal the surface. Remove from the pan and transfer to an ovenproof casserole. Heat 2 oz. butter in the frying pan, add the onions and cook slowly until soft. Add the mushrooms and quickly sauté; remove them while still crisp and place over the meat. Blend the flour into the pan juices, adding remaining $\frac{1}{2}$ oz. butter, and gradually add the stock and wine. Blend to a smooth consistency. Bring to the boil and simmer for 2–3 minutes. Adjust the seasoning and pour into the casserole. Cover and cook in the oven at 350°F, 180°C (mark 4) for about 1$\frac{3}{4}$ hours until the pork is fork tender. Serve sprinkled liberally with chopped parsley. Garnish with croûtons or sliced, toasted French bread.

Arista di maiale al latte

'Arista' (the chine or saddle) of pork tastes new and different when simmered in milk, with a slightly sweet milk glaze. When simmered in water in the oven it's known as Arista Alla Fiorentina. Served cold, it is tender and moist.

4 lb. loin of pork
3 cloves garlic, skinned
6 whole cloves
3 tbsps. oil
salt and freshly ground black pepper
1 level tsp. dried rosemary
1$\frac{1}{2}$ pt. milk

SERVES 8–10

The joint can be either chined and not boned, or boned and rolled into a sausage shape. Remove the rind and any excess fat; with point of a sharp knife make nicks in the fat and stud the meat with garlic and cloves. Heat the oil in a large saucepan and place the meat fat side down, to brown. Turn it and season the fat with salt, pepper and rosemary. Add the milk to the saucepan, bring to the boil and simmer gently, covered, for about 2 hours. During this time, the milk turns to a curd-like solid. Scrape this from the pan sides and stir into the cooking liquid. Simmer the pork for a further 2 hours until only the brown curd remains. Remove the meat to a serving dish and spoon the sauce, with all its grainy little pieces, over it. Serve hot or cold with a potato salad flavoured with a little fennel.

Pork with apricots

A pleasant choice for an informal dinner party, served with rice spiked with sautéed almonds and a little dressed watercress.

4 pork chops, about 5–6 oz. each
freshly ground black pepper
dry mustard
cooking oil
1 small onion, skinned and finely chopped
1 level tbsp. flour
1 chicken stock cube
8-oz. can apricot halves
1 tbsp. cider vinegar
parsley to garnish

SERVES 4

Trim the chops well and season on each side with pepper and mustard. Just cover the base of a large frying pan with oil; when it is hot, brown the chops quickly on each side. Keep on one side. To the pan fat, add the onion and cook for 5 minutes; drain off any excess fat. Stir in the flour, add a crumbled chicken cube and the juice from the apricots made up to ½ pt. with water, together with 1 tbsp. cider vinegar. Bring to the boil, stirring, add the chops and simmer gently, covered, for 45 minutes to 1 hour, turning the chops once. Five minutes before the end of the cooking time, add the apricots. The juices should be of a glaze consistency; if not, bubble to reduce them before adding the apricots. Garnish with parsley.

Pork and bean salad
(see picture page 23)

Grill, fry or bake an extra batch of sausages then enjoy this wonderful way to serve them cold.

2 tbsps. chopped parsley
1 small onion, skinned and very finely chopped
1 level tsp. dry mustard
1 level tsp. French mustard
1 level tsp. paprika pepper
1 level tsp. salt
freshly ground black pepper
¼ level tsp. grated nutmeg
2 level tsps. caster sugar
4 tbsps. salad oil
2 tbsps. tarragon vinegar
juice of 1 orange
7-oz. can red kidney beans, drained
2 large cooked potatoes, diced
1 lb. cold cooked pork sausages
2 eating apples, cored and finely diced
2 tomatoes, peeled, halved and seeded

SERVES 4

In a lidded container, shake together the first 12 ingredients to make a dressing. In a bowl lightly toss together the beans, potatoes, sausages cut into ¼-in. slices, apples and chopped tomato halves. Fold through the dressing and leave to marinade for 30 minutes before serving, giving an occasional stir.

Bacon in cider

2 lb. collar bacon joint
1 bayleaf
1 large onion, skinned and chopped
½ pt. dry cider
1 level tsp. cornflour

SERVES 6

String the bacon joint and soak it in cold water for about 4 hours. Drain, place in a saucepan and cover with cold water. Bring to the boil, pour off the water and cover again with fresh water. Add the bayleaf, bring to the boil, cover, reduce heat and simmer for half the cooking time, based on 20 minutes per lb. plus 20 minutes. Remove the joint from the liquid and peel away the rind. Place the bacon in an oven-proof casserole with the chopped onion and cider. Cover and cook in the oven at 375°F, 190°C (mark 5) for the rest of the cooking time. Baste 2 or 3 times with the cider mixture. Slice the bacon and keep it warm. Thicken the juices with the cornflour, cook for 1–2 minutes and pour over the bacon.

Bacon steaks

1 lb. lean stewing steak
2 oz. fresh white breadcrumbs
1 oz. cocktail onions, finely chopped
salt and freshly ground black pepper
1 egg
10 rashers streaky bacon
cooking oil
4 tomatoes
1½ lb. potatoes, peeled
oil or fat for deep frying

SERVES 4

Trim the steak and put it through a mincer. Combine the steak, breadcrumbs, onions, seasoning and egg together in a bowl. Divide it into 10 equal portions and shape into small burgers about 1 in. thick. Remove the rind and bones from the bacon. Stretch the bacon on a flat surface, using the back of a knife. Wrap 1 rasher round each burger like a collar. Place them in a shallow roasting tin, brush with oil and bake in oven at 400°F, 200°C (mark 6) for 50 minutes to 1 hour. Make a small cross with the point of a knife into the dome end of each

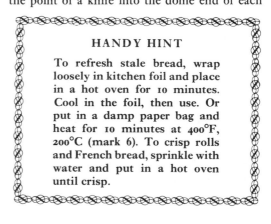

HANDY HINT

To refresh stale bread, wrap loosely in kitchen foil and place in a hot oven for 10 minutes. Cool in the foil, then use. Or put in a damp paper bag and heat for 10 minutes at 400°F, 200°C (mark 6). To crisp rolls and French bread, sprinkle with water and put in a hot oven until crisp.

tomato. Brush with oil. Bake in the bottom of the oven for 10 minutes when the steaks are nearly cooked. Cut the potatoes into small dice. Deep fat fry them at 350°F, 180°C, for 5 minutes. Remove from fat, increase the heat to 375°F, 190°C, and cook for a further 3 minutes until golden brown. Serve the diced potatoes in the centre of a serving dish. Arrange the burgers around the edge with the tomatoes.

∗ Beef goulash

A hearty stew from Hungary – thickened with potato and flavoured lightly with caraway.

1½ oz. lard
2 medium onions, skinned and finely chopped
2 lb. chuck steak
1–2 level tbsp. paprika pepper
1 level tsp. caraway seeds
½ raw potato, peeled and grated
2 level tbsps. tomato paste
½ pt. stock
1 lb. old potatoes, peeled
salt
1 small green pepper, thinly sliced

SERVES 5–6

Melt the lard in a saucepan and fry the onions until evenly brown. Trim the beef and cut into walnut-sized pieces. Stir the paprika into the onions and add the beef, caraway seeds and grated raw potato. Cover and cook slowly for 10 minutes. Stir in the tomato paste and stock. Cover and simmer gently until the meat is almost tender – about 1½ hours. Now add the 1 lb. potatoes, cut in small cubes. Simmer for a further 30 minutes. For a thicker consistency continue to cook with the lid off. Season with salt, if necessary. Add the green pepper. Serve with buttered noodles garnished with poppy seeds.

∗ Aberdeen sausage

1 lb. stewing beef
¼ lb. streaky bacon, rinded
4 oz. onion, skinned
4 oz. rolled oats
2 tsps. Worcestershire sauce
1 small egg, beaten
1 level tsp. salt
freshly ground black pepper
1 level tbsp. chopped parsley

SERVES 4

Trim the meat where necessary to remove surplus fat. Put the beef, bacon and onions twice through a mincer. Add the remaining ingredients and mix well. Shape into a long thick sausage and wrap in oiled foil. Fold the foil lightly across the top and twist the side edges together. Place on a baking sheet and bake at 300°F, 150°C (mark 2) for about 2 hours. Gently remove the foil and serve hot in thick slices.

∗ Swiss steak

This reasonable cut of steak makes a meaty main course, enriched by a nourishing tomato sauce with a hint of garlic. Serve with jacket potatoes and green beans.

3 level tbsps. flour
1–2 level tsps. salt
¼ level tsp. pepper
1½ lb. chuck or blade bone steak
2 oz. lard or dripping
2 medium sized onions, skinned and sliced
1–2 stalks celery, chopped
1 clove garlic, skinned and crushed
12½-oz. can tomatoes
3 level tsps. tomato paste

SERVES 4

Season the flour with salt and pepper. Trim the meat and rub in the flour until all is worked in. Cut the meat into 8 portions. Melt half the fat, add the onions and brown lightly. Remove the onions from the pan. Melt the rest of the fat in the pan and brown the steak on both sides. Reduce the heat, add the celery, garlic, tomatoes and paste. Stir, cover and simmer *very* gently for 1½ hours. Add the onion to the meat and continue cooking for a further 30 minutes.

∗ Beef double-crust pie

½ oz. butter
¾ lb. minced beef
1 pkt. onion sauce mix
¼ pt. milk
2 canned pimiento caps, sliced
salt and pepper
8 oz. shortcrust pastry (8 oz. flour, etc.)
beaten egg to glaze

SERVES 4

Melt the butter in a pan, add the mince and sauté gently for about 10 minutes. Sprinkle the sauce mix over the meat. Stir well, then stir in the milk. Bring it to the boil and simmer for 5 minutes. Add the pimiento and adjust the seasoning, simmer for a further 5 minutes and let it cool. Roll out two-thirds of the pastry thinly and line the base of a 7½-in. round deep pie plate. Fill this with meat mixture then roll out the remaining pastry and use to cover the pie. Trim and knock up the edges, brush with beaten egg and decorate with the pastry trimmings. Bake at 400°F, 200°C (mark 6) for about 1 hour till golden brown.

Pork and bean salad (*see page 21*)

✳ Curried beef balls

2 cloves garlic, skinned
1 level tsp. chopped stem ginger
1 level tsp. ground fennel
1 level tsp. ground cinnamon
¼ level tsp. ground cloves
freshly ground black pepper
1 lb. lean minced beef
4 oz. bread
¼ pt. milk
1 medium sized onion, skinned and chopped
1 level tsp. salt
1 egg, beaten
beaten egg and breadcrumbs for coating

For curry sauce
1 onion, skinned and chopped
1 tbsp. cooking oil
1 clove garlic, skinned and crushed
1 level tbsp. curry powder
1 level tsp. ground ginger
1 level tsp. turmeric
1 oz. desiccated coconut
1 pt. milk
salt and pepper
lemon juice

SERVES 4

Pound together the first 6 ingredients and add them to the beef. Soak the bread in milk, then squeeze it out. Work this into the beef with the onion, salt and egg. Make 14 balls, coat them in egg and breadcrumbs and refrigerate. To make the sauce, fry the onion in oil until soft, then stir in the garlic, curry powder, ginger and turmeric. Cook gently for 5 minutes, add the coconut and milk and simmer until creamy. Season with salt and pepper.

Fry the meat balls until brown all over in enough oil to just cover the base of the pan. Add them to the sauce, cook gently for about 20 minutes and flavour with lemon juice.

HANDY HINT

To add garlic to salads, a favourite way is to use a *chapon* – a hard crust of bread rubbed with cut garlic, then used to stir the dressing and left among the salad stuffs. Or simply rub the inside of the salad bowl with a cut clove of garlic before use.

Pimiento beef balls

2 lb. potatoes, boiled and creamed
1 lb. minced beef
4 oz. sage and onion stuffing mix
1 small clove garlic, skinned and crushed
1 egg, beaten
salt and pepper
4 tbsps. cooking oil
2 level tbsps. cornflour
14½-oz. can consommé with red wine
7-oz. can pimientos, drained and sliced
chopped parsley for garnish

SERVES 4

Pipe a potato border around an entrée dish; keep warm. Combine the beef, stuffing, garlic, egg and seasoning. With floured hands, shape the mixture into about 40 balls and fry them in oil for 20 minutes, turning. In a pan, combine the cornflour and consommé, bring to the boil and cook for 2 minutes. Add the sliced pimiento and beef balls and poach in the consommé for 10 minutes. Spoon into the potato-lined dish and garnish with chopped parsley.

✳ Battalian beef bake

3 tbsps. corn oil
¾ lb. onions, skinned and sliced
1 clove garlic, skinned and crushed
1½ lb. prime collar or slipper of bacon joint, rinded and cut into ½-in. cubes
2½ lb. lean minced beef
1 large orange
15-oz. can tomatoes
2 bayleaves
salt and freshly ground black pepper
½ tsp. Worcestershire sauce
4 lb. old potatoes
2 oz. butter or margarine
2 oz. plain flour
1¼ pt. milk
1 level tsp. made mustard
4 oz. mature Cheddar cheese, grated
2 tbsps. freshly grated Parmesan cheese

SERVES 10

Heat the oil in a large pan and sauté the onions and garlic until soft but not coloured. Add the bacon and cook gently for 10 minutes, then stir in the mince. Cook for a further 10 minutes, stirring frequently. Thinly pare the rind from the orange and cut it into fine julienne strips; cook it in boiling water for 5 minutes then drain.

Squeeze the juice from the orange. Add the orange strips and orange juice, tomatoes, bayleaves, salt, pepper and Worcestershire sauce to the meat and bring to the boil. Cover the pan and simmer gently for 45 minutes. Peel the potatoes and cook in salted water until almost tender; drain, cool and slice. Turn the meat into a shallow 6-pt. casserole (or two 3-pt. casseroles) and arrange the potato slices in an overlapping pattern over the meat. Melt the butter or margarine in a pan, stir in the flour and cook for 1 minute. Slowly add the milk and bring to the boil. Add salt and pepper to taste, with the mustard. Simmer for 3 minutes, remove from the heat and stir in the Cheddar cheese until it melts. Spoon the sauce over the potato and sprinkle with Parmesan cheese. Cook in the oven at 425°F, 220°C (mark 7) for about 45 minutes, until really hot and the cheese is brown. Serve immediately.

✳ Beef olives

1½ lb. rump steak or topside, cut into 8
   pieces about ¼ in. thick and 2½ in. by 3 in.
1 small onion, skinned
¼ lb. button mushrooms
2 oz. fresh breadcrumbs
1 level tsp. dried mixed herbs
2 tsps. chopped parsley
1 oz. shredded suet
1 large tomato, skinned and seeded
salt and pepper
1 egg yolk
dripping
¾ pt. stock or tomato juice
flour or cornflour for thickening
creamed potatoes

SERVES 4

Trim the steak free of any fat and beat it to flatten each piece. Mince or finely chop the onion with the mushroom skins and stalks, reserving the mushroom caps. Add to the breadcrumbs, herbs, suet and chopped tomato. Season and bind with the egg yolk. Divide this stuffing between the pieces of steak, roll them up carefully and secure with fine string or cocktail sticks. Brown each olive in a little melted dripping. Place them in a casserole, add the stock or tomato juice and cook in the oven at 375°F, 190°C (mark 5) for about 1 hour until tender. Strain off the gravy, thicken and check seasoning. Remove the string or sticks from olives and arrange them on a bed of creamy piped potatoes; garnish with sauté mushroom caps. Glaze the olives with a little gravy and serve the remainder separately.

Fondue bourguignonne

(*see picture page 27*)

French/Swiss beef-and-dip party dish, cooked at the table.

6–8 oz. fillet or rump steak per person
oil for frying
dips – see below
finely chopped onion or shallot
finely chopped parsley
chutney (optional)
roughly chopped pineapple (optional)

Cut the steak into 1-in. cubes with a sharp knife; arrange on individual serving plates. Place a metal container of oil over a spirit stove to heat; the ideal temperature is around 375°F. Give each guest a long-handled wooden skewer or two-prong fondue fork for spearing the meat, which they cook in the oil, cool a little and transfer to a second fork for eating. Dip each piece in one of the sauces (below), then in a mixture of onion and parsley. Chutney and pineapple are good, too. Offer crusty bread as an accompaniment.

Horseradish dip: whisk together 6 level tbsps. whipped cream, 3 level tbsps. horseradish sauce and freshly ground black pepper.

Curry dip: mix together 3 level tbsps. home-made mayonnaise, 3 level tbsps. whipped cream, 1 level tsp. curry powder and 1 tsp. chutney sauce.

Paprika dip: beat 3 oz. cream cheese until soft, combine with 4 level tbsps. home-made mayonnaise, 1 level tsp. paprika pepper and 3 gherkins, finely chopped.

Tomato dip: mix together 3 level tbsps. home-made mayonnaise, 3 level tbsps. whipped cream, 2 level tbsps. tomato ketchup, 2 level tsps. tomato paste and a good dash Worcestershire sauce

HANDY HINT

Eggs should be cracked into a cup before using unless you are absolutely sure they will not be bad.

Mustard dip: blend 1½ level tsps. dry mustard with 2 tsps. port. Add 3 level tbsps. home-made mayonnaise and 4–6 level tbsps. whipped cream.

Chicken French style

Crisp on the outside, tender on the inside, this is a really moist, flavoursome and juicy way with chicken.

4–4½ lb. roasting chicken
4 oz. butter
1 lemon

SERVES 6

Prepare the chicken, trussing in the usual way. Stuff the inside with 2 oz. butter, the chicken liver and half a wiped lemon. Rub the outside with the juice of the other ½ lemon and spread with 2 oz. softened butter. Cook, covered, in the oven at 425°F, 220°C (mark 7) allowing 25 minutes per lb., uncovering the bird for the last 10 minutes to brown it. Remove the chicken, add a little giblet stock to the juices, adjust seasoning and boil rapidly; serve as a gravy.

Chicken julienne

This recipe is equally successful with cold roast turkey.

1 lb. cooked roast chicken meat
1½ oz. butter
1½ oz. flour
½ pt. rich chicken stock
½ pt. milk
2 tbsps. lemon juice
1 oz. cheese, grated
pinch of dried rosemary
salt and pepper
1 oz. flaked almonds, toasted
6–8 oz. long grain rice
water
salt
1–2 tbsps. chopped parsley
lemon twist and parsley sprig for garnish

SERVES 4

Cut the carved chicken into long narrow strips and place them in a shallow ovenproof dish. Melt the butter, stir in the flour and cook for a few minutes. Slowly add the stock and milk, beating well. Bring to the boil, stirring and cook gently for 2–3 minutes. Add the lemon juice, cheese and rosemary. Adjust the seasoning,

remembering that the chicken meat will dilute the sauce flavour. Pour it over the chicken and sprinkle with nuts. Cover and place in the oven at 350°F, 180°C (mark 4) for 40 minutes. Serve in a border of parsley rice (below) garnished with a lemon twist and a parsley sprig.

Parsley rice: Cook rice in boiling salted water until tender. If wished, this can be done early in the day or the day before, the cold, well separated rice parcelled in kitchen foil with a few shavings of butter and reheated at 350°F, 180°C (mark 4) for 40 minutes alongside the chicken dish. Add parsley and toss lightly.

Arroz con pollo

A top-of-the-stove chicken dish from Mexico.

3-lb. oven-ready roasting chicken
2 level tbsps. seasoned flour
4 tbsps. vegetable oil
1 medium sized onion, skinned and finely chopped
16-oz. can tomatoes
water
6-oz. can pimientos, drained and sliced
2 chicken stock cubes
8 stuffed olives
6 oz. long grain rice
salt and pepper
½ lb. pork sausages, cut in ½-in. slices
a small pkt. frozen peas

SERVES 4

Prepare the chicken and cut it into 8 pieces. Coat the joints with seasoned flour. Heat the oil in a 7-pt. saucepan, brown the joints, then drain and keep them warm. Add the chopped onion to the saucepan and cook until golden brown. Drain tomatoes and make up the liquid to ¾ pt., with water. To the onion in the pan add the tomatoes, tomato liquid, pimientos, crumbled stock cubes, olives, rice, seasoning and sausages. Mix well together and arrange the chicken joints on top. Cover and simmer for 30 minutes, occasionally lifting the rice with a fork to prevent it from sticking. Add the thawed peas and simmer for a further 15 minutes.

HANDY HINT

Eight tablespoonfuls of water equal ¼ pint.

Fondue bourguignonne (*see page 25*)

✳ Fried salami chicken

20 chicken drumsticks, skinned
6–8 oz. salami, skinned and sliced (40 slices)
4–5 large eggs, beaten
1 large white loaf made into breadcrumbs
oil for frying
2 15-oz. cans grapefruit segments, drained
¼ cucumber, sliced

SERVES 10

Make an incision to the bone along one side of

each drumstick and loosen the flesh around the bone. Place 2 slices salami around the bone, pull the chicken flesh together and secure with cocktail sticks. Dip the chicken first into beaten egg and then breadcrumbs and pat the crumbs in well. Repeat the egg and breadcrumb process to give a good coating. Deep fry in hot oil (360°F) for 7–10 minutes until golden brown and the flesh is cooked through. Drain on absorbent paper and cool. Decorate the drumsticks with cutlet frills and garnish with grapefruit and sliced cucumber.

Baked lemon chicken

You may get better value from a whole bird jointed at home.

4 chicken portions, thawed
4 rashers lean streaky bacon
½ oz. butter
2 tbsps. cooking oil
1½ tbsps. lemon juice
salt and pepper
chopped parsley

SERVES 4

Pull away and discard the chicken skin, if necessary using a sharp knife. Rind the bacon and snip it into small pieces. Heat the butter and oil in a flameproof shallow casserole which just takes the chicken. When hot, brown the chicken. Keep the chicken on one side, add the bacon and fry until beginning to brown. Pour off the surplus fat, return the chicken to the casserole, spoon the lemon juice over and season with salt and freshly ground pepper. Cover tightly and cook in the oven at 350°F, 180°C (mark 4) for about 1 hour. To serve, spoon the bacon and reduced juices over the chicken and add parsley.

Swedish chicken salad
(*see picture page 30*)

3½-lb. oven-ready chicken, roasted
6 oz. long grain rice
1 green eating apple
1 red eating apple
2 bananas
lemon juice
¼ pt. double cream
⅓ pt. mayonnaise
1 level tsp. curry powder
salt and pepper
watercress for garnish

SERVES 6

Carve the freshly cooked cold chicken into slices and then cut into strips. Meanwhile, cook the rice, drain and cool. Core and thinly slice the apples, peel and thickly slice the bananas; dredge both with lemon juice. Whip the cream to the same consistency as the mayonnaise and lightly fold it into the mayonnaise. Add the curry powder. Fold in the chicken, apple and banana, add more lemon juice and adjust the seasoning. Pile the chicken mixture on a bed of rice or combine with the rice. Garnish with watercress.

Poulet en cocotte bonne femme

A pot roast with a succulent flavour.

4 oz. sausage meat
2 level tbsps. fresh white breadcrumbs
1 chicken liver, chopped
2 tbsps. chopped parsley
3–3½ lb. oven-ready roasting chicken
salt and pepper
2½ oz. butter
4 oz. lean bacon, rinded and diced
1 lb. potatoes, peeled and diced
chopped parsley or chives for garnish

SERVES 6

Work together the sausage meat, breadcrumbs, liver and parsley. Stuff the chicken at the neck end with the sausage stuffing, secure with a skewer and season. Melt the butter in a 4–5-pt. flameproof casserole and brown the chicken all over. Add the bacon, cover and cook for 15 minutes. Baste the chicken then add the potatoes, turning them in the fat. Cover and continue cooking in the oven at 350°F, 180°C (mark 4) for 1½ hours or until tender. Serve, sprinkling the potatoes with more chopped parsley – or chives, if available.

Chicken liver sauté

Rich and nutritious, serve with buttered leaf spinach.

2 oz. streaky bacon, rinded
salt and freshly ground black pepper
3 level tbsps. flour
8 oz. chicken livers
1½ oz. butter or margarine
4 oz. long grain rice
1 level tbsp. tomato paste
1 tbsp. sherry
pinch mixed dried herbs
½ chicken stock cube
chopped parsley and tomato slices for
  garnish

SERVES 2–3

Scissor-snip the bacon into a small frying pan and fry until fat starts to run. Season the flour, spoon it into a polythene bag, add the chicken livers and coat evenly. Add the butter to the bacon and, when melted, add the livers. Cook for 5–10 minutes over a gentle heat. Pour ½ pt. water into a small saucepan, add ½ level tsp. salt and the rice, bring to the boil, stir once, cover, reduce heat and simmer for about 15 minutes or until the rice is tender and the water absorbed.

✳ Ragout of oxtail

3 level tbsps. flour
salt and freshly ground black pepper
3 lb. oxtail, jointed
1½ oz. white fat or dripping
3 celery stalks, trimmed and sliced
½ lb. carrots, pared and sliced
½ lb. onions, skinned and chopped
¼ lb. bacon in a piece, rinded and diced
bouquet garni
1 stock cube
1½ pt. water
chopped parsley

SERVES 4–6

Combine the flour and seasonings in a plastic bag. Add half the oxtail and shake to coat evenly before removing. Repeat with the rest of the meat. Melt 1 oz. fat in a large open frying pan and brown the oxtail on all sides – about 15 minutes. Drain the meat on absorbent paper before adding it to a 6-pt. flameproof casserole. To the meat juices in the pan, add the remaining fat and sauté the prepared vegetables and bacon for 10 minutes. Add the bouquet garni and any surplus flour from the plastic bag. Dissolve the stock cube in the boiling water, pour it over the vegetables and bubble together before adding to the oxtail. Cook covered in the oven at 425°F, 220°C (mark 7) for 1 hour. Reduce the temperature to 300°F, 150°C (mark 2) for a further 2½–3 hours, until the meat is fork tender. Discard the herbs, cool rapidly and chill overnight. One hour before serving remove all surface fat. Reheat in a flameproof casserole on top of the cooker for about 40 minutes. Adjust seasonings if necessary, sprinkle with chopped parsley and serve with wedges of freshly boiled cabbage.

HANDY HINT

One egg can be replaced in custards, salad dressings and pie fillings by 2 yolks; in yeast doughs, biscuits and cookies by 2 egg yolks and 1 tbsp. water.

Remove the liver sauté from the heat. Stir in the tomato paste, sherry, herbs and ¼ pt. boiling water in which stock cube is dissolved. Return to the heat and simmer for 5 minutes. Pile the rice into one dish and the liver into another. Garnish the rice with chopped parsley, the liver with tomato slices.

Rognoni tripolata

¾ lb. sheeps' kidneys
1 oz. butter
grated rind of ½ lemon
¼ level tsp. salt
freshly ground black pepper
1 level tbsp. cornflour
¼ pt. beef stock (make from a cube)
2 tbsps. Marsala
2 tsps. lemon juice
chopped parsley

SERVES 2

Skin the kidneys, cut them in half, remove the cores and slice thinly. Melt the butter in a pan, add lemon rind, salt and pepper. Sauté gently for 2–3 minutes. Cream the cornflour with 3 tbsps. stock until smooth, then add the remaining stock and blend together before adding to the kidneys. Cook gently for about 10 minutes, stirring occasionally. Increase the heat to thicken the sauce and cook for 2–3 minutes. Remove from the heat, stir in the Marsala and lemon juice and serve on hot noodles, sprinkled over with chopped parsley.

Liver and spaghetti casserole

(*see picture page 31*)

Economical and nutritious, canned tomatoes are a good standby at the in-between time for vegetables.

¾ lb. lamb's liver
2 oz. dripping
2 onions, skinned and thinly sliced
2 rashers lean streaky bacon, rinded
15-oz. can whole tomatoes
¾ oz. flour
salt and pepper
4 oz. spaghetti
grated cheese
tomato slices and chopped parsley for garnish

SERVES 4

Swedish chicken salad (*see page 28*)

Cut the liver into slices, brown on both sides in hot fat, drain and arrange in an ovenproof dish or casserole. Fry the onions and bacon (cut in pieces) until beginning to colour and add to the liver. Drain the tomatoes. Stir the flour into the drippings in the pan, brown for 2–3 minutes then gradually stir in the tomato juice, made up to $\frac{1}{2}$ pt. with water. Bring to the boil and add to the liver with the whole tomatoes. Season well. Cover and cook at 350°F, 180°C (mark 4) for $\frac{3}{4}$–1 hour. Cook the spaghetti in boiling, salted water for 10–12 minutes, drain and arrange it round the edge of the casserole. Top with grated cheese. Alternatively, turn the liver mixture and spaghetti into a heatproof dish, top with grated cheese, grill lightly and garnish with tomato slices and chopped parsley.

✳ Casseroled heart

A dish that looks after itself – orange and walnut give a new twist to an old favourite.

1 ox heart, weighing 2½–3 lb.
2–3 oz. white fat or butter
2 onions, skinned and sliced
1 oz. flour
½ pt. potato water or stock
salt and pepper
½ lb. carrots, pared and grated
1 small swede, peeled and grated
1 orange
6 shelled walnut halves

SERVES 6

Trim the heart and cut it into ½-in. slices. Wash well. Melt the fat in a large frying pan, and sauté the meat until slightly browned. Remove the meat, sauté the onion, then put both in a casserole. Stir the flour into the remaining fat and brown slightly. Pour in the potato water or stock, bring to the boil and simmer for 2–3 minutes. Adjust the seasoning and strain the stock over the sliced heart. Cover and cook for 3½–4 hours at 300°F, 150°C (mark 1–2).

Add the grated carrot and swede after 2½–3 hours. Remove the rind from the orange, free from pith, shred finely and cook in boiling water for 10–15 minutes, drain and refresh in cold water. Add with the walnuts to the casserole 15 minutes before cooking is completed.

✳ Pigeons in cream

Plump pigeons are succulent and tender cooked in this 100-year-old way from Denmark. Serve with plainly boiled whole potatoes and crisp lettuce.

6 pigeons
4 oz. butter
¼ pt. stock
2 level tbsps. redcurrant jelly
½ pt. double cream
salt and pepper
1 tbsp. brandy
chopped parsley

SERVES 6

Wash the pigeons and trim away the claws and undercarriage bones with scissors. Fry in melted butter until well browned on each side of the breast. Place in a casserole, breast side down, with the pan juices. Add the stock and cook, tightly covered, in the oven at 325°F, 170°C (mark 3) for about 2 hours, until really tender. Remove the birds from the casserole and keep warm. Reduce pan juices by half by fast bubbling

Liver and spaghetti casserole (*see page 29*)

in a small pan, then stir in the redcurrant jelly and cream. Adjust the seasoning, bring to the boil and add the brandy, flamed. Pour the sauce over the birds and serve with plenty of chopped parsley.

Fish pie Manitoba

Fish and bacon are natural partners, golden corn brings a splash of colour.

1 lb. cod, haddock or coley fillet
¼ lb. streaky bacon rashers, rinded
1 oz. butter or margarine
salt and freshly ground black pepper
7-oz. can corn kernels, drained
½ pt. milk
sliver of lemon rind
1 level tbsp. cornflour
1 level tbsp. chopped parsley
1½ lb. old potatoes, boiled and creamed

SERVES 4

Skin the fish and cut the bacon into small pieces. Fry the bacon lightly until it begins to brown and the fat runs, add the butter and when it melts add the fish and fry for a further 5–10 minutes. Flake the fish, add the corn, stir and turn into a 2½-pt. pie dish. Heat ½ pt. milk, less 2 tablespoonfuls, with the lemon rind. Pour it on to the cornflour which has been blended with the reserved milk. Add this to the pan and bring to the boil, stirring. Discard the lemon rind, season the sauce well, add the parsley and pour it over the fish in the pie dish. Use freshly cooked potatoes as a topping. Place the dish on a baking sheet and cook towards the top of the oven at 425°F, 220°C (mark 7) for about 30 minutes until golden brown and crisp.

Cheese and onion soufflé

1 oz. butter or margarine
2 oz. onion, skinned and chopped
1 oz. plain flour
¼ pt. milk
3 oz. mature Cheddar cheese, grated
3 eggs, separated
salt and freshly ground black pepper

SERVES 2–3 *(make 2 to serve 4 people)*

Grease a 7-in. soufflé dish. Melt the butter, stir in the onion and cook for 2–3 minutes until transparent. Add the flour and cook the roux

for a few minutes. Gradually stir in the milk and bring to the boil, stirring all the time. Set aside to cool. When cool, fold in the grated cheese and add the egg yolks one at a time, beating well. Sprinkle over the seasoning. Stiffly whisk the egg whites, fold these into the mixture and turn it into the soufflé dish. Bake at 400°F, 200°C (mark 6) for about 30–35 minutes until well risen and brown. Serve at once with fingers of hot buttered toast.

Baked eggs and cheese potatoes

Sliced tomatoes with chives makes a tasty accompaniment to this quick-to-cook meal.

2 lb. potatoes, peeled and cooked
8 oz. Cheddar cheese, grated
4 eggs
salt and pepper
4 tbsps. top of the milk

SERVES 4

Slice the potatoes fairly thickly and make a bed of them in a buttered ovenproof dish. Sprinkle over half the grated cheese. Break the eggs one at a time on to a saucer and slide carefully on top of the cheese and potatoes. Season and cover with the remaining grated cheese. Spoon over the milk and bake uncovered in the centre of the oven at 375°F, 190°C (mark 5) for about 20 minutes. Serve hot.

Country vegetable skillet

This is warming and just right with chunky slices of toasted French bread. Serve in bowls to catch all the delicious natural juices.

2 oz. butter
½ lb. onions, skinned and finely sliced into rings
4 oz. celery, trimmed and sliced
½ lb. courgettes, trimmed and sliced
½ lb. tomatoes, skinned and thickly sliced
salt and pepper
4 oz. Cheddar or Lancashire cheese, grated
chopped parsley

SERVES 4

In a lidded (preferably easy-clean) frying pan, melt the butter and layer the onions, celery, courgettes and tomatoes in the base. Season, cover and cook on top of the cooker over a moderate to low heat for about 30 minutes until the vegetables are tender but still a little crisp. Remove the lid, toss the cheese over them and return to the heat just long enough for the cheese to melt, but take care not to boil or over-cook. Garnish with chopped parsley.

Spring side-dishes

Red cabbage and sweetcorn salad

1 red cabbage (approx. 3 lb.)
¼ pt. French dressing
1 cucumber, diced
salt and freshly ground black pepper
2 11-oz. cans sweetcorn kernels, drained
½ level tsp. finely grated lemon rind
1 tbsp. clear honey

SERVES 16

Quarter the cabbage, discard any coarse stems and shred the cabbage very finely. Place in a large bowl with the dressing, toss and leave for 2 hours. Place the diced cucumber in a bowl, season with salt and pepper and leave for 2 hours. Drain off any excess moisture from the cucumber and add with the corn, lemon rind and honey to the cabbage. Toss thoroughly.

Bacon-topped tomatoes

1½ lb. tomatoes, skinned
1 medium sized onion, skinned
4–6 oz. streaky bacon, rinded
salt and pepper
2 tsps. chopped parsley

SERVES 6

Slice the tomatoes thickly and arrange in a shallow ovenproof serving dish. Very finely chop the onion. Mince or finely chop the bacon and lightly fry until the fat starts to run. Season tomatoes and sprinkle with onion and bacon. Bake, uncovered, at 350°F, 180°C (mark 4) for 10–15 minutes. Garnish with parsley.

HANDY HINT

Potatoes are best stored in a cool, dry, dark place with plenty of air circulating.

Dressed leeks

3 lb. leeks
9 tbsps. salad oil
3 tbsps. cider vinegar
1 level tsp. French mustard
1 oz. onion, skinned and finely chopped
2 level tsps. caster sugar
½ level tsp. salt
freshly ground black pepper

SERVES 16

Trim about half the green part from the leeks. Cut the remainder of the leeks into ⅛-in. slices and wash thoroughly in water. Drain, blanch in boiling salted water for 3–4 minutes then cool quickly in cold water. Drain well. In a lidded container shake together the remaining in-gredients. Pour the dressing over the leeks and toss together.

Dressed macaroni and mushrooms

1 lb. quick-cooking macaroni
½ lb. button mushrooms
1 clove garlic, skinned and crushed
4 tbsps. lemon juice
2 tbsps. wine or cider vinegar
salt and freshly ground black pepper
1 large red pepper, seeded and chopped
1 large green pepper, seeded and chopped
¼ pt. thick mayonnaise
¼ pt. natural yoghurt
chopped parsley

SERVES 16

Cook the macaroni in boiling salted water. Drain and then rinse it under cold running water. Thinly slice the mushrooms and place them in a bowl with the garlic, lemon juice, vinegar, salt and pepper. Leave to marinade for 30 minutes, stirring frequently. Blanch the peppers for 1 minute, rinse them in cold water and drain. Blend together the mayonnaise and yoghurt. Add to the mushrooms and mix well, then stir in peppers. Toss through the macaroni till well coated in dressing. Turn into a serving dish.

Whole beans with pimiento

1 lb. frozen haricots verts
1 cap canned pimiento
butter
lemon juice
freshly ground black pepper

SERVES 6

Cook the beans as directed on the packet, do not overcook. Drain thoroughly, melt a little butter in the pan and add a squeeze of lemon juice. Return beans and toss lightly. Turn into a hot serving dish and garnish with thin strips of pimiento and freshly ground black pepper.

Peanut slaw

12 oz. white cabbage
1 tbsp. wine vinegar
3 tbsps. salad oil
2 tbsps. chopped parsley
1 level tsp. French mustard
grated rind of 1 lemon and juice from half
  the lemon
$\frac{1}{4}$ level tsp. salt
freshly ground black pepper
2 oz. salted peanuts

SERVES 4

Discard the thick cabbage stem and shred the rest finely. Shake together the vinegar, oil, parsley, mustard, lemon rind, juice, salt and pepper. Pour over cabbage, add the peanuts, toss and chill for 30 minutes before serving.

Buttered cucumber

1 large plump cucumber
water
salt
knob of butter
freshly ground black pepper

SERVES 6

Thinly pare the skin from the cucumber using a potato peeler. Cut the cucumber into about 2-in. lengths and each piece into 4 lengthwise; remove some of the seed area. Place in a saucepan with just enough water to barely cover, add salt and cook for about 7 minutes, making sure

they remain crisp. Drain off the liquid and, just before serving, add a knob of butter and some freshly ground pepper.

Casseroled sweet-sour onions

Pop this dish in with the roast joint and potatoes, for a special extra vegetable.

1 lb. onions, skinned and sliced
1 level tsp. salt
3–4 tbsps. cider vinegar
2 oz. butter, melted
2–3 level tbsps. caster sugar
3 tbsps. boiling water

SERVES 3–4

Put the onions in a casserole. Blend together the salt, vinegar, butter, sugar and water. Pour over the onions, cover and bake at 375°F, 190°C (mark 5) for about 1 hour.

Carrots Vichy

A flavour-saving way – for variety, cut the carrots in strips, chunks or diagonally; leave new carrots whole and omit the blanching.

1 lb. carrots, pared
water
1 level tsp. sugar
butter
salt
freshly ground black pepper
chopped parsley

SERVES 4

Cut the carrots into $\frac{1}{4}$-in. slices. Blanch in boiling salted water for 2–3 minutes, then drain. Return the carrots to the pan with $\frac{3}{4}$ pt. water, sugar, a knob of butter and very little salt. Bring to the boil, reduce the heat and boil gently without the lid for about 45 minutes, by which time the liquid should be evaporated. If not, reduce by fast boiling. To serve, add another knob of butter, a dusting of pepper and chopped parsley.

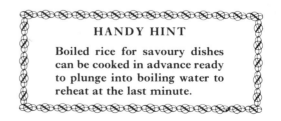

HANDY HINT

Boiled rice for savoury dishes can be cooked in advance ready to plunge into boiling water to reheat at the last minute.

Risotto

½ lb. lean streaky bacon
½ lb. onions, skinned and thinly sliced
10 oz. long grain rice
1½ pt. stock or water
2 chicken stock cubes, optional
salt and pepper

SERVES 6

Rind the bacon and cut it into small pieces with a pair of scissors. Cook in a frying pan until crisp and the fat is extracted. Drain the bacon from the fat and keep the bacon on one side. Fry the onion and rice in the bacon fat until well coloured. Pour in the stock or water and crumbled stock cubes. Bring to the boil and adjust seasoning. Turn into a casserole with a close-fitting lid. Cook in the lower part of the oven set at 375°F, 190°C (mark 5) for about 40 minutes. Stir in the finely chopped bacon pieces, check the seasoning and serve warm.

Spring desserts

Jamaican crunch pie

4 oz. gingernuts
2 oz. butter, melted
¼ pt. double cream
1 can sweetened condensed milk (approx. 7 oz.)
6 tbsps. lemon juice
grated rind of 1 lemon
glazed slices of lemon for decoration

SERVES 6

Crush the gingernuts with a rolling pin or a few at a time in an electric blender. Blend with the melted butter. Use the gingernut mixture to line a 7½-in. pie plate or flan ring placed on a flat plate. Work the crumbs with the back of a metal spoon to form a shell; the edge should appear just above the plate rim. Lightly whip the cream, fold in the condensed milk, lemon juice and rind and beat until smooth. Pour this into the biscuit shell and chill overnight in the refrigerator.

Glazed lemon slices for decoration: Put 8 thick lemon slices (free of pips) in a frying pan, in enough water to cover, and poach until tender. Keep the water level up by adding extra if necessary. Drain the slices and add 3 oz. sugar to the liquid in the pan. When the sugar has dissolved, boil it to reduce to a glaze. Pour over the slices and cool before using.

✳ Lemon fluff

A light, refreshing easy-to-make dessert. If a refrigerator is used to set this sweet, do not leave for any length of time as over-chilling will spoil the texture.

2 large lemons
3 eggs, separated
5–6 oz. caster sugar
2 level tsps. powdered gelatine
3 tbsps. water
3–4 tbsps. double cream
angelica or grated chocolate for decoration

SERVES 4

Grate the rind of the lemons and squeeze out the juice (about 6 tbsps.). Whisk the yolks and sugar together in a large deep bowl. Gradually whisk in the lemon juice and continue to whisk until the mixture begins to thicken. Dissolve the gelatine in the water, in a bowl over hot water. Cool it slightly and quickly whisk into the lemon mixture. When it is beginning to set, fold in the stiffly beaten egg whites and lemon rind, using a metal spoon. Divide between 4 sundae glasses. Leave to set. Serve decorated with swirls of lightly whipped cream and angelica or grated chocolate.

✳ Bakewell tart

Adapted from a traditional recipe, this has a light moist topping with a crisp pastry base; serve dusted with sifted icing sugar.

4 oz. shortcrust pastry (4 oz. flour, etc.)
1 tbsp. raspberry jam
2 oz. butter
2 oz. caster sugar
1 egg
2 oz. ground almonds
1–2 drops almond essence

SERVES 4

Roll out the pastry and use it to line an 8-in.

diameter pie plate. Decorate the edges and roll out any off-cuts to form a lattice pattern on top. Spread the jam over the pastry. Cream the butter and sugar until light and fluffy. Beat in the egg and fold in the ground almonds and almond essence. Spread this mixture evenly over the jam and decorate with lattice strips of pastry. Bake in the centre of the oven at 375°F, 190°C (mark 5) for about 1 hour. Eat warm or cold.

Orange buttered apples

(*see picture opposite*)

For a change of flavour try half sugar and half golden syrup, a pinch of powdered ginger goes well too.

4 cooking apples, all of even size
2 oz. butter
2 oz. caster sugar
grated rind and juice of 1 small orange

SERVES 4

Core the apples, and make a cut through the skin round the centre of each. Cream together the butter and sugar until pale and light, beat in the orange rind and as much juice as it will take. Place the apples in a baking dish, fill centres with orange butter and bake at 350°F, 180°C (mark 4) for about 30 minutes. Serve from the dish with pouring custard or cream.

✳ Oranges in caramel syrup

(*see picture page 41*)

9 oranges
water
1 lb. caster sugar
2 cloves

SERVES 4–8

Thinly pare the rind from 2 oranges, free of white pith. Cut the rind into very thin julienne strips with a sharp knife. Put into a small pan, cover with water, then cover with a lid and cook until the rind is tender. Strain off the liquid. Cut away all the pith from the 2 oranges and the rind and the pith from another 6 oranges. Squeeze the juice from the remaining orange. Dissolve the sugar in $\frac{2}{3}$ pt. water with the cloves. Bring to the boil, remove the cloves and boil until a deep caramel colour. Remove the pan from the heat, slowly add the orange juice and return to a very low heat to dissolve the caramel. Arrange the whole peeled oranges in a single

layer in a serving dish. Top with the julienne strips and spoon the caramel syrup over. Lightly cover and leave in a cool place overnight, by which time the caramel should have softened. To serve, spoon the juices over the oranges and serve thick pouring cream separately. A small sharp knife is needed for cutting the oranges, or they may be pre-sliced.

✳ Peach and apple soufflé

1¼ lb. cooking apples, peeled, cored and sliced
15½-oz. can peach slices, drained
6 eggs, separated
10 oz. caster sugar
2 tbsps. lemon juice
5 level tsps. powdered gelatine
3 tbsps. water
2 tbsps. orange liqueur
¼ pt. single cream
½ pt. double cream
few frosted black grapes

SERVES 10

Stew the apples in 6 tbsps. peach juice until soft; cool. Sieve or liquidise the apples with the drained peaches. Place the egg yolks, sugar and lemon juice in a bowl over a pan of hot water and whisk until very thick and creamy and the whisk leaves a trail. Remove from the heat and whisk until cool. Dissolve the gelatine in 3 tbsps. water in a basin over a pan of hot water and cool slightly. Whisk the fruit purée into the egg mixture, followed by the softened gelatine and liqueur. Whisk the creams together until thick but not stiff and fold into the mixture. Finally fold in the stiffly beaten egg whites. Turn into a prepared 2½-pt. soufflé dish and chill in the refrigerator until set. Using a round-bladed knife remove the collar from the soufflé and decorate the top with grapes.

To frost grapes: First dip into egg white then coat thoroughly in caster sugar. Leave to dry.

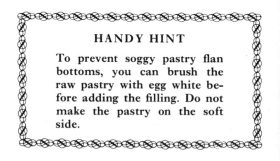

HANDY HINT

To prevent soggy pastry flan bottoms, you can brush the raw pastry with egg white before adding the filling. Do not make the pastry on the soft side.

Pineapple meringue Torte

1-lb. 4-oz. can pineapple segments
4 egg whites
8 oz. caster sugar
pinch cream of tartar
4 oz. blanched almonds, finely chopped

For filling
½ pt. double cream
3 tbsps. milk
icing sugar

SERVES 6–8

Several hours before required, turn the contents from the can of pineapple into a saucepan and boil until the juice is reduced almost entirely and the pineapple looks opaque. Cool. Whisk the egg whites in a deep bowl until stiff, add 2 tbsps. of the measured sugar and the cream of tartar and whisk again until stiff. Fold in the remainder of the sugar and the finely chopped nuts. Spread the meringue in two 8–9-in. discs over non-stick baking paper placed on baking sheets. Dry in the oven at 300°F, 150°C (mark 2) for about 1¼ hours, until the almond meringue is crisp and the paper peels away easily. Cool and store in an airtight tin or in kitchen foil.

Orange buttered apples (*see page 36*)

Whip the cream and milk together until thick enough to spread. Use about two-thirds to sandwich the meringue discs together, along with almost all the pineapple. Place the meringue on a serving plate. Dust with icing sugar. Using a fabric forcing bag and a medium vegetable rose nozzle, pipe whirls of cream round the top edge of the torte. Finish with the reserved pineapple and leave to stand in a cool place, preferably the refrigerator, for several hours, to make the final cutting easier.

Shortcake gâteau

10 oz. plain flour
2 oz. ground rice
8 oz. butter
4 oz. caster sugar
finely grated rind of 1 lemon
2 oz. shelled walnuts, finely chopped
1 egg yolk
$\frac{1}{2}$ pt. whipping cream
2 $15\frac{1}{2}$-oz. cans loganberries or raspberries, well drained
icing sugar

SERVES 8

Place the flour, ground rice, butter, sugar and lemon rind in a bowl and rub in until the mixture resembles breadcrumbs. Add the walnuts and egg yolk and knead together to give a soft dough. Chill, wrapped in a polythene bag, for 30 minutes. Roll two-thirds of the dough into a rectangle 12 in. by 6 in. and place carefully on a baking sheet. Roll out the remainder of the pastry and cut into six 3-in. rounds with a fluted pastry cutter. Cut each in half to form semi-circles. Place on a baking sheet. Cook in the oven at 350°F, 180°C (mark 4) until light brown and firm to the touch, allowing about 30 minutes for the rectangle and about 20 minutes for the semi-circles. Whilst it is still on the baking sheet, cut the rectangle in half lengthwise with a sharp knife and cool. Remove to a wire rack. Wrap in foil to store. About 1 hour before required, whip the cream until stiff and, with a fabric forcing bag fitted with a large rose vegetable nozzle, pipe two-thirds in a thick line down the centre of one walnut shortbread. Spoon $1\frac{3}{4}$ cans of fruit over the piped cream. Arrange the second walnut shortbread over the berries, press down lightly and pipe the remaining cream in whirls down the centre. Arrange shortbread semi-circles along the cream and mount a whole berry in between each.

Jellied lemon syllabub

1 pt. lemon jelly tablet
grated rind and juice of 1 lemon
2 oz. caster sugar
3–4 tbsps. Cointreau
$\frac{1}{2}$ pt. double cream

SERVES 6

Dissolve the jelly tablet in $\frac{1}{2}$ pt. boiling water; make up to 1 pt. with cold water. Divide between six stemmed glasses and put in a cool place to set. Combine the grated lemon rind and juice with the sugar and liqueur. Whip the cream until stiff, fold in the lemon mixture and divide between the six glasses. Chill lightly.

Pineapple pudding

2 oz. butter
4 oz. caster sugar
2 eggs, separated
1 oz. plain flour
8-oz. can pineapple rings
$\frac{3}{4}$–1 pt. milk
cherries and angelica to decorate

SERVES 4

Cream the butter and 2 oz. sugar until light and fluffy. Beat in the egg yolks and flour. Drain the pineapple and measure the juice; make up to 1 pt. with milk. Warm the milk and juice but do not boil (do not worry if it curdles) and gradually pour it on to the creamed mixture. Return to the pan and cook until thick and creamy without boiling, stirring all the time. Pour the custard into a 2-pt. ovenproof pie dish and arrange 4 pineapple rings on top of the custard.

Whisk the egg whites until stiff. Add $1\frac{1}{2}$ oz. sugar and whisk again until stiff. With a large star nozzle, pipe the meringue in 4 whirls on top of the pineapple. Sprinkle with the remaining sugar. Put in oven at 300°F, 150°C (mark 2) for about 30 minutes until meringue is pale golden in colour. Decorate.

Raspberry whip

15-oz. can raspberries
$\frac{1}{2}$ pt. single cream
1 pkt. raspberry quick-whip dessert mix
crystallised rose petals for decoration

SERVES 4

Drain the fruit and combine the syrup and cream in a bowl. Sprinkle in the mix and whip for 1 minute with a rotary whisk. Spoon half the mixture into stemmed glasses, cover with two-thirds of the fruit, the rest of the mix and top with the remaining fruit. Chill for 30 minutes. Decorate with crystallised rose petals.

Rhubarb meringue

Forced rhubarb is tender and a refreshing change.

1 lb. rhubarb
4 individual sponge cakes
2 oz. sugar
juice and grated rind of 1 large orange
2 egg whites
4 oz. caster sugar

SERVES 4

Cut rhubarb in $\frac{1}{2}$-in. pieces and slice the sponge cakes. In a 2-pt. ovenproof pie dish, put alternate layers of sponge, rhubarb, sugar, orange juice and rind. Cover and bake for 30 minutes at 375°F, 190°C (mark 5). Make a meringue with the egg whites and caster sugar and pipe or spoon it on to the baked mixture. Return to the oven, just below the centre, and bake for a further 10–12 minutes. Serve warm.

Banana en croûte

1 lemon
4 large bananas
1 level tbsp. caster sugar
$\frac{1}{4}$ level tsp. ground cinnamon
8 slices brown bread from a ready-sliced small loaf
$1\frac{1}{2}$ oz. butter
1 oz. shelled walnuts, roughly chopped

SERVES 4

Grate the rind from the lemon and squeeze out the juice. Peel and halve the bananas lengthwise. Toss in the lemon juice and leave to soak for

HANDY HINT

An emergency way to make a piping bag is to improvise with a small (not gusseted) plastic bag – just cut the top off one corner, insert icing nozzle and secure with sticky tape.

1 hour. Blend together the caster sugar and cinnamon. Remove the crusts from the brown bread. Melt $\frac{1}{2}$ oz. butter in a frying pan and fry the bananas on both sides until golden. Toast the bread until golden, butter liberally, sprinkle with the cinnamon sugar, top with the bananas, sprinkle with the nuts and serve warm.

Lemon freeze

For crumb layer
2 oz. cornflake crumbs
2 level tbsps. caster sugar
1 oz. butter, melted

For lemon layer
2 eggs, separated
small can sweetened condensed milk
4 tbsps. lemon juice
3 level tbsps. caster sugar

SERVES 8

In a bowl blend together the crumbs, sugar and butter until well mixed. Press all but 4 tbsps. into the base of a $1\frac{1}{2}$ pt. ice-tray or other dish suitable for the freezer. Beat egg yolks in a deep bowl until really thick and creamy, combine with the condensed milk and add the lemon juice; stir until thickened. Beat the egg whites until stiff but not dry. Gradually beat in the caster sugar and fold through the lemon mixture. Spoon into the ice-tray and sprinkle with the remaining crumbs. Freeze until firm. To serve, cut in 8 bars.

Lemon frosted apricot pies

8 oz. rich shortcrust pastry (8 oz. flour, etc.)
15-oz. can apricot halves
$1\frac{1}{2}$ level tsps. arrowroot
grated rind of $\frac{1}{2}$ lemon

For lemon icing
2 oz. icing sugar
lemon juice
double cream for serving

SERVES 4

Roll out the pastry and use about half to line a 4-cup sheet of Yorkshire pudding tins. Drain the apricots and divide between the pastry cases. Blend $\frac{1}{4}$ pt. fruit juice with the arrowroot in a small pan, bring to the boil and boil until clear, stirring. Add the lemon rind and spoon over the apricots. Make lids from the remaining pastry and slit the centre of each. Bake in the oven and, while still hot, brush with lemon icing made by blending 2 oz. icing sugar with enough lemon juice to give a thick coating consistency. Serve just warm with lightly whipped cream. oven at 400°F, 200°C (mark 6) for about 30 minutes until golden. Take the pies from the

Apricot crisp

A fresh fruit flavour just right to follow a heavier first course – the topping is crisp and buttery.

15-oz. can apricot halves
½ tablet orange jelly
¼ pt. boiling water
¼ pt. double cream
1 oz. butter
1 level tbsp. golden syrup
2 oz. cornflakes

SERVES 4

Pulp the apricots with their juice. Dissolve the jelly in boiling water. Cool it slightly and stir it into the apricot pulp. Divide the jelly between 4 sundae glasses and put it in a cool place to set. Whip the cream until it holds its shape and put a layer over the apricot mixture. Heat the butter and golden syrup, stir in the lightly crushed cornflakes and pile on top of the cream. Leave to harden before serving.

Norwegian omelette

Hidden away under the hot meringue is firm ice-cream. Swap the flavours for variety – pineapple, raspberry or coffee ripple are particularly good.

4 trifle sponges
2 tbsps. sherry
8 oz. granulated sugar
4 fl. oz. water
4 egg whites
few drops vanilla essence
17 fl. oz. block vanilla ice-cream

SERVES 6

Cut the trifle sponges in half lengthwise and place side by side to line the base of a shallow oval ovenproof dish. Moisten the sponges with sherry. In a saucepan, dissolve the sugar in the water then boil to bring it to soft ball stage (250°F). In a deep bowl, whip the egg whites until forming soft peaks but not looking dry. Pour the syrup into the egg whites in a steady stream, whisking all the time. Add vanilla essence

and continue to whisk until the mixture is stiff and fluffy. Place the block of ice-cream on the soaked sponge and cover with half the meringue mixture, spreading with a palette knife, ensuring that the meringue is sealed at the edge of the dish. Put the remainder of the meringue in a piping bag fitted with a large star vegetable nozzle and pipe swirls over the top of the spread meringue. Bake towards the top of the oven at 450°F, 230°C (mark 8) for 2–3 minutes to brown lightly. Serve immediately.

Note: To 'flame' Norwegian omelette/Baked Alaska, warm a tablespoonful or two of brandy, ignite it and sprinkle around the edge of meringue – not on top or it will char.

Cinnamon-apple pancakes

Have a store of pancakes in the freezer; here's a way to zip up purée of apples and enjoy a quick hot pudding too.

For basic batter
4 oz. plain or self-raising flour
¼ level tsp. salt
1 egg
½ pt. milk, approx.

For filling
4 oz. fresh white breadcrumbs
3½ oz. butter
grated rind and juice of 1 lemon
1½ lb. cooking apples, peeled and sliced
2 oz. caster sugar
1 level tsp. ground cinnamon
icing sugar

SERVES 4–8

Sift the flour and salt into a bowl. Break an egg into the centre, add 2 tbsps. milk and stir well. Gradually add the rest of the milk, stirring continuously. Beat until the consistency of single cream. Heat a 6½–7 in. frying pan, preferably one with slightly sloping sides. Brush the surface of the heated pan with a little lard or corn oil. Raise the handle-side of the pan slightly. Pour the batter in from the raised side, so that a very thin skin of batter flows over the pan; move to and fro to achieve this. Place the pan over a moderate heat and leave until the pancake is golden brown. Turn pancake over and cook the second side until golden. Turn the pancakes on to a clean tea towel. Repeat, greasing the pan each time. Makes 8 pancakes.

For the filling: Fry the crumbs in 2½ oz. butter

Oranges in caramel syrup (*see page 36*)

until golden, turning often. Place the remaining butter, lemon rind, juice, apples, sugar and cinnamon in a pan, cover and cook gently until puréed. Add the fried crumbs. Divide the mixture between the pancakes and roll up. Place them side by side in a single layer in a hot oven-proof dish, cover with foil and heat in the oven at 325°F, 170°C (mark 3) for about 20 minutes. Dust heavily with icing sugar before serving.

✳ Lemon cheesecake pie

A no-bake pie – rich and delicious.

6 oz. digestive biscuits
3 oz. caster sugar
3 oz. butter, melted
1½ 1-pt. pkts. of lemon jelly
3 tbsps. water
2 eggs, separated
¼ pt. milk
grated rind of 2 lemons
4 tbsps. lemon juice
12 oz. cottage cheese
½ oz. caster sugar
¼ pt. double cream, whipped

For decoration
¼ pt. double or whipping cream, optional

SERVES 6–8

Crush the digestive biscuits, place the crumbs in a bowl and combine them with the sugar and butter. Use the crumb mixture to line a 9-in. (2-pt.) shallow open pie plate. Press the shell into place with the back of a spoon and chill it. In a small pan over a low heat, dissolve the jelly in the water. Beat together the egg yolks and milk, pour on the jelly, stirring, and return the mixture to the saucepan. Heat it for a few minutes without boiling, then remove from the heat and add the lemon rind and juice. Cool the jelly until it begins to set. Stir in the sieved cottage cheese, or blend the jelly mixture and unsieved cheese

---

HANDY HINT

Persimmons – a fruit which may be new to you – must be yellowish-red in colour; when green they are very astringent. Wine may be used to flavour the fruit, or serve it with wedges of lemon or lime.

---

in an electric blender. Whisk the egg whites stiffly, add ½ oz. sugar and whisk again until stiff. Fold this quickly into the cheese mixture, followed by the ¼ pt. whipped cream. Spoon the cheesecake into the crumb crust, piling it up slightly. Chill it until set, then top with whipped cream.

Rhubarb flake bake

A more homely dessert – and easy to make – uses delicate pink forced rhubarb.

1½ lb. rhubarb
4 oz. sugar
2 oz. butter or margarine
2 oz. Demerara sugar
2 oz. cornflakes

SERVES 4

Trim the rhubarb and cut it into ½-in. pieces. Place with 4 oz. sugar in a casserole dish suited to table serving. Melt the butter, add the Demerara sugar and cornflakes. Turn this on to the rhubarb and cook in the oven at 350°F, 180°C (mark 4) for 25–30 minutes until golden and crisp. Serve with pouring custard.

Pears marguerite

Brandy and raisins make a happy pair; introduce pears and you have a certain winner. Start 2 hours before you want to eat.

4 oz. seedless raisins
3 tbsps. brandy
¼ pt. double cream
1 oz. glacé cherries, chopped
1 oz. angelica, chopped
1-lb. 13-oz. can pear halves, drained
angelica for decorating

SERVES 4

Place the raisins in a small pan with the brandy, bring to the boil then leave to get cold. Whisk the cream until it begins to thicken, stir in the raisins and brandy, cherries and angelica. Pile the cream mixture on the pear halves, placed hollow side up on a serving dish. Decorate with angelica leaves. Chill for 30 minutes.

Lemon layer sponge

A great favourite – a light lemon-flavoured pudding with its own built-in sauce.

2 large eggs, separated
6 oz. caster sugar
2 oz. butter
2 oz. plain or self-raising flour
½ pt. milk
3 tbsps. lemon juice
grated rind of 1 lemon

SERVES 4

Beat the egg yolks with the sugar and softened butter in a large basin. Beat the flour into the egg yolk mixture with the milk, lemon juice and rind. Whisk the egg whites until stiff and fold evenly into the mixture. Turn the mixture into a buttered 2-pt. pie dish. Bake in a water bath at 350°F, 180°C (mark 4) for 40–50 minutes until golden brown and lightly set. Serve hot.

Gipsy tart

A reminder of school days – delicious but rather sweet – and a great favourite with young people.

small can evaporated milk
6 oz. shortcrust pastry (6 oz. flour, etc.)
7 oz. soft brown sugar

SERVES 4–6

Place the unopened can of evaporated milk in a refrigerator overnight, if possible. Line a shallow baking tin 11 in. by 7½ in. with pastry, knock up the edge, and bake blind for about 10 minutes at 400°F, 200°C (mark 6).

Whisk the evaporated milk until thick and frothy. Stir in the brown sugar and pour into the pastry case. Bake at 350°F, 180°C (mark 4) for a further 20–25 minutes, until the filling is set. Serve warm or cold.

Banana condé

For extra speed use a can of creamed rice instead of making your own.

2 oz. pudding rice
2 level tbsps. custard powder
1 pt. milk
1–2 level tbsps. sugar
2 bananas
sieved apricot jam
1 level tsp. instant coffee powder
1 level tsp. Demerara sugar

SERVES 4

Cook the rice in boiling water for 15 minutes. Drain. Blend the custard powder with a little of the milk. Heat the rest of the milk and when just boiling, pour over the blended powder, add sugar, stir and return to the pan, together with the rice. Bring back to the boil and boil gently for 2–3 minutes. Cool, stir occasionally and divide between 4 individual dishes. Just before serving, peel the bananas and slice them. Arrange, overlapping, on top of the rice. Brush with warm sieved apricot jam. Sprinkle lightly with a mixture of instant coffee powder and Demerara sugar.

*Streusel pear flan

The rich pastry case makes all the difference to the morish filling.

6 oz. pâte sucrée (6 oz. plain flour, etc.)

For filling
2 1-lb. 13-oz. cans pear halves
2 oz. fresh white breadcrumbs
2 oz. soft dark brown sugar
2 oz. chopped mixed peel
2 oz. glacé cherries, halved
2 tbsps. warm apricot glaze

SERVES 6–8

Roll out the pastry and use it to line an 8-in. fluted flan dish. Drain the pears. Remove a thin slice from the rounded surface of 8 pears so that they will sit evenly. Chop these pieces along with the rest of the pears; place the chopped pear in the flan base. In a bowl blend together the breadcrumbs, sugar and peel. Scatter this over the chopped pears. Arrange the pear halves hollow side up on the crumb mixture with cherries between. Bake in the oven at

HANDY HINT

If you use the saucepan method to cook a steamed pudding, remember to add a piece of lemon or a little vinegar to the water to prevent discoloration of an aluminium pan during cooking; and it's a good idea to sit the basin on crossed skewers, an old upturned ovenproof plate or saucer, or a metal ring such as a shallow pastry cutter, to raise the basin off the base of the saucepan.

400°F, 200°C (mark 6) for about 1 hour – cover the pastry with foil if beginning to over-brown. Glaze the pears with apricot glaze and serve warm or cold with thick or soured cream.

Velvet refrigerator cake

A make-ahead dinner party dessert.

24–26 soft sponge fingers
6 oz. caster sugar
2 level tbsps. cornflour
¾ pt. milk
½ pt. double cream
2 oz. unsweetened chocolate
2 egg yolks
1 oz. butter
1 level tsp. powdered gelatine
2 tsps. water
toasted flaked almonds for decoration

SERVES 4–6

Line the sides of a loaf tin measuring 7 in. by 5 in. by 2½ in. (top measurement) with a strip of non-stick paper. Arrange some sponge fingers to cover the base and sides. In a saucepan blend together the sugar and cornflour, gradually stir in the milk and ¼ pt. cream. Break the chocolate into pieces, add to the milk and bring slowly to the boil, stirring all the time. Boil gently for 2–3 minutes, stirring. Cool for a few minutes then beat in the egg yolks. Return to the heat and cook for 1 minute more. Beat in the butter. Sprinkle the gelatine over 2 tsps. water and stir this into the chocolate mixture. Cool, stirring occasionally. When beginning to thicken, pour half the mixture over the sponge fingers. Cover with another layer of sponge fingers. Spoon over the remainder of the chocolate mixture and cut the sponge fingers level with the chocolate mixture. Use the bits to place over the chocolate in a final layer. Leave overnight in the refrigerator. To serve, turn out on to a flat dish and remove the paper. Whip the rest of the cream. Cover the top of the cake with cream and strew with almonds.

Velvet refrigerator cake (*see above*)

Simnel cake (see below) and Hot Cross buns (see page 47)

Spring cakes

Oregon prune cake

This one has a sugary prune topping.

4 oz. plain flour
$\frac{1}{2}$ level tsp. baking powder
$\frac{1}{2}$ level tsp. salt
2 oz. butter or block margarine
4 oz. caster sugar
1 egg, beaten
1 tbsp. milk

For topping
$15\frac{1}{2}$-oz. can prunes, drained and stoned
$\frac{1}{4}$ level tsp. ground cinnamon
1 level tbsp. sugar
2 oz. shelled walnuts, chopped
1 oz. butter, melted

Grease and base-line a shallow $7\frac{1}{2}$-in. square tin.
Sift together the flour, baking powder and salt
into a bowl. Rub in the butter until the mixture
resembles fine breadcrumbs. Stir in the sugar
and mix to a softish consistency with egg and
milk. Turn into the tin, level the surface and
lightly press the prunes into the mixture. Combine the cinnamon, sugar, walnuts and butter.
Spoon over prunes. Bake in the centre of the
oven at 375°F, 190°C (mark 5) for 40–45 minutes.
Cool slightly; turn out. Eat warm.

Simnel cake

For tea at Easter-time; a traditional pleasure in
whichever month it falls

8 oz. plain flour
pinch of salt
$\frac{1}{2}$ level tsp. grated nutmeg
$\frac{1}{2}$ level tsp. ground cinnamon
8 oz. currants, cleaned
4 oz. sultanas, cleaned
3 oz. chopped mixed peel
4 oz. glacé cherries, quartered
6 oz. butter
6 oz. caster sugar
3 eggs

For the almond paste
8 oz. ground almonds
4 oz. icing sugar, sifted
4 oz. caster sugar
1 egg
lemon juice
egg white or melted jam

Grease and line a 7-in. diameter round cake
tin. Make the almond paste in the usual way,
take a third of it and shape into a circle slightly
smaller than the tin. Sift together the dry cake
ingredients, add the fruit, peel and glacé

cherries. Cream the butter and sugar until doubled in volume. Beat in each egg separately. Fold the flour into the creamed mixture, adding a little milk if required to give a dropping consistency. Put half the mixture into the prepared cake tin, spreading it a little up the sides of the tin. Place the round of almond paste on top. Cover with the rest of the mixture, spreading evenly. Bake at 300°F, 150°C (mark 1–2) for $2\frac{1}{2}$–3 hours. Cool on a wire rack.

Brush the top of the cake with a little egg white or melted jam, and coat with almond paste. Decorate with 11 small almond paste balls, or mark a pattern on the surface; brush the surface of the paste with egg white. Tie a band of greaseproof paper round the sides and put the cake in a moderate oven to brown the paste evenly. Run a little glacé icing in a circle in the centre, and add a fluffy yellow chicken and ribbon bow.

✳ Chocolate fudge cake

A really dark mixture with a cup-cake icing, this keeps well for up to 1 week.

3 oz. butter or block margarine
3 oz. caster sugar
1 large egg
2 oz. golden syrup
5 oz. plain flour
1 oz. cocoa
$\frac{1}{2}$ level tsp. bicarbonate of soda
2 level tsps. baking powder
few drops vanilla essence
$\frac{1}{4}$ pt. buttermilk

For frosting
2 oz. plain chocolate
3 tbsps. water
1 oz. butter
7 oz. icing sugar, sifted

Cream together the fat and sugar until light and fluffy. Beat in the egg and syrup. Sift together the flour, cocoa, bicarbonate of soda and baking powder and add alternately with the essence and buttermilk, beating lightly. Turn the mixture into a greased and lined 7–$7\frac{1}{2}$ in. deep sandwich tin, or use a shallow tin and raise the sides with a greaseproof paper collar to give a total depth of about 2 in. Bake in the centre of the oven at 375°F, 190°C (mark 5) for about 30 minutes. Turn out to cool on a wire rack. Fix a band of double greaseproof paper round the cake to come $\frac{3}{4}$–1 in. above the highest part of the cake; secure it with a paper clip or pin. Spoon the frosting (below) over the top when beginning to

set and swirl with a knife. Leave until firm but not hard before removing paper and cutting.

To make frosting: In a small pan, melt the chocolate with the water; do not boil. Off the heat, add the butter in small pieces. When melted, gradually beat in the icing sugar.

✳ Easter biscuits

This lightly spiced mixture eats well at any time of the year.

4 oz. butter
5 oz. caster sugar
2 egg yolks
6 oz. plain flour
2 oz. rice flour
1 level tsp. mixed spice
2 oz. currants
milk to mix

For glaze
egg white
caster sugar

MAKES ABOUT 24

Cream the butter and sugar until light and fluffy. Beat in the egg yolks one at a time. Sift together the flours and spice and work them into the creamed ingredients. Lastly add the currants and a little milk if needed. Knead lightly. Roll out between sheets of non-stick paper to $\frac{1}{4}$–$\frac{1}{8}$ in. thickness. Cut into 2-in. rounds with a fluted cutter. Lift the rounds with a palette knife on to a baking-sheet lined with greaseproof paper or non-stick paper. With the back of a knife indent lines across the biscuits about $\frac{1}{4}$–$\frac{1}{2}$ in. apart. Bake in the oven centre or just above at 350°F, 180°C (mark 4) for 15–20 minutes. After 10 minutes brush the biscuits evenly with unbeaten egg white and dredge lightly with caster sugar.

✳ Lemon loaf cake

Good to make and eat whilst fresh – though this cake does keep and mellow, wrapped in kitchen foil for 2 or 3 days. The very thin lemon glaze drooled over the warm cake makes it moist and gives the crust a delicious flavour.

4 oz. block margarine
6 oz. caster sugar
2 large eggs
grated rind and juice of 1 lemon
6 oz. self-raising flour
2 oz. icing sugar, sifted

By hand, cream together the margarine and sugar. Beat in the eggs one at a time with the grated lemon rind. Lightly beat in the flour. Turn the mixture into a loaf tin, top measurement 8½ in. by 4½ in., lined with greaseproof paper. Level the surface and bake in the centre of the oven at 350°F, 180°C (mark 4) for 50–60 minutes. A slight dip may form in the centre of the cake but it will not spoil the texture. Turn out upside down on to a wire rack. Combine 2 tbsps. lemon juice with the icing sugar. Prick the cake all over with a fine skewer and whilst still hot brush evenly all over with the lemon glaze, reverse and repeat on the top crust until all the glaze is absorbed. Cool on the rack.

Ginger nuts

Old time favourites with traditional cracked tops. Use the low measure if you prefer a light ginger flavour.

4 oz. self-raising flour
½ level tsp. bicarbonate of soda
1–2 level tsps. ground ginger
2 level tsps. caster sugar
2 oz. butter
3 oz. golden syrup

MAKES ABOUT 24

Sift together the flour, bicarbonate of soda, ginger and sugar. Melt the butter, stir in the syrup. Add to the dry ingredients and stir well. Roll the mixture into small balls and place them well apart on greased baking sheets. Flatten them slightly and bake just above the centre of the oven for 15–20 minutes at 375°F, 190°C (mark 5). Cool for a few minutes before lifting carefully from the baking sheet. Cool. Store in an airtight tin.

Coconut wafers

Crisp and wafer-thin, these store well in an airtight tin. They are handy as a crunchy partner to soft textured fruit desserts and ice-cream as well as with tea, coffee and chocolate.

2 oz. butter
2 oz. caster sugar
1 level tbsp. golden syrup (1½ oz.)
2 tsps. lemon juice
2 oz. plain flour
1 oz. desiccated coconut, very finely chopped

MAKES ABOUT 16

Cream together the butter and sugar until light and fluffy. Beat in the syrup. Fold in the lemon juice, flour and coconut and mix thoroughly. Place in 1 tsp. at a time on a greased baking sheet, keeping them apart as the wafers spread. Bake at 350°F, 180°C (mark 4) for about 15 minutes, when the edges should be golden brown and the centres lightly coloured. Cool slightly before lifting carefully from the tray with a palette knife on to a wire rack.

✳ Hot cross buns

(*see picture page 45*)

Served for breakfast fresh from the oven – on the evening before, make the dough as far as *. Cover the tray with aluminium foil and store it in a refrigerator.

Before baking remove foil, lightly cover with a cloth and leave the buns in a warm place until double their size. Do this when you make the early cup of tea. Now brush with milk and bake as directed.

14 oz. plain strong bread flour
pinch of salt
1 level tsp. ground cinnamon
1 level tsp. ground nutmeg
3 oz. currants, cleaned
1 oz. chopped mixed peel
½ oz. fresh bakers' yeast
¼ pt. milk, good measure
3 oz. sugar
2 oz. butter, melted
1 large egg
milk and sugar to glaze

MAKES 14

Sift together the flour, salt and spices. Add the fruit. Dissolve the yeast in tepid milk and add the sugar, melted fat and beaten egg. Pour into a well made in the centre of the flour. Beat with the hand until smooth, then cover and set to rise until doubled in size. Knead lightly on a floured board. Divide into 14 pieces, and shape into buns. Place on a well-greased baking sheet (allowing room to spread). Mark a cross on each, using the back of a knife * (stop here if making overnight). Put them in a warm place lightly covered with a clean tea towel to prove for about 20–30 minutes. Glaze with milk before putting the buns in the oven at 450°F, 230°C (mark 8) for 10–15 minutes. Bring to the boil 2 tbsps. milk, 2 tbsps. water and 1½ oz. sugar; boil this for 2 minutes and then use it to glaze the buns just before the end of the baking. Cool on a wire rack or serve warm.

Lunch from a fork (*see page 9*)

CHAPTER TWO

SUMMER

The fruits of Summer are at their best served simply. Apricots, home-grown cherries and gooseberries each make a delightful compote. They're a good buy for pies and flans too, with a hint of spice or a vanilla pod added to the syrup. There will be large dessert gooseberries to eat without cooking, and it's strawberry time, so make the most of a short season. A little goes a long way in shortcakes, as a filling in a sweet pastry case glazed with warm redcurrant jelly and the odd few brighten up a fresh fruit salad. Enjoy those large imported yellow peaches gently poached with lemon and cinnamon or flavour the syrup with orange liqueur. Do you like olives? Buy them loose – they're cheaper.

Salad vegetables are plentiful. Juicy, peppery garden radishes for picnic munching, a variety of crisp lettuces, cool cucumbers and firm deep-coloured tomatoes are just a few. For cooking, choose tender broad beans, fresh green peas, home-grown corn on the cob and a little bit of a luxury – asparagus. Fresh shellfish, crab, lobster, prawns and shrimps are at their best and, in August, the 12th heralds the beginning of the game season.

School holidays, visitors and picnics can make this a wicked season for housekeeping. Don't underestimate the value of eggs along with that of cheese, especially for family catering when days are warmer. Egg and bacon pie or poached eggs on fried bread with a cheese and mushroom sauce is a great choice for high tea or supper. Cottage cheese is high in protein but needs seasoning with perhaps French mustard or lemon juice. Lancashire and Leicestershire cheeses toast well. Always have grated cheese on the table with salads.

The cold meat counter offers some sound buys if pre-cut to an economical thickness. Meaty brawns, chopped pork and ham, Frankfurters and aromatic continental sausages have little or no cereal filler; a selection makes an attractive and filling platter. Home-made pâtés, terrines and quiches are good standbys too. From the kitchen, cut-and-come-again cold joints for warm weather salad meals are the wisest choice. A bacon joint, collar or forehock, and a boned shoulder of lamb lend themselves to economical carving, or a piece of salt beef, slowly simmered, can be sliced wafer thin. For unbeatable flavour and value buy an ox-tongue to press at home. A big chicken cooked in a roasting bag makes succulent cold eating; use the juices as a base for a light summer soup. Make Scotch eggs – sausagemeat costs less than sausages. Introduce black pudding as a hot dish – cut it in thick slices, sauté for 10 minutes and serve with a sauce of lightly browned onion, raisins and apple.

For the freezer
Capture Summer for the Winter and stow away the soft fruits and others. Open-freeze raspberries, loganberries, currants red and black (don't worry if there is not time to remove the stems – they come away easily when frozen), cooking gooseberries (whole without sugar or puréed to save valuable space) and a few stoned red cherries for pies. Some farms offer pick-your-own facilities where you should pay less than in the shops. Strawberries with their high percentage of water tend to collapse on thawing but strawberry purée has an excellent flavour. Pop in the odd summer pudding or two as well.

Don't miss out on year-round herbs; freeze a 'nest egg' at their peak. Perennials like chives, fennel, mint and parsley, which are constantly needed for use later, don't take much space chopped and packed in small amounts.

Tomatoes are at their cheapest towards the end of the season and can be frozen whole in a polythene bag. Remember they have a high water content so when thawed are not suitable for salad use, but are valuable additions for stews and made-up dishes in the winter, likewise concentrated purée or sauce. Beans are in abundance now, catch them young and really fresh from the garden. Track down limes and pack juice and slivers of peel separately for round the year Daiquires. There may be some early apple windfalls in August, though under-ripe they purée quite satisfactorily.

Summer fruits
Apart from those which are available the year round, apricots, cherries, gooseberries, limes, lychees, mangoes, nectarines, peaches, persimons, plums, pomegranates, raspberries, rhubarb (end of the season), strawberries, blackcurrants, redcurrants, figs (fresh), loganberries, blackberries (arrive end of season).

Summer vegetables
Apart from those which are available the year round, aubergines (end of their season), asparagus, avocados, carrots (young), green beans, broad beans, endive, fennel, globe artichokes, courgettes, new potatoes (home grown), peas (home grown), salsify, shallots, spinach, chillies, vegetable marrow, corn on the cob, okra, turnips (young).

Poultry and game
Apart from those which are available the year round:

Guinea fowl	(all the year but best November–January)
Venison	(July 1st–February 28th)
Black game (capercaillie, black cock)	(August 20th–December 20th)
Grouse	(August 12th–December 10th)
Hare	(August 1st–February 28th)

Ptarmigan (August 20th–December 10th)
Wood pigeon (all the year but best August–September)
Snipe (August 12th–January 31st).

Summer menus

*(Dishes marked * are included in the recipes on pages 52 to 89)*

Dinner for 6
*Smoked haddock ramekins
Brown bread and butter

*Lamb oysters
Potato croquettes
Minted peas

*Melon and grapefruit jelly

Dinner for 6
Orange and walnut salad

*Bacon and mushroom pie
Lemon dressed carrots

*Blackcurrant cream slice

Picnic for 6
Fruit juice cocktail

*Bumper sausage roll
*Picnic tomatoes
Sliced cucumber and onion salad
Lettuce wedges

*Almond bars
Whole sugared strawberries

Supper for 4
*Salad niçoise

*Summer lamb casserole

*Cherry pie
Pouring cream

Teenagers' eightsome
Chilled grapefruit juice

*Pork and pimiento kebabs
*Pitta bread
Tomato and onion salad

*Banana creole

Supper for 4
Tomato salad
Brown bread and butter

*Kulebyaka
Runner beans with butter sauce

*Compote of peaches

Sunday evening for 6
Chilled fruit cup

*Lemon chicken double crust pie
*Noodles rusticana
*Tomato coleslaw

*Pineapple and grape salad

Lunch for 4
Chilled grapefruit juice

*Glazed collar bacon with apricots
Pan-cooked potatoes
Garden peas

*Queen of puddings

Supper for 2
*Egg mayonnaise

*Herring parcels with mustard
butter
Grilled tomatoes
Fingers of bread and butter
Dressed watercress sprigs

*Ice cream fiesta

Garden lunch for 4
Grapefruit with ginger

*Salmon and cheese flan
New potato mayonnaise
Sliced tomatoes

*Norwegian cream
Cigarette wafers

Summer evening for 6
*Smoked trout pâté
Melba toast

*Lamb cutlets paprika
Buttered corn kernels
Leaf spinach
Fluffy rice

*Grapefruit sorbet
Fan wafers

Cut the cost menus

*Spiced shoulder of lamb
Whole new potato salad
Sliced tomatoes with onion and
watercress

*Frosted gooseberry plate pie

*Bobotie
Runner beans
Stuffed tomatoes

Fresh fruit salad

*Cream of cucumber soup

*Pasta niçoise
Oven-fresh French bread

*Summer sponge pudding

*Picnic pies
*Mushroom salad
Tossed salad greens

*Gooseberry fool

Summer starters

Smoked haddock ramekins

8 oz. smoked haddock
1 level tbsp. aspic jelly crystals
$\frac{1}{4}$ pt. natural yoghurt
8 capers, chopped
2 hard-boiled eggs, chopped
salt and freshly ground black pepper
paprika pepper and parsley sprigs for
    garnish

SERVES 6

Poach the haddock in water to cover until the flesh flakes easily. Drain, skin and mash the flesh until smooth. Dissolve the aspic jelly crystals in 2 tbsps. boiling water, stir in the yoghurt, fish, capers, hard-boiled egg and seasoning to taste. Divide the mixture between 6 ramekin dishes and chill. Garnish with paprika and parsley.

Egg mayonnaise

Mayonnaise offers endless possibilities; for a change omit the curry powder and add a teaspoonful of snipped chives or a few finely chopped shrimps or prawns.

2 eggs
2 tbsps. thick mayonnaise
2 tbsps. soured cream
$\frac{1}{2}$ level tsp. curry powder
lettuce
paprika pepper

SERVES 2

Boil the eggs for 10 minutes then drain and plunge into cold water; when they are cool enough to handle, remove the shells and for quick cooling leave the eggs in water until cold. In a small bowl, combine the mayonnaise, soured cream and curry powder; leave to stand for 30 minutes. Put a lettuce leaf on each plate and top with the eggs, cut lengthwise and yolk

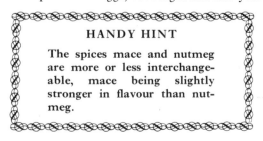

HANDY HINT

The spices mace and nutmeg are more or less interchangeable, mace being slightly stronger in flavour than nutmeg.

uppermost. Spoon the mayonnaise over and garnish with paprika.

✳ Smoked trout pâté

8 oz. smoked trout
2 oz. butter
3 oz. fresh white breadcrumbs
finely grated rind and juice of 1 lemon
salt and freshly ground black pepper
pinch grated nutmeg
$\frac{1}{4}$ pt. single cream
$\frac{1}{4}$–$\frac{1}{2}$ pt. aspic jelly

SERVES 6

Remove the skin and bones from the trout and finely chop the flesh. Melt 2 oz. butter in a small pan and pour it on to the breadcrumbs with the lemon rind and juice. Season well with salt, pepper and nutmeg. Add the fish to the breadcrumbs and fold the cream through. Spoon the mixture into 6 ramekins (4 fl. oz. each). Make up aspic jelly and when it is on the point of setting, spoon it over the fish mixture. Chill.

Dressed tomato with avocado

A clean-tasting starter to a meal, garnished with onion rings and dressed in an unusual vinaigrette that's seasoned with paprika and tomato paste.

6 firm tomatoes, skinned
1 small onion, skinned
2 avocados
juice of 1 lemon
4 tbsps. salad oil
2 tbsps. red wine vinegar
1 level tsp. tomato paste
1 level tsp. paprika pepper
salt and freshly ground black pepper
$\frac{1}{2}$ clove garlic, skinned and crushed

SERVES 4

Thinly slice the tomatoes and cut the onion into thin rings. Halve the avocados and carefully ease out the stones with the point of a knife. Remove the skin by placing them cut side downwards and running the point of a knife along the centre of the skin, then carefully peel back the skin from the narrow end. Cut the flesh into dice and turn gently in lemon juice. In a tightly lidded container, combine the oil, vinegar,

tomato paste, paprika, salt, pepper and garlic. Arrange the tomatoes and onion rings in overlapping circles around the edge of four small plates. Pile diced avocado in the centre and spoon the dressing over.
Note: Prepare within 1 hour of serving.

Courgettes à la grecque

Home produced courgettes are in season so make the best of them while they are less expensive. Serve as a starter or salad course.

2 small onions
3 tbsps. olive or corn oil
1 clove garlic, skinned and crushed
¼ pt. dry white wine
salt and freshly ground black pepper
1¼ lb. courgettes
1 lb. tomatoes
chopped fresh chervil

SERVES 4–6

Skin and thinly slice the onions and sauté them in oil until soft but not coloured. Add the garlic, wine and plenty of seasoning. Wipe courgettes, discard end slices and cut remainder into rings. Peel and quarter the tomatoes and discard the seeds. Add the courgettes and tomatoes to the pan and cook gently without covering, for 10 minutes; cool. Garnish with chervil.

Sweet-sour onions

Still crunchy and deliciously juicy, these onions are just right as part of an hors d'oeuvre selection.

1 lb. small even-sized onions, skinned
½ pt. water
¼ pt. malt vinegar
2½ oz. granulated sugar
2 oz. sultanas
2 level tbsps. tomato paste
2 tbsps. corn oil
salt and freshly ground black pepper
cayenne pepper
chopped parsley

SERVES 6

Place the onions, water, vinegar, sugar, sultanas, tomato paste and oil in a saucepan with salt, pepper and cayenne to season. Heat slowly to dissolve the sugar, bring to the boil, reduce the heat, cover and simmer for about 45 minutes. Drain off the juice, reduce a little by fast boiling

and pour it over the onions before leaving them to go cold. Serve garnished with chopped parsley.

Cucumber portugaise

This looks pretty on the table with its delicate green colour; double the quantity for a salad for a buffet table.

2 large cucumbers
4 oz. onion, skinned and finely chopped
4 tbsps. cooking oil
4 medium sized firm tomatoes, peeled, seeded and diced
2 level tsps. tomato paste
2 tbsps. garlic vinegar
pinch dried thyme
salt and freshly ground black pepper

SERVES 6

Thinly pare the cucumbers using a potato-peeler, then cut into 1-in. lengths. Cut each piece into quarters along the length. Remove the centre seeds with the point of a knife and discard. Plunge the cucumber into boiling salted water for 5 minutes, drain and refresh under cold running water. Sauté the onion in the oil until tender, add the tomatoes, the paste, vinegar and thyme. Blend the cucumber with the tomato. Season well and turn into a serving dish. Chill and serve with crusty bread.

Salad niçoise

A substantial salad starter to balance a one-pot main course.

1 medium sized green pepper
1 small onion, skinned
2-oz. can anchovy fillets
milk
7-oz. can tuna steak
½ lb. French beans, cooked
8 stoned black olives
3 tbsps. French dressing
1 egg, hard-boiled
1 tomato, sliced

SERVES 4

Cut the stem end off the pepper, discard the seeds and membrane and slice the flesh finely. Slice the onion wafer thin. Drain the oil from the anchovies, turn them on to a saucer, just cover with milk and leave for 10 minutes. Drain on kitchen paper. Drain the tuna and flake.

In a bowl toss together the beans, green pepper, onion, tuna and olives. Add the French dressing and toss again. Serve on individual plates. Cut the egg into eight and slice the tomato, use these to garnish the salad, along with a lattice of anchovy fillets.

Melon and grape cocktail

1 medium sized honeydew melon
1 lb. black grapes
4 tbsps. French dressing (made with garlic vinegar)
½ oz. flaked almonds

SERVES 6–8

Halve the melon and discard the seeds. Make melon balls, using a potato ball scoop, or cut the flesh into large dice. Remove the pips from the grapes, using the rounded end of a clean hair grip. Marinade the melon and grapes in dressing for at least 1 hour before spooning into glasses. Garnish with toasted flaked almonds.

✳ Chilled watercress soup

This is a popular and economical cold soup for a crowd which can be made a day ahead, but do not incorporate the cream until the day you intend serving it.

4 bunches watercress, washed and trimmed
2 oz. butter
6 oz. onion, skinned and chopped
3 pt. chicken stock
¼ level tsp. salt
freshly ground black pepper
1 tbsp. lemon juice
2 bayleaves
2 oz. plain flour
1 pt. creamy milk
¼ pt. single cream

SERVES 12

Finely chop the watercress sprigs. Melt 1 oz. butter, add the onion and sauté until soft and transparent. Add the watercress and sauté for a further 5 minutes, covered. Pour over the stock (check seasoning if stock cubes are used) and add the salt, pepper, lemon juice and bayleaves. Bring to the boil, reduce the heat, cover and simmer gently for 45 minutes. Discard the bayleaves and blend or sieve the soup to give a fine even texture.

In a clean pan, make a roux with 1 oz. butter and the flour. Add the milk and sieved mixture

and slowly bring to the boil, stirring. Adjust seasoning. Chill until quite cold. Stir in the cream and serve garnished with tiny watercress sprigs or chopped parsley.

✳ Gazpacho

Spanish delight, the choice of garlic lovers; enjoy gazpacho when tomatoes are deep red and sun ripened.

1 lb. fully ripe tomatoes
1 small onion, skinned
1 small green pepper, seeded
1 clove garlic, skinned
3 tbsps. wine vinegar
3 tbsps. olive oil
15-oz. can tomato juice
1–2 tbsps. lemon juice
salt and pepper
¼ cucumber
toast croûtons

SERVES 6

Wash the tomatoes, dry and roughly slice them. Slice the onion and green pepper. Place the tomatoes, onion, green pepper, garlic, vinegar and olive oil in an electric blender goblet and purée. Turn the mixture into a basin and add tomato and lemon juice and seasoning to taste. Chill thoroughly. Serve with diced cucumber and croûtons.

✳ Cream of cucumber soup

This is a clear tasting soup to partner most main courses. A touch of curry powder added with the butter makes a change.

1½ pt. chicken stock
1 large cucumber
1 tsp. finely chopped shallot or onion
1 oz. butter
¾ oz. flour
salt and pepper
green colouring
2 egg yolks
4 tbsps. milk
freshly grated cucumber and chopped mint for garnish

SERVES 6

If home-made chicken stock is not available, use 1½ pt. water with 1 chicken stock cube. Peel the cucumber and cut it into ½-in. slices.

In a saucepan, bring to the boil the stock, cucumber and shallot. Reduce the heat and simmer for 15–20 minutes until the cucumber is soft, then either rub it through a fine sieve or put it in the electric blender. Melt the butter in the pan, stir in the flour and cook over a low heat for a few minutes. Slowly stir in the sieved cucumber and stock. Bring to the boil, check the seasoning and simmer for 5 minutes more. Cool and use a mere drop of colouring to make the mixture a delicate green. Blend the egg yolks and milk together, add a little soup, stir well and pour back into the pan. Reheat but *do not boil*. Garnish and serve.
Note: If preferred serve chilled; thin with a little milk if required.

Chilled avocado soup
(*see picture page 57*)

Whipped up in an electric blender, this soup takes only seconds to prepare.

2 avocados
15-oz. can vichyssoise soup
½ pt. milk
¼ pt. chicken stock
2 tbsps. lemon juice

SERVES 4–6

Halve, stone and peel the avocados. Roughly chop them and put in a blender with the vichyssoise, milk, stock and lemon juice. Blend at high speed until smooth. Pour into a jug and chill, covered, for up to 4 hours. Serve in small bowls and garnish with chives.

Lemon and mushroom soup

This soup is quick to prepare and makes good use of any available chicken stock.

2 oz. butter
1½ oz. flour
1 pt. chicken stock
½ pt. milk
½ lb. mushrooms, wiped and finely chopped or minced
2 tbsps. chopped parsley
salt and freshly ground black pepper
lemon juice
¼ pt. single cream

SERVES 6

Heat the butter in a saucepan and stir in the flour, cook for a few minutes then stir in the chicken stock and bring to the boil, stirring. Add the milk, mushrooms and the chopped parsley. Season with salt, pepper and lemon juice to taste. Cook gently for 5 minutes then stir in the single cream and reheat without boiling.

Chilled prawn soup
(*see picture page 56*)

1 large can evaporated milk, chilled
4 tbsps. lemon juice
2 level tsps. finely grated onion
1 level tsp. made mustard
2 tbsps. double cream
salt
6 oz. peeled prawns, finely chopped
3 tbsps. finely chopped parsley
paprika

SERVES 4–6

Combine the evaporated milk, lemon juice, onion, mustard, cream and salt to taste. Gently stir in the prawns and parsley. Pour into glasses or soup cups and sprinkle the tops with paprika. Chill for about 1 hour. Accompany with Melba toast.

Grapefruit and walnut mayonnaise

An appetiser salad, lightly dressed and so easy to put together; ring the changes with fresh orange segments.

3 large grapefruits
2 oz. shelled walnut halves
4 tbsps. thick mayonnaise
mint

SERVES 4

Using a stainless steel knife, over a plate to collect the juice, peel the skin from the fruit. Remove all traces of white pith. Segment the grapefruit and arrange the slices on 4 small side plates. Spoon 1–2 tsps. of the collected juice over the fruit. Roughly break the walnuts and sprinkle at one end of each plate. Place 1 tbsp. well seasoned mayonnaise beside the walnuts and decorate with a small sprig of mint.

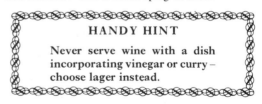

HANDY HINT

Never serve wine with a dish incorporating vinegar or curry – choose lager instead.

✳ Peter's pâté

There is just a hint of garlic in this pleasant all-rounder, which should be sliced rather than spooned.

1 lb. pig's liver
2 oz. butter
1 onion, skinned and chopped
¼ lb. streaky bacon, rinded and diced
¼ lb. belly pork, diced
1 clove garlic, skinned
1½ level tbsps. tomato paste
⅛ level tsp. freshly ground black pepper
⅛ level tsp. garlic salt
⅛ level tsp. dried basil
⅛ level tsp. salt
4 tbsps. red wine
grated rind of ¼ lemon
1 bayleaf
lettuce, cucumber and tomatoes for garnish

SERVES 8

Remove the skin and gristle from the liver. Melt the butter in a saucepan, fry the onion then add all the ingredients except the garnish. Cover and cook slowly for about 1½ hours. Discard the bayleaf and drain the meat, retaining the liquor. Mince the meat finely and stir in the liquor; for a very smooth pâté, purée the meats and liquor in an electric blender. Turn the pâté into a 1½-pt. pie dish, cover with foil and cook at 350°F, 180°C (mark 4) for 30 minutes. Leave in a cold place until cold, then refrigerate. To serve, turn out and garnish.

Chilled prawn soup (*see page 55*)

Chilled avocado soup (*see page 55*)

✳ Cold cheese soufflé

Season this light and frothy soufflé mixture well to bring out the flavour.

$\frac{1}{8}$ level tsp. each salt, black pepper and cayenne pepper
$\frac{1}{2}$ level tsp. French mustard
2 tsps. tarragon vinegar
$\frac{1}{2}$ pt. aspic jelly
2 oz. Parmesan cheese, grated
2 oz. Gruyère cheese, finely grated
$\frac{1}{2}$ pt. double cream
$\frac{1}{4}$ pt. thick mayonnaise
2 oz. toasted breadcrumbs
mustard and cress

SERVES 6

Tie collars of greaseproof paper round 6 $2\frac{3}{4}$-in. diameter soufflé dishes, to extend 2 in. above the rims of the dishes. Place the salt, pepper, cayenne and mustard in a bowl. Add the vinegar and aspic, which should be cold but not quite set. Beat until frothy then add the cheeses and mix well. Whip the cream until almost stiff and fold it in, along with the mayonnaise. Blend the mixture thoroughly then spoon it into the prepared soufflé dishes and allow to set in a cool place. Remove the paper collars. Decorate each soufflé with toasted breadcrumbs pressed around the sides and a sprig of mustard and cress in the centre.

Avocado mousse

A subtle balance of flavours, this ring salad looks attractive on the table. Make and eat on the same day.

1 level tbsp. powdered gelatine
$\frac{1}{4}$ pt. water
3 avocados
lemon juice
1 level tsp. finely chopped onion
2 tsps. Worcestershire sauce
$\frac{1}{4}$ pt. rich chicken stock
salt and freshly ground black pepper
$\frac{1}{4}$ pt. double cream, whipped
$\frac{1}{4}$ pt. thick mayonnaise
2 egg whites

For dressing
1 small green pepper
4–6 spring onions
2 oz. black olives
$\frac{1}{4}$ pt. French dressing

SERVES 8

In a small bowl, sprinkle the gelatine over the water. Place the bowl over a pan of hot water and leave until dissolved. Cool but do not allow the gelatine to set. Halve, stone and peel the avocados and mash the flesh with a little lemon juice until smooth. Add the onion, Worcestershire sauce, chicken stock and gelatine; season well and leave in a cold place until it begins to set. Whisk the cream to the same consistency as the mayonnaise, fold both through the gelatine mixture. Stiffly whisk the egg whites and fold these in. Turn the mousse into a $2\frac{1}{2}$-pt. oiled ring mould and refrigerate.

For dressing: Seed and blanch the pepper; cool it under running water and cut it into fine strips. Trim and finely snip the spring onions. Add the pepper, onion and whole olives to the dressing. Unmould the mousse. Drain some of the flavourings from the dressing and use to garnish the mousse, serving the remaining dressing separately.

Summer main course dishes

Lemon chicken double crust pie

Think ahead and cook the chicken for this pie the day before in a roaster bag. Strip the flesh from the carcass and refrigerate when cold with the juices stored separately.

3-lb. oven-ready chicken
$1\frac{1}{2}$ oz. butter
3 level tbsps. flour
1–2 oz. cheese, grated
2 tbsps. chopped parsley
grated rind and juice of 1 lemon
salt and freshly ground black pepper
12 oz. shortcrust pastry (12 oz. flour, etc.)
beaten egg or milk to glaze
8-oz. pkt. frozen asparagus spears

SERVES 6

Remove the chicken giblets and cook the bird in a roaster bag with the oven set at 375°F, 190°C (mark 5) for about $1\frac{1}{2}$ hours. Drain off the chicken juices and make up to $\frac{1}{2}$ pt. with water. Skin the chicken, strip the meat from the bones and roughly chop it. Melt 1 oz. butter in a pan, stir in the flour and cook for 1–2 minutes. Blend in the chicken juices to make a sauce; simmer for a few minutes, then stir in the cheese, chopped chicken, parsley, lemon rind and 2–3 tsps. lemon juice. Adjust the seasoning and allow to cool. Roll out the pastry and use half to line a 10-in. metal or foil pie plate. Spread the filling over, damp the edges and top with a pastry lid, sealing the edges. Make a slit in the centre, brush with egg or milk, and bake at 400°F, 200°C (mark 6) for about 45 minutes. Garnish with freshly cooked asparagus glazed with melted butter.

Chicken mille feuilles

Quick and right for a buffet party. The secret, here, is to buy a chicken larger than you need, roast it for the family meal one day and keep some of the flesh for the party session the next.

7½-oz. pkt. frozen puff pastry, thawed
8 oz. full fat cream cheese
2 tsps. lemon juice
4 level tsps. thick mayonnaise
¼ level tsp. salt
freshly ground black pepper
12 oz. cooked chicken flesh
3–4 lettuce leaves, finely shredded
¼ lb. firm tomatoes, skinned

SERVES 4

Roll out the pastry into a rectangle 12 in. by 11 in. (¼ in. thick) and prick well. Place it on a dampened baking sheet, divide equally into three, crosswise, and separate the pieces slightly. Bake at 400°F, 200°C (mark 6) for 20–25 minutes until well risen. Cool on a wire rack. Using a rotary whisk or an electric blender, blend the cheese, lemon juice, mayonnaise and seasonings together. Cut the chicken flesh into small manageable pieces, add two-thirds to the creamed cheese mixture and spread lightly over the pastry layers. Sprinkle shredded lettuce on top. Slice the tomatoes thinly, cut in half again and arrange over lettuce. Layer up to form a 'loaf'. Top with the remaining chicken flesh and tomatoes. Cut with a really sharp knife. Eat fresh, on the day of making.

Chicken Elizabet

Deliciously succulent Chicken Elizabet is golden-skinned, meaty chunks of roast bird lightly dressed with wine-marinaded button mushrooms and garnished with tomatoes.

3½-lb. oven-ready chicken
½ lb. button mushrooms
4 tbsps. red wine
4 tbsps. salad oil
1 tbsp. red wine vinegar
½ level tsp. sugar
¼ level tsp. mustard
few grains cayenne pepper
3 cocktail onions, finely chopped
2 small gherkins, chopped
2 tsps. chopped parsley
salt and freshly ground black pepper
lettuce leaves, watercress and tomatoes to
    garnish

SERVES 6

Roast the chicken and leave to cool before carving. Meanwhile wipe the mushrooms and trim the stalks down to the caps. Place in a sauce-pan with the wine and simmer for about 15 minutes, until the wine evaporates and the mushrooms are pink. Turn into a bowl. Shake or whisk together the oil, vinegar, sugar, mustard, cayenne, onions, gherkins and parsley. Adjust seasoning, spoon over the warm mushrooms and leave until cold. Cut the chicken flesh from the carcass in large pieces, retaining the skin. Arrange the chicken on a bed of lettuce with sprigs of watercress round the edge, pile mushrooms in the centre and garnish with tomatoes.

✳ Chicken and banana curry

Holiday time is perhaps the best period to introduce new flavours to the younger folk. Lightly spiced, this curry is specially created with them in mind, and can be served with side dishes for the family to dip into and try: chutney, sliced tomato, cucumber with soured cream are just a few.

4-lb. oven-ready chicken
giblets
1 tbsp. corn oil
1½ oz. butter
1 lb. firm bananas
½ lb. onions, skinned and thinly sliced
4 oz. lean bacon, rinded and diced
2 level tsps. curry powder
1 oz. flour
2 level tsps. tomato paste
4 tbsps. single cream
salt and freshly ground black pepper

SERVES 6

Joint the chicken into 12 pieces and discard the skin. Place the giblets in a small pan, cover with cold water. Bring to the boil and simmer for about 30 minutes. Heat the oil in a thick based pan, add 1 oz. butter and, when it is on the point of browning, add the chicken pieces, flesh-side down. Fry for about 10 minutes until golden. Remove the chicken and place fleshy side upper-most in a casserole. Add a further ½ oz. butter to the pan. Peel and thickly slice the bananas, add to the pan and fry briefly until golden. Drain and add to the chicken. Fry the onion and bacon until tender in the reheated pan juices. Stir in the curry powder and flour and cook for 1 minute. Strain the giblet stock, pour it over the onion and bring to the boil. Stir in the tomato paste and cream and season well. Pour the sauce over the chicken, cover and cook at 325°F, 170°C (mark 3) for about 1¼ hours.

Chicken and avocado salad

A main course salad. Serve with oven-fresh crusty bread.

$3\frac{1}{2}$-lb. oven-ready chicken, roasted
8 tbsps. salad oil
4 tbsps. tarragon vinegar
$\frac{1}{4}$ level tsp. dry mustard
$\frac{1}{4}$ level tsp. salt
$\frac{1}{2}$ level tsp. sugar
1 level tsp. finely chopped onion
$\frac{1}{2}$ level tsp. snipped chives
$\frac{1}{2}$ level tsp. chopped parsley
$\frac{1}{2}$ level tsp. fresh thyme
1 lb. courgettes
$\frac{1}{2}$ lb. cooked French or round green beans
2 avocados
$\frac{1}{2}$ lb. firm tomatoes, sliced

SERVES 6

Carve the chicken flesh in large pieces. Combine the oil, vinegar, mustard, salt, sugar, onion, chives, parsley and thyme. Shake well and spoon a little over the chicken. Wipe and trim the courgettes, slice, then cook in boiling salted water for about 5 minutes. Drain and cool quickly under running water. Marinade the courgettes and beans in the remaining dressing. Halve, stone, peel and dice the avocados a short time before arranging the salad. Fold through the courgettes and pile in the centre of a serving dish. Surround with sliced tomatoes and top with chicken.

Barbecued roast stuffed chicken

4 oz. onion, skinned and chopped
4 oz. bacon, rinded and chopped
2 oz. butter
4 oz. fresh white breadcrumbs
1 lb. pie veal, minced
pinch of fresh thyme
salt and freshly ground black pepper
1 large egg, beaten
$3\frac{3}{4}$–4-lb. oven-ready chicken, boned
6 oz. sliced tongue
barbecue sauce (see below)

SERVES 8

Fry the onion and bacon in 1 oz. butter. Add to the breadcrumbs with the veal and thyme. Season and bind with egg. Lay out the chicken, skin side down. Cover it with half the veal forcemeat; cut the tongue into strips, place it over the forcemeat and cover with the remaining forcemeat. Draw the sides of the chicken together and sew up with fine string. Place in a roasting tin, brush with 1 oz. melted butter and cook at 400°F, 200°C (mark 6) for 1 hour. Brush the chicken with barbecue sauce, return it to the oven and baste every 15 minutes for a further 1 hour – cover loosely with kitchen foil if it starts to overbrown.

For barbecue sauce: Combine 5 tbsps. red wine, 4 tbsps. chicken stock, 2 tbsps. red wine vinegar, 1 tsp. each soy and Worcestershire sauce, 1 level tsp. each tomato paste and French mustard and 1 level tbsp. sugar. Boil to reduce by half.

✳ Bobotie

A family favourite from Rhodesia, Bobotie is a popular main course recipe for all ages.

lard or dripping
1 medium sized onion, skinned and finely chopped
1 slice white bread
little milk
1 oz. stoned raisins, finely chopped or minced
1 lb. lean minced beef
1 oz. chopped almonds
2 tsps. vinegar
3 level tsps. Demerara sugar
3 level tsps. curry powder
1 egg, well beaten
1 egg
$\frac{1}{4}$ pt. milk
salt and freshly ground black pepper

SERVES 4

Melt a little fat in a frying pan and fry the onion gently until well browned. Soak the bread in the milk and squeeze out the excess moisture. Add the raisins, meat and bread to the onion, then add the almonds, vinegar, sugar, curry powder and the beaten egg. Stir well. Turn the mixture into a $2\frac{1}{2}$-pt. pie dish. Beat the other

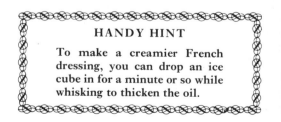

HANDY HINT

To make a creamier French dressing, you can drop an ice cube in for a minute or so while whisking to thicken the oil.

Steak Diane (*see below*)

egg with the milk, season and pour over the meat mixture. Stand the pie dish in another container with hot water to come half-way up and cook in the oven at 375°F, 190°C (mark 5) for about 1 hour, until set. Serve hot with fluffy rice and mango chutney, or cold, thickly sliced with a mixed salad.

Beef salad

This is a super way with the cold joint.

½ level tsp. dried basil
2 tbsps. French dressing
about half a lettuce, washed and dried
½ lb. juicy cold roast beef, cubed
1 eating apple, peeled, cored and sliced
1 oz. black olives, stoned

SERVES 2

Marinade the basil in the French dressing for 1 hour. Line two individual salad dishes with the lettuce. Combine the beef, the apple and the olives with the basil dressing and pile on the lettuce leaves.

Steak Diane

(*see picture above*)

4 fillet steaks (about 4 oz. each, ½ in. thick)
1 oz. butter
2 tbsps. cooking oil
2 tbsps. Worcestershire sauce
1 tbsp. lemon juice
1 tbsp. grated onion
2 tsps. chopped parsley

SERVES 4

Fry the steaks in the butter and oil for about 2

minutes each side. Remove and keep hot. Add the Worcestershire sauce and lemon juice to the pan juices, stir well and warm through. Add the onion and parsley and cook gently for 1 minute. Serve the sauce spooned over the steaks. Garnish with parsley sprigs and lemon slices.

Meat mould

A marvellous standby to have in the refrigerator, and this mould uses up bits and pieces from the weekend round of family eating.

½ lb. cold roast beef, preferably slightly underdone
½ lb. cold cooked bacon
¼ lb. liver, fried until firm
2 oz. onion, skinned
2 oz. carrot, pared
4 oz. fresh white breadcrumbs
2 tbsps. water
2 tbsps. chopped parsley
2 eggs, beaten
salt and freshly ground black pepper

SERVES 6

Mince together the beef, bacon, liver, onion and carrot. Moisten the breadcrumbs in the water and add to the meat mixture together with the parsley and the eggs. Season well and turn into a 2-pt. pudding basin. Cover with greased foil and place in a roasting dish with 1 in. water. Cook at 325°F, 170°C (mark 3) for about 1 hour. Cool in the basin. When cold, turn out and slice.

Beef in red wine jelly

3–3½ lb. silverside beef
few crushed parsley stalks
2 bayleaves
thinly pared rind of 1 lemon
1 clove garlic, skinned and crushed
4 oz. onion, skinned and sliced
1 celery stalk
1 medium sized carrot, pared and sliced
½ pt. red wine
1 lb. lean back bacon in a piece
2 lb. veal bones
½ pt. water
2 tbsps. port

SERVES 10–12

Place the joint in a polythene bag with the parsley, bayleaves, lemon rind, garlic, onion, celery, carrot and red wine. Put inside a deep bowl and marinade overnight. Next day remove the beef and dry it on absorbent paper. Remove the rind and fat from the bacon, heat the fat until it runs enough to use it to brown the beef evenly over the surface. Place the chopped bones in the base of a large casserole, add the browned meat and pour over the marinade, ½ pt. water and the diced lean bacon. Cover with foil and cover closely with a lid. Cook in the oven at 300°F, 150°C (mark 2) for about 4 hours. The meat must be very tender. Cool the meat and strained juices separately. Lift the fat from the jellied juices, melt the jelly, add port and make up to 1 pt. with cold water. Slice the meat and arrange overlapping in a shallow dish. Adjust the seasoning and spoon the half-set jelly juices over the meat. Chill.

Ginger glazed lamb nuggets

1 lb. boned leg or shoulder lamb

For the marinade
3 level tbsps. chopped stem ginger
1 tbsp. soy sauce
1 level tbsp. tomato paste
2 spring onions, chopped
salt and freshly ground black pepper
6 tbsps. white stock

SERVES 4

Cut the meat into bite-sized pieces and place it in a small shallow dish. Combine all the marinade ingredients in a small pan, using the white part only from the onion. Heat gently for 5 minutes, cool and pour over the meat. Cover and leave to marinade overnight in the refrigerator.

The next day, drain the meat, thread on 4 skewers and grill under a moderate heat for 30 minutes, brushing over with a little of the marinade. Turn several times to ensure the meat is cooked on all sides. Arrange the skewers in a serving dish. Heat the marinade, add any meat juices from the grill pan, avoiding fat, and pour over the meat. Serve garnished with the snipped green of the spring onions.

Lamb cutlets paprika

12 lamb cutlets
4 oz. butter
1 level tsp. paprika pepper
½ level tsp. ground ginger
2 tbsps. capers
watercress for garnish

SERVES 6

Trim the cutlets or get the butcher to do this for you. Place in a single layer in a baking dish and cook in the oven at 425°F, 220°C (mark 7) for about 20 minutes. Meanwhile, cream together the butter, paprika, ginger and capers. Drain the juices from the cutlets, spread the seasoned butter over them and return the dish to the oven to cook the cutlets for a further 10–15 minutes until they are crisp, golden and bubbly. Serve garnished with sprigs of crisp watercress.

Spiced shoulder of lamb

Rosemary and spices mingled give an unusual lift to this popular cold cut of lamb.

1 boned shoulder of lamb
1 level tbsp. fresh rosemary
2 level tbsps. brown sugar
1 level tbsp. flour
1 level tsp. salt
½ level tsp. ground allspice
½ level tsp. ground ginger
pinch of nutmeg
2 oz. butter, melted
1 tbsp. vinegar
1 level tbsp. tomato ketchup

SERVES 6

Flatten the lamb, make slits in the flesh and skin and insert spikes of rosemary. Combine the remaining ingredients and spread half over the fleshy surface. Roll up neatly and tie with fine string. Place the lamb in a roasting tin, pour the remaining spice mixture over and bake in the oven at 350°F, 180°C (mark 4) for about 1½ hours. Serve cold with mint jelly.

Summer lamb casserole

An effortless one-dish meal for cooler evenings. Made earlier in the day, it doesn't suffer from reheating if you add the potatoes and peas only at this late stage.

2 lb. neck of lamb
salt and freshly ground black pepper
1 lb. new carrots, scraped and sliced
1 lb. small new potatoes, scraped
8-oz. pkt. frozen peas or fresh shelled peas
1 level tbsp. tomato paste
fresh mint, chopped

SERVES 4

Place the meat in a shallow flameproof casserole. Cover with cold water and bring to the boil.

Pour off the water and rinse the meat. Return it to the casserole with 1 pt. cold water, to which 2 level tsps. salt and ½ level tsp. pepper have been added. Bring to the boil. Add the carrots, cover and cook in the oven at 325°F, 170°C (mark 3) for about 1½ hours, until the meat is fork tender. Add the potatoes to the casserole, cover and cook for a further 20 minutes. Remove the meat and strip off the flesh from the bones, roughly cut and return to the casserole with the peas and tomato paste. Adjust the seasoning and return it to the oven for a further 10–15 minutes. To serve, sprinkle with chopped mint.

Lamb oysters

6 lamb chump chops
1 oz. butter or margarine
½ small onion, skinned and grated
3 oz. mushrooms, chopped
1 tbsp. chopped parsley
grated rind of 1 lemon
1 egg yolk
salt and freshly ground black pepper
cooking oil
2 tbsps. sherry

SERVES 6

Trim the chops, discard the bones, and cut a 'pocket' in the side of the meat. Melt the butter or margarine, sauté the onion until soft, then add the mushrooms. Off the heat, stir in the parsley, lemon rind, egg yolk and seasonings. Use the mixture to fill the pockets and secure with wooden cocktail sticks. Brush a frying pan with oil, brown the chops quickly on both sides, lower the heat and cook for 15–20 minutes, turning once. Arrange the chops on a serving plate. Add the sherry to the pan juices, bubble, season and spoon over the chops.

Peperoni ripieni

½ oz. butter
2 medium sized onions, skinned and minced
1½ lb. lean pork, minced
1 pkt. mushroom sauce mix
¼ pt. milk
salt and freshly ground black pepper
4 tomatoes, skinned and chopped
6 medium even-sized green peppers

SERVES 6

Melt the butter and sauté the onions till beginning to brown. Stir in the pork and sauté it for about

10 minutes. Stir in the sauce mix, then ¼ pt. milk and bring to the boil. Simmer for 3 minutes, then season well and add the tomatoes. Wipe the peppers and cut a thin slice from the stem end of each pepper; discard the seeds and fill each one with some of the pork mixture. Place them in an ovenproof dish and bake at 350°F, 180°C (mark 4) for about 45 minutes.

✳ Pork chops in orange-pepper sauce

(*see picture opposite*)

4 trimmed loin chops
salt and pepper
1 oz. sugar
1 oz. butter
1 clove garlic, skinned and sliced
1 oz. cornflour
½ level tsp. dried rosemary
½ pt. water
3 tbsps. lemon juice
3 tbsps. orange juice
½ green pepper, seeded and chopped
6 thick slices fresh orange

SERVES 4

Season both sides of the chops with salt, pepper and a little of the sugar. Melt the butter in a frying pan and brown the chops well on both sides. Place the chops on one side. Add the rest of the sugar, garlic, the cornflour and rosemary to the drippings. Stir well and gradually add the water. Cook, stirring, until glossy. Add the fruit juices and green pepper. Return the chops to the pan and place a slice of orange on each chop. Cover with a lid, plate or foil. Simmer over a low heat for 40 minutes until the chops are tender, basting occasionally; uncover for the last 10 minutes. Serve garnished with fresh half slices of orange.

HANDY HINT

Dry, rubbed in pastry mixture may be stored in an airtight container in a refrigerator for several weeks. Let it 'warm up' for a short time, then add water in the usual way. When a recipe asks for 4 oz. shortcrust pastry, weigh out 6 oz. ready mix and use about 4 teaspoonfuls water for mixing.

Pork and pimiento kebabs

For outdoor cooking lay the kebabs on the barbecue grid and add to the smoky scent of the charcoal fire a handful of herbs, spices or citrus peel. Allow one meaty kebab for each person, with Pitta bread, a salad and a glass of wine.

1½ lb. fillet of pork
1 level tbsp. grated onion
2 tbsps. finely chopped parsley
¼ level tsp. dried oregano
½ level tsp. each ground cummin, ground
   coriander and ground mace
¼ level tsp. ground ginger
¼ level tsp. salt
freshly ground black pepper
¼ level tsp. cayenne pepper
4 oz. small onions
7½-oz. can pimientos, drained
cooking oil

SERVES 8

Trim the meat, removing any excess fat. Prick all over with a fork and cut into 1-in. pieces. In a bowl, combine the grated onion, parsley and all the spices, add the meat and turn to distribute the pieces. Leave covered in a cool place for 3 hours. Pour boiling water over the small onions and leave for 2–3 minutes before draining off and skinning. Cut the pimiento into large pieces and fold over if necessary to give a neat shape. Thread 8 skewers with meat, onion and pimientos alternately. Brush liberally with oil. Place under a pre-heated grill or rotary spit at full heat for 5 minutes to seal the surface. Reduce to medium heat and cook for about 40 minutes until well browned, turning at intervals. Baste frequently using the pan drippings to keep well moistened.

Picnic sandwich box

1 small uncut crusty Bloomer loaf
3 oz. butter, melted
½ lb. pork sausagemeat
¼ lb. cooked ham, finely chopped
¼ lb. pressed tongue, finely chopped
2 oz. onion, skinned and chopped
2 eggs
¼ pt. milk
salt and freshly ground black pepper
2 hardboiled eggs, shelled

SERVES 8

Cut horizontally across the loaf, two-thirds of the way up, and remove the 'lid'. Gently ease

Pork chops in orange-pepper sauce (*see opposite*)

away the bread from around the crust edge and make about 4 oz. breadcrumbs from the dough. Brush the cavity of the loaf and lid with some of the melted butter. Combine the sausagemeat, chopped meats, breadcrumbs and onion together. Beat the two eggs and milk together, season well and mix with the forcemeat. Place one-third of the filling down the centre of the loaf. Arrange the halved, boiled eggs lengthwise on top. Pack around with more filling and top with the lid. Secure the loaf like a parcel with string. Use the remaining melted butter to brush all over the loaf. Place it on a baking sheet and bake at 400°F, 200°C (mark 6) for 15 minutes; cover with foil and continue cooking for 45 minutes. Serve either hot or cold, in thick slices.

Tivoli salad

The soured cream makes this main-meal salad distinctive.

12-oz. can chopped ham with pork
6 oz. Samsoe cheese
2 tsps. finely chopped onion
4 tbsps. soured cream
1 tbsp. lemon juice
pepper
1 avocado
lettuce
4 small slices fried bread
chopped chives for garnish

SERVES 4

Cut the chopped ham with pork and cheese into small cubes. Add the onion. Blend together the soured cream and lemon juice and season with pepper. Halve, stone, peel and roughly dice the avocado, fold it into the soured cream with the ham mixture. Pile it on to a dish lined with lettuce, scatter diced fried bread on top and garnish with snipped chives.

✳ Picnic pies

½ oz. butter
¾ lb. streaky bacon, rinded and minced
¾ lb. pie veal, minced
1 level tbsp. flour
¼ pt. water
2 tbsps. chopped parsley
freshly grated nutmeg
freshly ground black pepper
¼ level tsp. dried thyme

For shortcrust pastry
1 lb. plain flour
6 oz. block margarine
6 oz. lard
salt
cold water
beaten egg to glaze

MAKES 24

Melt the butter in a frying pan and add the minced bacon and veal. Fry gently until the fat begins to run – about 7 minutes. Stir in the flour, cook for a further minute then stir in the water with the parsley, nutmeg, pepper and thyme. Salt may be needed after tasting. Leave the mixture to cool while making up the pastry, using the flour, margarine, lard, salt and water. Line 24 lightly greased small patty tins (approx. capacity 2½ tbsps. water) with the pastry, reserving enough for lids and leaves. Brush beaten egg around the rims of the pastry cases, spoon in the meat, cover with pastry and decorate. Brush with beaten egg and bake at 400°F, 200°C (mark 6) for about 30 minutes.

HANDY HINT

Stuffings are best made with fresh breadcrumbs. If only dry crumbs are available, soak them in a little milk or stock for 1 hour and squeeze out the excess moisture before use.

✳ Osso buco

3 lb. shin of veal (6 pieces)
salt and pepper
3 oz. butter
1 medium onion, skinned and finely chopped
2 carrots, pared and thinly sliced
2 stalks celery, trimmed and thinly sliced
¼ pt. dry white wine
1½ level tbsps. flour
¾ pt. stock
1 lb. tomatoes, skinned and quartered
pinch of dried rosemary
3 tbsps. chopped parsley
1 small clove garlic, skinned and finely chopped
grated rind of 1 lemon

SERVES 6

Ask your butcher to saw the veal into 6 1½–2 in. thick slices. Season the meat with salt and pepper. Melt the butter in a saucepan large enough to take the veal in one layer. Brown the veal, then put it aside. If necessary, add a little more butter before gently frying the onion, carrot and celery until they are just beginning to brown. Pour off the excess fat, return the meat to the pan and add the wine. Cover and cook gently for 1 hour. Transfer the meat to a large shallow casserole. Blend the flour with a little stock to a smooth paste and stir in the remainder of the stock. Pour round the veal. Add the tomatoes and rosemary. Cover and continue to cook gently in the oven at 350°F, 180°C (mark 4) for a further 1 hour, until the meat is tender. Sprinkle with a mixture of parsley, garlic and lemon rind.
Note: If it is more convenient, do the initial cooking on top of the stove the day before. Cool quickly and refrigerate.

Glazed collar bacon with apricots

A useful standby for serving hot or cold and it will keep well in the fridge for several days after the first meal.

4 lb. joint prime collar bacon
3 oz. Demerara sugar
cloves
spiced apricots (see below)

SERVES 12

String the bacon joint firmly in shape and soak

it for 3–4 hours. Drain and put it into a large saucepan and cover with cold water. Bring to the boil and throw away the water. Add fresh cold water to cover, bring to the boil, reduce the heat, cover and simmer allowing 20 minutes per lb. plus 20 minutes. 15 minutes before the end of the cooking time, drain the bacon from the stock and strip off the rind. Using a sharp knife, score the fat in a criss-cross design. Press the sugar into the fat until it is well coated, then stud with cloves. Place the joint in a baking tin and brown in the oven at 425°F, 220°C (mark 7) for about 15 minutes until golden. Serve hot or cold with a garnish of spiced apricots.

Spiced apricots: Combine the drained syrup from a 15-oz. can of apricot halves with 4 tbsps. vinegar and 2 level tbsps. Demerara sugar. Add 4 cloves and a pinch of cinnamon. Over a low heat dissolve the sugar then boil gently for 5–7 minutes, add the apricot halves and leave until cold.

✳ Bumper sausage roll

For a picnic occasion, carry this roll whole or in thickly sliced portions that have been individually wrapped in foil.

3½-oz. pkt. sage and onion stuffing
13-oz. pkt. frozen puff pastry, thawed
4 oz. lean streaky bacon
1½ lb. pork sausage meat
salt and freshly ground black pepper
1 small egg
poppy seeds (optional)

SERVES 6

Make up the stuffing following the packet instructions and leave until cold. Roll out the pastry to about 15 in. square. Rind the bacon and snip into a small frying pan using scissors, and cook slowly until golden. Work into the sausage meat and season well with salt and pepper. Shape the sausage meat in an oblong and place in the centre of the pastry, mound the stuffing over the sausage. Brush the pastry edge with beaten egg, fold the pastry over to overlap and seal it. Turn over, tuck the ends under and decorate with thinly rolled pastry trimmings cut in long narrow strips. Brush with beaten egg and sprinkle with poppy seeds. Bake at 425°F, 220°C (mark 7) for about 45 minutes. When light golden brown, cover with a double sheet of wetted greaseproof paper. Serve hot with vegetables or cold with a picnic salad.

Bacon and mushroom pie

1½ lb. back rashers of bacon
2 oz. butter or margarine
2 oz. onion, skinned and sliced
6 oz. button mushrooms
1 oz. flour
½ pt. milk
5 oz. frozen peas
freshly ground black pepper
13-oz. pkt. frozen puff pastry, thawed

SERVES 6

Rind the bacon and cut in ½-in. strips. Melt the butter or margarine in a large frying pan, add the bacon and cook for 5–7 minutes. Remove the bacon using a draining spoon and place it in a 3-pt. pie dish. Fry the onions and mushrooms until tender, drain and add to the bacon. Stir the flour into the pan juices, cook for 1–2 minutes, gradually add the milk and bring to the boil, stirring. Add the peas and pour into the pie dish, stir and season with pepper. Cool slightly, then cover with a pastry lid. Bake at 425°F, 220°C (mark 7) for 30 minutes, then reduce the temperature to 375°F, 190°C (mark 5) and cook for about a further 25 minutes.

Iscas a Portuguesa

(*see picture page 69*)

Liver sauté, Portuguese style, with garlic and wine vinegar.

1 lb. calves' or lambs' liver
1 clove garlic, skinned and crushed
4 tbsps. white wine vinegar
1 bayleaf
few peppercorns
lard
¼ pt. stock
2 level tsps. cornflour

SERVES 4

Slice the liver very thinly. Marinade it overnight with the garlic, vinegar, bayleaf and peppercorns then drain the liver very thoroughly and strain the marinade. Melt just enough lard in a frying pan to cover the base; when hot, fry the liver until lightly browned and just cooked through. This should be done quickly. Keep the liver warm on a serving dish. To the pan drippings, add the marinade and stock blended with cornflour, loosening the drippings from the pan. Bring to the boil, boil for 1–2 minutes then pour over the liver. Serve at once, with boiled onions, carrot sticks and sliced boiled or fried potatoes.

Prawn chartreuse

1 lb. haddock fillet, skinned
1 medium sized onion, skinned
1 bayleaf
½ pt. milk
salt and pepper
1 oz. butter
1 oz. flour
anchovy essence
3 level tsps. powdered gelatine
2 tbsps. hot water
¼ pt. thick mayonnaise
¼ pt. single cream
1 egg white
½ lb. frozen prawns, thawed
cucumber slices
a few fresh prawns in the shell for garnish

SERVES 8

Place the haddock in a saucepan with the onion, bayleaf, milk, salt and pepper and poach for 10–15 minutes until cooked and creamy. Drain the fish from the stock. Measure the stock and make it up to ½ pt. with more milk if necessary. Flake the fish finely, discarding any small bones, or purée in a blender. Melt the butter in a saucepan, add the flour, then off the heat stir in the fish liquor. Return to the heat and stir until boiling, lower the heat and simmer for 3 minutes. Add the fish and season with salt, pepper and anchovy essence.

Dissolve the gelatine in 2 tbsps. water in a small bowl over a pan of boiling water. Add the gelatine to the fish mixture and mix very thoroughly. Leave until almost cold but still soft. Stir in the mayonnaise and cream and lastly the whisked egg white. Decorate the base of an 8½-in. spring-release cake tin, fitted with a tubular fluted base, with a few whole prawns and the sides with cucumber slices. Roughly chop the remaining prawns. Quickly fold the chopped prawns into the fish mixture and carefully spoon into the decorated mould. Chill

---

HANDY HINT

To give maximum flavour to dishes which are cooked for a long period of time, add herbs only in the last half hour.

---

until set – but do not over chill. Unmould about 1 hour before serving. Garnish with whole prawns in the shell.

Buttery lemon plaice

1 lemon
3 oz. butter
1 oz. shallot, skinned and finely chopped
12 fillets plaice
chopped parsley

SERVES 6

Using a potato peeler, finely pare the rind from half the lemon and shred it finely. Halve and squeeze out the juice from the pared half and reserve. Cut the remaining half into slices and reserve. Melt 1 oz. butter in a small pan and sauté the shallot and shredded lemon rind until soft but not coloured. Butter the base of a shallow ovenproof serving dish. Fold each fillet in half and arrange in pairs, one black and white skin per person, in a single layer. Spoon over the sautéed lemon rind and shallot. Cover with foil and bake at 325°F, 170°C (mark 3) for about 25 minutes. Just before serving, melt the remaining 2 oz. butter in a small pan. When it is on the point of turning brown, carefully add the juice of half the lemon which you have reserved. Remove the foil from the fish, pour the butter over it and garnish the plaice with the reserved lemon slices and a sprinkling of chopped parsley.

Smoked salmon mousse

1 bayleaf
2 oz. onion, skinned and chopped
3–4 white peppercorns
2 strips lemon rind
¾ pt. milk
1 oz. butter
1 oz. flour
3 level tsps. powdered gelatine
3 tbsps. lemon juice
¼ pt. soured cream
grated rind ½ lemon
4 oz. smoked salmon trimmings
salt and freshly ground black pepper
2 egg whites
parsley sprigs

SERVES 6

Place the first 5 ingredients in a pan. Bring to the boil, remove from the heat and infuse for 15 minutes. Melt the butter in another pan and

Iscas a Portuguesa (*see page 67*)

stir in the flour. Cook the roux for 1–2 minutes then gradually add the strained milk, stirring. Bring to the boil, stirring. Cook for a few minutes then pour into a bowl, cover with wetted grease-proof paper and cool. Dissolve the gelatine in the lemon juice, in a basin over a pan of hot water. Remove from the heat and stir in the soured cream. Whisk the cream into the cooled sauce to combine them evenly. Add the lemon rind and 3 oz. salmon, finely chopped. Adjust season-ing. Stiffly whisk the egg whites and when the sauce is nearly set, fold the whites in evenly. Divide between six 6-fl. oz. moulds or small cups and chill until set. Unmould the mousses on to individual plates. Make 6 small salmon rolls from the remaining salmon and use as garnish, with parsley sprigs. Serve with rolled brown bread and butter.

Herring parcels with mustard butter

Herrings are at their best from June–December. In Spring, vary this recipe by using mackerel.

3 oz. butter, softened
2 level tbsps. Dijon mustard
1 tbsp. chopped parsley
salt and freshly ground black pepper
2 herrings or mackerel, cleaned and heads
 removed
½ lemon

SERVES 2

Combine the softened butter with the mustard, parsley, salt and pepper. Shape two pieces of foil, each 9 in. by 9 in., into 2 boat shapes suitable to hold the fish. Spread a little of the savoury butter in the base of the foil. Fill the cavity of each fish with the savoury butter, reserving two tsps. Score the fish with 3 slits, at a slant, on each side. Place each fish in a foil boat and top with the reserved butter. Grill under a moderate heat for about 10–15 minutes, turning once during cooking. Serve in the foil boats to retain the juices. Garnish with more parsley and lemon wedges.

HANDY HINT

Vegetable cooking fats and lard are excellent for greasing as they do not contain water or salt.

✳ Salmon and cheese flan

Leave on the tin base for outdoor eating, don't remove the ring if it has to travel.

6 oz. shortcrust pastry (6 oz. plain flour, etc.)
1 large egg, beaten
¼ pt. milk
2 oz. onion, skinned and grated
salt and pepper
7½-oz. can pink salmon
3½ oz. cheese, grated
parsley for garnish

SERVES 4

Roll out the pastry and use to line an 8½-in. loose-bottomed French fluted flan tin. Whisk together the egg, milk and onion. Season lightly with salt and pepper. Drain the salmon, discard any dark skin and bone, flake the fish and spoon it into the bottom of the pastry case. Scatter the cheese evenly over the fish. Spoon the egg custard mixture over. Bake in the centre of the oven at 400°F, 200°C (mark 6) for 15 minutes, reduce the temperature to 350°F, 180°C (mark 4) for about a further 25 minutes until the flan is golden brown and set. Remove the flan ring and leave to cool. Garnish with parsley.
Note: If preferred make in 4 individual 4-in. flan rings.

✳ Kulebyaka

A traditional Russian dish, easy to make because you can use bought pastry and do the preparation in advance. Do eat Kulebyaka warm and oven fresh.

1 lb. fresh spinach
1½ oz. butter
salt and freshly ground black pepper
1 egg, beaten
2 oz. long grain rice
4 oz. onion, skinned and chopped
½ lb. tomatoes, skinned
¼ lb. button mushrooms
13-oz. pkt. frozen puff pastry, thawed
7½-oz. can red salmon, drained and flaked
melted butter
lemon wedges

SERVES 4

Wash the spinach well and remove any coarse stalks. Melt ½ oz. butter in a pan and cook the

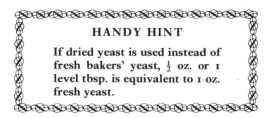

spinach, covered, turning it often. Drain it well, chop roughly and season. When cool, add half the egg. Boil the rice in the usual way. Sauté the onion in $\frac{1}{2}$ oz. butter until golden. Cut tomatoes in half, remove the seeds and cut into dice. Trim, wipe and slice the mushrooms and sauté in $\frac{1}{2}$ oz. butter. Season well and leave to one side. Roll out the pastry to a rectangle 11 in. by 16 in. and brush it with beaten egg. In the centre of the pastry, layer up the onion, tomato, mushroom, rice, spinach and salmon, with seasoning, keeping away from the edges. Brush the pastry edge with beaten egg, fold both long sides over the filling and roll it up like a Swiss roll. Tuck the final end under the roll. Slash across the top 3–4 times, place the roll on a damp baking sheet and bake at 450°F, 230°C (mark 8) for 30 minutes until golden brown.

Before serving, pour melted butter down the slash marks. Serve with lemon wedges.

Pasta niçoise

8 oz. twisted pasta
4 firm tomatoes
4 eggs, hard boiled
7-oz. can tuna steak, drained
1 red pepper, seeded and finely sliced
4 oz. French beans, cooked
16 black olives
few capers
5 tbsps. garlic flavoured French dressing

SERVES 4

Cook the pasta in boiling salted water until tender but not soft. Drain it well and rinse at once in cold water, then let it cool. Quarter the tomatoes and shell and cut the hard-boiled eggs lengthwise into quarters. Flake the tuna. Place pasta, fish, tomatoes, sliced red pepper, French beans, olives and capers in a bowl and mix gently. Add French dressing and toss, using two forks. Spoon the salad on to a serving dish or 4 individual plates and garnish with the quartered hard-boiled eggs.

Summer extras

Noodles rusticana

A help-yourself type supper dish; spicy red sauce trickles down through hot, buttery egg noodles.

6 small onions, skinned
10 oz. back bacon rashers, rinded
4 oz. butter
10 oz. noodle nests
2 oz. Parmesan cheese, grated
2 tbsps. chopped parsley
2 level tsps. dried mixed herbs
freshly ground black pepper
6 oz. mature Cheddar cheese, grated
2 9-oz. cans Buitoni tomato sauce

SERVES 6

Parboil the onions in salted water for about 5 minutes. Drain them and cut in half. Cut the bacon into small pieces and gently fry until cooked; leave to one side. Melt 1 oz. butter and fry the onion halves until golden brown, turning them carefully to retain their shape. Keep them warm. Cook the noodles in fast boiling salted water for 3–4 minutes, drain well, then melt the remaining butter and add noodles, bacon, Parmesan cheese, parsley, herbs and pepper. Toss lightly to combine the ingredients. Pile into a heated shallow serving dish and garnish with onion halves. Sprinkle with more parsley. Serve with a bowl of well-flavoured cheese and hot tomato sauce.

Pitta bread

This is hollow, Arab bread, traditionally served with meats from the skewer. Bake as individual, flattish round 'baps', then make a pouch inside. When ready to serve, gently ease the top open and slip the kebab contents into the hollow and top with chopped raw tomato and grated onion. Eat as you would a sandwich, with plenty of large paper napkins to hand.

$\frac{1}{2}$ oz. fresh bakers' yeast
about $\frac{1}{2}$ pt. water
1 lb. plain strong bread flour
$\frac{1}{2}$ level tsp. salt
oil

MAKES 8

Blend the yeast until smooth with a little water; when smooth add the remainder of the water. Sift the flour and salt into a bowl and make a well in the centre. Pour in the yeast liquid and stir, gradually incorporating the flour to make a firm but not hard dough. Knead on a lightly floured board until smooth and elastic – about 10 minutes. Sprinkle a plastic bag with oil and put the dough in it, turning it to cover with oil. Leave in a warm place for about 2 hours until double in size. Turn the dough out of the bag and knead again for a short time. Divide it into 8 pieces, knead each into a ball and flatten them to about $\frac{1}{4}$ in. thick. Place on a flat tray inside a plastic bag and leave to rise again until spongy. Meanwhile preheat the oven to 450°F, 230°C (mark 8) and heat oiled baking sheets. Lift the risen rounds of dough on to the baking sheets, brush with cold water and bake for about 10 minutes towards the top of the oven. Lift from the baking sheets and cool on wire racks. The bread is pale in colour, with a soft inside.

Summer salads

Picnic tomatoes

6 large even-sized tomatoes
$\frac{1}{4}$ pt. stiff mayonnaise
2–3 level tbsps. piccalilli
1 tsp. double cream, optional
salt and freshly ground black pepper
$\frac{1}{2}$ lb. corned beef
mint for garnish

SERVES 6

Cut a thin slice from the end opposite the stem of each tomato. Carefully remove the seeds and centre membrane using a teaspoon. Turn the shells upside-down to drain. Fold together the mayonnaise, piccalilli and cream and season well. Chop the corned beef and combine with the mayonnaise mixture. Use to fill the tomato shells and use tomato slices as 'lids', cut-side uppermost. Serve on rounds of bread and butter and garnish with mint sprigs.

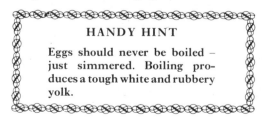

HANDY HINT

Eggs should never be boiled – just simmered. Boiling produces a tough white and rubbery yolk.

Note: For outdoor packing either use lidded containers and pack the tomatoes closely together to avoid movement, or wrap individually in a twist of foil or self-clinging plastic film.

Tomato coleslaw

1 lb. crisp green eating apples
juice of 1 lemon
1 lb. white cabbage
3 oz. seedless raisins
$\frac{1}{2}$ pt. thick mayonnaise
salt and freshly ground black pepper
1 lb. tomatoes

SERVES 6–8

Wipe the apples, core and dice them, leaving the skin on. Place the dice in a basin with the lemon juice and toss lightly to coat evenly with the juice. Finely shred the cabbage. In a large bowl, combine the cabbage with the raisins, mayonnaise, and drained apple. Season well. Place two-thirds of the cabbage mixture in a deep serving dish, levelling the surface. Slice the tomatoes crosswise, season, and place half in a layer over the slaw. Cover with remaining cabbage mixture, making a cone shape in the

centre. Arrange a circle of overlapping tomatoes around the top edge. Keep in a cool place.
Note : If the slaw is made in advance, omit the apple and add before serving.

Potato salad

A good potato salad is a mark of a good cook.

1–1½ lb. potatoes
1 tbsp. finely chopped onion, optional
¼ pt. mayonnaise
1 tbsp. chopped parsley or mint

Boil the potatoes in their jackets. Peel and slice or dice them, then add the chopped onion. When cold, mix with sufficient mayonnaise to moisten. Make well in advance, so that the flavours have time to blend. Sprinkle with parsley or mint before serving.
Note : New or waxy potatoes give the best results. Tiny new potatoes may be left whole. Potatoes dressed while hot will need more mayonnaise.

Oriental salad bowl

(see picture above right)

Crisp, cool and colourful, glistening with French dressing, Chinese cabbage looks rather similar to a Cos lettuce but is much larger; its crisp juicy leaves can be knife-shredded and make an interesting salad.

1 lb. Chinese cabbage leaves, washed, dried
    and shredded
4 oz. carrot, coarsely grated
2 red apples, chopped
15-oz. can crushed pineapple
1 bunch watercress, washed and sprigged

For dressing
6 tbsps. salad oil
2 tbsps. vinegar
4 tbsps. pineapple juice
salt and freshly ground black pepper
1 level tsp. French mustard

SERVES 4–6

In a bowl combine the Chinese cabbage leaves, carrot and apple. Drain the pineapple, reserving the juice, and add the crushed fruit to the Chinese leaves mixture. Place all the dressing ingredients in a tightly lidded container and shake well. Add to the salad and toss lightly. Pile it into a serving bowl and arrange watercress sprigs around the edge.

Oriental salad bowl (*see left*)

Mushroom salad

Uncooked mushrooms have a wonderful flavour; serve this as an hors d'oeuvre, or as an accompaniment salad for fish.

4 oz. open mushrooms
1 tbsp. lemon juice or cider vinegar
3 tbsps. salad oil
1 tbsp. finely chopped parsley
little freshly ground black pepper
salt

SERVES 4

Wipe mushrooms, if necessary. Do not peel.

Avocado and tomato salad (*see page 74*)

Remove the stalks and slice the caps very thinly into a serving dish. Add lemon juice, oil, parsley and pepper and marinade in the dressing for 30 minutes, turning occasionally. Salt lightly just before serving.

Cucumber chartreuse

A jellied salad, cool and refreshing, with a sharpness which gives a good balance to rich fish such as salmon.

1 pt. lime jelly tablet
hot water
¼ pt. cider vinegar
2 level tsps. sugar
a drop of green colouring
8 oz. diced skinned cucumber (½ a large cucumber)

SERVES 6

Place the jelly cubes in a 1-pt. measure and make up to ¾ pt. with hot water. Stir until the jelly has melted. Add the vinegar and sugar and a drop of colouring. Leave to cool until of the consistency of unbeaten egg white. Fold in the cucumber and when this is evenly suspended, pour the mixture into a 1½-pt. mould. Leave until set. Unmould in the usual way.

Caesar salad

This is a favourite salad in America.

French dressing, or packet type garlic-cheese dressing (bought from a delicatessen)
1 head Cos lettuce
1 raw beaten egg, or 1 coddled egg
2-oz. can anchovy fillets, drained and chopped
2 oz. Parmesan cheese, grated
salad oil
2 cloves garlic, skinned and cut
3 slices French bread, cut into cubes

SERVES 4–6

Prepare the dressing. Wash the lettuce and drain it thoroughly. Break or pull it to pieces, toss it in the dressing and mix in the egg, anchovy and cheese. Make sure that all ingredients are well blended. Heat the oil in a pan with the garlic and fry the croûtons until golden. Discard the garlic and drain the croûtons on kitchen paper. Just before serving, add the croûtons to the salad.

Green salad

The simplest of all, crisp and chilled. Serve with cold or hot foods as an alternative to a cooked vegetable; it is especially good with steaks.

1 lettuce
1 bunch watercress
1 head chicory, when in season
French dressing

SERVES 4

Prepare the lettuce and shred it lightly. Tiny leaves may be left whole. Sprig the cress and slice the chicory finely. Toss the vegetables together lightly with the dressing.

Avocado and tomato salad

(*see picture page 73*)

A colourful favourite to partner a juicy steak, a succulent grilled cutlet or even the ever-popular banger.

½ medium sized green pepper
2 tomatoes
1 small onion
1 avocado
juice of ½ lemon
snipped parsley

For dressing
4 tbsps. salad oil
2 tbsps. wine vinegar
½ level tsp. caster sugar
¼ level tsp. salt
¼ level tsp. dry mustard
¼ level tsp. Dijon mustard
freshly ground black pepper

SERVES 4

Seed and very thinly slice the pepper. Skin and slice tomatoes. Skin the onion and cut into paper-thin rings. Shake together all the dressing ingredients. Just before serving, halve, stone, peel and slice the avocado and squeeze a little lemon juice over it. Arrange the pepper, tomatoes, onion and avocado on four small plates, moisten with dressing and garnish with snipped parsley.

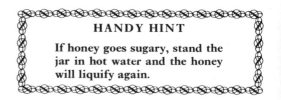

HANDY HINT

If honey goes sugary, stand the jar in hot water and the honey will liquify again.

Orange dressed beetroot

An interesting way to make a salad of young tender garden beets.

10 small, cooked globe beetroots

For dressing
1 large spring onion, finely chopped
salt and pepper
2 level tsps. sugar
1 level tsp. continental mustard
2 tbsps. tarragon vinegar
3–4 tbsps. salad oil
2 tbsps. orange juice
grated rind of ½ orange

Cut the beetroots in half and place in a dish. Shake all the dressing ingredients vigorously together in a screw-topped jar. Pour the dressing over the beetroots and leave for several hours, preferably overnight, in a cool place. Turn occasionally in the dressing.

Jellied gazpacho salad

The cool gleaming shapes of jellied salads are well suited to party occasions.

3 level tsps. powdered gelatine
1 pt. water
1 chicken stock cube
2 tbsps. malt vinegar
½ level tsp. salt
1 level tsp. paprika pepper
½ level tsp. dried basil
few drops Tabasco sauce
4 oz. green pepper, seeded and finely diced
1 clove garlic, skinned and crushed (optional)
2 oz. onion, skinned and finely chopped
2 oz. celery, trimmed and finely chopped
12 oz. tomatoes, skinned and chopped
soured cream

SERVES 6

Sprinkle the gelatine into ¼ pt. cold water in a bowl. Place the bowl over a pan of hot water until the gelatine is dissolved. In another pan, heat the remaining water, add the stock cube and stir until dissolved. Remove from the heat and add the vinegar and seasonings. Blend in the gelatine and chill till it is the consistency of unbeaten egg white. Blanch the peppers in fast-boiling water for 1 minute, drain and cool. Fold in the garlic, onion, celery, pepper and tomatoes. Pour into a 2-pt. ring mould and chill until set. Unmould on to a serving plate and serve with soured cream.

Cherry salad

Fresh cherries are still very much with us. In a pie or just *en branche* they are always a firm favourite. But have you tried a Cherry Salad as an out-of-ordinary accompaniment to cold gammon and tongue?

cherries
flaked almonds
water
French dressing

Stone some cherries using a special stoner so as to keep the fruit whole. Soak a few flaked almonds in water for about 30 minutes and then drain. Toss the cherries and almonds together with a French dressing.

Guernsey salad

(*see picture page 76*)

8 medium sized tomatoes
salt
3 tbsps. single cream
2–3 tsps. lemon juice
⅛ level tsp. freshly ground black pepper
¼ level tsp. sugar
2 tsps. chopped mint

SERVES 4

Skin the tomatoes, cut them in half and remove the seeds. Chop the flesh roughly and lightly sprinkle with salt. Blend the cream with the lemon juice, pepper, sugar and mint. Coat the tomatoes with the dressing.

Beans lyonnaise

¾ lb. frozen or shelled fresh broad beans
6 oz. ⁤⁤⁤⁤⁤, skinned and sliced
1 o⁤⁤⁤⁤
sa⁤⁤⁤⁤shly ground black pepper
po⁤⁤⁤⁤s

SERVE⁤⁤ 3

Cook the beans in plenty of boiling salted water for about 7 minutes or 15–20 minutes if fresh. Sauté the onion in the butter until tender. Drain the beans thoroughly. Fork the beans through the onion. Season. Transfer to a serving dish and dust lightly with poppy seeds.

Guernsey salad (*see page 75*)

Summer desserts

Summer sponge pudding

An up-dated version of an old time favourite.

2 pkts. boudoir biscuits (28 fingers)
$\frac{1}{4}$ pt. milk
2 oz. sugar
$\frac{1}{4}$ pt. water
$\frac{1}{2}$ lb. blackcurrants, stalked
$\frac{1}{2}$ lb. raspberries
$\frac{1}{2}$ pt. thick, sweetened apple purée
6 fl. oz. double cream
1 tbsp. milk
crushed crystallised rose petals

SERVES 8

Dip the boudoir biscuits, one at a time, into the milk, just long enough to soften them sufficiently to mould around the inside of a 2-pt. pudding basin. Line the base first, then work round the sides. Keep back 4–5 fingers for the top. In a saucepan, dissolve the sugar in the water, add the currants and raspberries and stew for about 5 minutes. Remove the fruit from the pan with a draining spoon. Bubble down the juices to about 4 tbsps., add to the stewed fruit and combine with the apple purée. Turn the fruit into the biscuit-lined basin. Cover with remaining boudoir biscuits soaked in milk. Turn any protruding biscuits down. Cover with a piece of greaseproof paper and a small weighted saucer and leave overnight in the refrigerator. Just before serving, unmould on to a serving plate, mask with cream whipped with milk. Sprinkle with the rose petals.

Coffee cream refrigerator cake

A rich almost instant dessert – bought crisp sponge fingers dunked in really strong coffee that has brandy added, and layered up with whipped cream *in situ* on a serving plate.

$\frac{1}{4}$ pt. strong black coffee
2–3 tbsps. brandy
28 crisp sponge fingers or boudoir biscuits
$\frac{1}{2}$ pt. double cream
2 tbsps. milk
pistachio nuts, blanched

SERVES 6–8

In a shallow dish combine the coffee and brandy. Dip the sponge fingers one at a time in the coffee and arrange seven side by side on a serving plate. Whip $\frac{1}{4}$ pt. chilled cream and 1 tbsp. milk together until it just holds its shape. Use a little to layer over the sponge fingers. Repeat using the remaining sponge fingers, all the coffee and the whipped cream, using seven sponge fingers for each layer. Chill in the refrigerator, covered, for several hours. Whip the remaining $\frac{1}{4}$ pt. cream and 1 tbsp. milk until it holds its shape and spread a little over the top of the layered sponge fingers. Turn the remainder into a fabric piping bag fitted with a star vegetable nozzle. Use this to pipe 'shells' of cream across the top. Decorate with halved pistachio nuts. Chill until required.

Iced zabaione

A soft velvet-textured iced dessert with a rich but subtle flavour.

4 egg yolks
4 oz. sugar
6 fl. oz. Marsala

SERVES 4

Beat the yolks to a cream and mix in the sugar and Marsala. Heat gently in a double saucepan, stirring all the while, until the custard coats the back of a spoon. Pour the custard into 4 individual

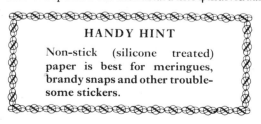

```
HANDY HINT
Non-stick (silicone treated)
paper is best for meringues,
brandy snaps and other trouble-
some stickers.
```

soufflé dishes, cool and then freeze until firm. Serve with crisp wafers or boudoir biscuits.

Queen of puddings

Revive this aristocrat of puddings that slips down so easily after a substantial main course; as a change try ginger cake instead of breadcrumbs.

$\frac{3}{4}$ pt. milk
1 oz. butter
1 oz. granulated sugar
3 oz. fresh white breadcrumbs
2 eggs, separated
grated rind of 1 lemon
2 tbsps. raspberry jam
approx. $1\frac{1}{2}$ oz. caster sugar

SERVES 4

Warm the milk with the butter and granulated sugar and add the breadcrumbs. Off the heat, add the beaten egg yolks and lemon rind. Pour the custard into a buttered 2-pt. pie dish and cook in the oven at 350°F, 180°C (mark 4) for about 20 minutes. Take it out of the oven and spread the top with raspberry jam. Whisk the egg whites until stiff, add 1 oz. caster sugar and whisk again. Spread this meringue over the jam and dredge with more caster sugar. Return the pudding to the oven at 300°F, 150°C (mark 1–2) for about 40 minutes.

Norwegian cream

Prepare the custard base several hours in advance for this light rich classic dessert.

stiff apricot jam
3 large eggs
1 level tbsp. sugar
few drops vanilla essence
$\frac{3}{4}$ pt. milk
2 oz. plain chocolate
4 tbsps. double cream

SERVES 4

Cover the base of a 2-pt. soufflé dish with apricot jam. In a bowl fork together 2 whole eggs and 1 extra yolk (reserving the white), the sugar and vanilla essence. Heat the milk until hot but not boiling and pour it over the eggs, stirring. Strain this custard on to the jam and cover the dish with kitchen foil. Stand the dish in a roasting tin with water to come half-way up and cook in the oven at 325°F, 170°C (mark 3) for about $1\frac{3}{4}$

hours until the custard is set. Lift the dish from the tin and leave it to go quite cold.

Before serving cover the top with a thick layer of curled or coarsely grated chocolate. Whisk the reserved egg white until stiff, whip the cream until it holds its shape and fold in the egg white. Spoon this on to the chocolate and spread it out to cover the top of the pudding. Then decorate with more chocolate.

Cherry pie

6 oz. shortcrust pastry (6 oz. flour, etc.)
raspberry jam
2 oz. ground almonds
2 oz. caster sugar
1 large egg, beaten
¾ lb. fresh red cherries, stoned
icing sugar

SERVES 4

Roll out about two-thirds of the pastry and use it to line a 7-in. flan ring placed on a baking sheet. Spread jam over the base. Blend the ground almonds with the caster sugar and beaten egg. Spread half the almond mixture over the jam, add the cherries, then the remainder of the almond mixture. Cover with a pastry lid and seal the edges. Bake at 375°F, 190°C (mark 5) for 30–40 minutes. Serve warm, dredged with icing sugar.

✳ Peach and lime mousse

Fruit balances well with most main dishes and this way it's easy to prepare.

1-lb. 13-oz. can peach halves
1 lemon
6 oz. lime marmalade
4 level tsps. powdered gelatine
¼ pt. double cream
2 egg whites

SERVES 6

Drain the peaches well and set three halves aside for decoration. Purée the remainder in an electric blender. Grate the lemon rind finely and add it to the puréed fruit with the squeezed lemon juice and marmalade. Purée again. In a small basin over a pan of hot water, dissolve the gelatine in 4 tbsps. peach syrup. Add a little fruit purée to the dissolved gelatine, blend it to a smooth cream and combine it evenly with the rest of the mixture. Chill until on the point of setting. Whip the cream until thick enough to just hold its

shape and fold it into the fruit mixture. Whisk the egg whites until firm but not dry, fold them into the fruit and cream mixture to give a light, even texture and turn it into a 2½-pt. glass dish. Chill until set. To decorate: with a small, sharp knife cut each reserved peach cap into 6–7 slices but do not completely separate, open into a fan shape and arrange on the mousse.

Note: If a blender is not available, pass the fruit and marmalade through a sieve. (The texture will not be so smooth.)

Strawberry gâteau

4 oz. butter
4 oz. caster sugar
2 large eggs, beaten
4 oz. self-raising flour
½ lb. fresh strawberries
1 tbsp. orange liqueur
1 orange
½ pt. double cream
1 tbsp. milk
1 level tbsp. caster sugar

Grease and line an 8½-in. diameter deep sandwich tin with paper a little above the rim. Beat the butter, add the sugar and cream until light and fluffy. Beat in the eggs. Lightly beat in the flour and turn the mixture into the tin. Level the surface and bake at 350°F, 180°C (mark 4) for about 20 minutes. Turn the cake out and cool on a wire rack. 1 hour before serving, reserve 5 even-sized strawberries with stalks attached and cut them in half lengthwise. Chop the remainder of the hulled strawberries and place them in a bowl with the liqueur, grated rind of orange and 3 tbsps. orange juice. Cut out a 4-in. round from the centre of the cake and make this into crumbs. Combine the crumbs with the chopped strawberries. Put the cake ring on a flat serving plate, fill the centre with the moistened strawberry crumbs. Whip the cream with the milk until it holds its shape, fold in the caster sugar and 1 tbsp. orange juice. Spoon the fluffy cream on to the cake surface to cover it. Top with a circle of halved strawberries.

HANDY HINT

Scoring pork rind deeply and rubbing well with oil and salt gives a really crunchy crackling.

Strawberry marquise

(see picture page 80)

1 lb. strawberries, hulled and sliced
1 level tbsp. caster sugar
2 tbsps. Kirsch
16-oz. can pineapple titbits
$\frac{3}{4}$ pt. double cream
1 oz. sugar
1 egg white

SERVES 6

Put the strawberries in a dish with the sugar and Kirsch and leave for 1–2 hours. Drain the pineapple titbits and purée the fruit. Whip the cream with 1 oz. sugar until stiff and fold in the stiffly beaten egg white and pineapple pulp. Turn the pineapple cream into a serving dish and chill. Just before serving, layer the strawberries over the cream mixture.

Glazed strawberry flan

A fruit flan is a must for summer. The continental type pastry has good cutting qualities.

8 oz. plain flour
5 oz. butter at room temperature
$2\frac{1}{2}$ oz. icing sugar, sifted
2 egg yolks
1 lb. strawberries, hulled
$\frac{1}{2}$ lb. redcurrant jelly
1 orange
$\frac{1}{4}$ pt. double cream
2 tbsps. milk

SERVES 6–8

Sift the flour on to a board or working surface or into a wide bowl. Make a well in the centre and put in the butter, icing sugar and egg yolks. With the fingertips, gradually work together the ingredients, incorporating the flour to give a malleable dough. Chill to a rolling consistency then roll out the pastry to fit the base of a 10-in. loose-bottomed French fluted flan tin and with the fingertips work the dough up the sides. Prick all over with a fork. Bake in the oven at 350°F, 180°C (mark 4) for 20 minutes. Cool before removing the flan tin.

Slice the strawberries lengthwise and arrange them in the flan. Place the redcurrant jelly in a saucepan. Thinly pare the rind from the orange and place it in the saucepan with the juice, bring to the boil and reduce to a glaze consistency. Strain, cool to lukewarm and brush it over the fruit. Whip the cream with the milk until just firm enough to hold its shape, then spoon it on to or pipe it round the flan. Serve fresh, preferably the same day.

Strawberries Romanoff

(see picture page 81)

A smart way to serve summer berries.

$\frac{3}{4}$ lb. strawberries, hulled
3 tbsps. port
1 level tbsp. caster sugar
1 tbsp. milk
$\frac{1}{4}$ pt. double cream
vanilla sugar
feuilles royales for decoration (see below)

SERVES 4

Put 4 whole strawberries on one side. Thickly slice the remainder. Place the sliced fruit in a bowl with the port and caster sugar. Turn lightly and leave to marinade for 1 hour, then spoon the strawberries into 4 stemmed glasses. Add the milk to the cream with vanilla sugar to sweeten. Whisk until the cream just holds its shape then spoon it over the strawberries. Before serving, decorate with whole berries and feuilles royales.

To make feuilles royales: Gradually stir 6 oz. sifted icing sugar into 1 large egg white; beat well. Make a piping bag in the usual way from greaseproof paper. Spoon the royal icing into the bag, snip off the tip to allow icing to flow through and pipe free-hand into leaf shapes on kitchen foil, starting with the outline and then filling in the leaf itself. Allow the leaves to dry for about 1 hour then pipe in the centre vein. Place the leaves on foil under a low grill for about 10 minutes until dried out and tinged brown. The leaves should now come away from the foil easily, so turn them over and dry for a little longer. Cool on a wire rack. Feuilles royales will store wrapped in foil for 2–3 weeks.

Strawberry mille feuilles

If it's easier to bake the pastry layers for this delicious dessert ahead, wrap them carefully in

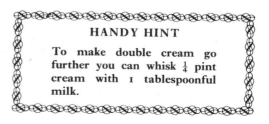

HANDY HINT

To make double cream go further you can whisk $\frac{1}{4}$ pint cream with 1 tablespoonful milk.

Strawberry marquise (*see page 79*)

kitchen foil and then refresh in the oven at 375°F, 190°C (mark 5) for about 10 minutes, cool and assemble just before serving.

13-oz. pkt. frozen puff pastry, thawed
½ lb. strawberries, hulled
1 level tbsp. caster sugar
½ pt. double cream
¼ pt. single cream
½ lb. strawberry jam
1 tbsp. lemon juice

SERVES 6–8 (make 2 for our party menu)

Roll out the pastry into a rectangle 16 in. by 13 in. Trim ½ in. off the edges. Mark into three down the long sides and cut into equal pieces 5 in. by 12 in. Prick the surface well. Place the pastry on a damp baking sheet and chill for 30 minutes then bake at 425°F, 220°C (mark 7) for 10–12 minutes. Cool on a wire rack. Leave four strawberries whole and cut the remainder into small pieces. Sprinkle the sugar over and leave for 10 minutes. Whip the creams together until they hold their shape. In a bowl, combine the jam and lemon juice.

To assemble the mille feuilles spread 5 tbsps. whipped cream over one pastry layer. Halve the jam and lightly spread it on top of the cream. Scatter with half the berries. Repeat with another layer then place one on top of the other, filling side uppermost. Position the last pastry layer on top, spread a little of the remaining cream over and place the bulk in a forcing bag fitted with a large star vegetable nozzle. Pipe cream as

decoration and add the remaining berries cut in half. Serve on a flat plate or board.

Compote of peaches

4 yellow peaches
4 oz. sugar
½ pt. water
piece of vanilla pod
1 tbsp. lemon juice
flaked almonds

SERVES 4

To skin the peaches, place them in boiling water, count 10, plunge them into cold water and carefully remove the skin. Dissolve the sugar in the water with the vanilla pod. Bring to the boil and boil for 3 minutes. Halve the peaches, discard the stones and thickly slice the fruit. Add the peaches to the syrup, discard the vanilla pod and cook gently for 5 minutes. Remove the pan from the heat, add the lemon juice and leave the fruit until cold. Brown a few flaked almonds under the grill and sprinkle over the peaches in a serving dish. Serve with thin crisp biscuits or soft sponge fingers.

✳ Raspberry mousse

Smooth and silky, simple yet sophisticated, this mousse has a light set rather similar to a soufflé.

3 whole eggs
2 egg yolks
4 oz. caster sugar
3 level tsps. powdered gelatine
3 tbsps. water
½ pt. unsweetened raspberry purée
red colouring, optional
½ pt. double cream

For decoration
crystallised violets

SERVES 6

Put the whole eggs and the yolks in a large deep bowl with the sugar. Place the bowl over a pan of hot, not boiling, water and whisk until thick and fluffy, not allowing the mixture to get too hot. Take the bowl from the pan and continue to whisk frequently until cool. Dissolve the gelatine in the water in a small bowl or cup standing in a little hot water. Stir a little of the fruit purée into the gelatine and then back into the bulk. Fold the purée evenly into the cool egg mixture. Add colouring if desired. When

Strawberries Romanoff (*see page 79*)

the raspberry mixture is starting to set fold in the lightly whipped cream; when evenly blended turn into a 2½-pt. serving dish. Chill in a refrigerator. To serve, decorate with crystallised violets.

Note: With 3 level tsps. gelatine this mousse has a very light creamy texture; for a firmer texture use 4 tsps. gelatine.

✻ Raspberry cream ring

A luscious, cream-filled, light as air sponge; raspberries add just the right sharpness and glycerine helps to keep the cake moist.

3 large eggs
3 oz. caster sugar
3 oz. plain flour, sifted
2 tsps. glycerine
2 level tbsps. sugar for syrup
2 tbsps. water
2 tbsps. sherry
½ pt. whipping cream
½ lb. fresh raspberries
icing sugar

Grease and flour a 3½-pt. ring mould. Whisk together the eggs and sugar over a bowl of hot (not boiling) water until the mixture is thick and pale in colour. Remove from the heat and continue whisking until cool. Resift half the flour over the egg mixture and fold in quickly and lightly. Repeat with the remaining flour and add the glycerine. Turn the mixture into the mould and bake above the oven centre at 375°F, 190°C (mark 5) for about 30 minutes. Turn the ring out and cool on a wire rack.

Prepare a thin syrup by boiling the 2 tbsps. sugar and water together; add the sherry. Split the cake in half and moisten the cut surface with the sherry syrup. Whisk the cream until it holds its shape, spoon it over the sponge halves and embed the raspberries in the cream on the base part. Top with the lid and dust with icing sugar.

HANDY HINT

If you lightly grease the cup, spoon or scale pan when measuring honey or syrup, it really will pour more easily. (Or lightly dust with flour to prevent sticking.)

Pineapple and grape salad

Served in the natural 'shell', these salads can be prepared several hours ahead and kept covered, but don't add the syrup until the last minute.

2 medium sized ripe pineapples
8-oz. can pineapple rings
8 oz. white grapes, peeled, halved and pipped
2 oz. trifle sponge cakes
2 tbsps. Kirsch
3 tbsps. lemon juice
2 level tbsps. caster sugar

MAKES 6

Cut away the top and bottom of each pineapple. Slice each in three crosswise. Scoop out almost all the flesh from the 'cases' leaving a base of fruit intact. Stand each 'case' on a small plate. Cut the pineapple flesh into small pieces. Drain the canned pineapple, reserving juice, shred the fruit and add it to the fresh pineapple. Combine with the grapes. Crush the sponges and divide between the pineapple cases. Mix 6 tbsps. reserved pineapple juice with the Kirsch and spoon it over the sponge. Heat the remaining pineapple juice in a small saucepan with the lemon juice and sugar. Bring it to the boil and continue to boil until a syrup is formed; remove it from the heat and set aside to cool. Fill the pineapple cases with the prepared fruit and spoon the syrup over.

Eight-fruit salad

Nobody says no to a home-made fruit salad; if time allows prepare it a day ahead but don't include the raspberries and apple until just before serving.

1 lb. fresh ripe apricots
juice of 2 lemons
4 large ripe eating pears
3 bananas
4 oz. green grapes
4 oz. black grapes
10½-oz. can lychees
1-lb. 13-oz. can yellow peach halves
4 oz. caster sugar
1 pt. water
3 tbsps. Cointreau
¾ lb. raspberries
1 red eating apple

SERVES 8

Place the apricots in boiling water for 1 minute, plunge them immediately into cold water then remove the skins, halve and stone them. Brush the surfaces lightly with lemon juice. Peel and core the pears and cut them into thin slices. Peel and slice the bananas. Toss both in lemon juice. Combine these three fruits in a large bowl. Skin grapes, if wished; halve and pip them. Add to the bowl with the contents of the can of lychees. Cut the peaches into quarters and add with their syrup to the salad. In a saucepan, slowly dissolve the sugar in the water. Bring to the boil, remove the pan from the heat and allow the syrup to get cold before adding the liqueur. Fold the syrup through the salad. Chill for 3–4 hours before serving or make the day before and keep covered in the refrigerator. Just before serving, scatter the raspberries over; core the apple, leaving the skin on, and arrange thin slices in a fan shape over the top of the salad. Coat the surface with syrup.

Banana creole

Choose a dish suitable for cooking and serving; pouring cream is a good accompaniment.

$2\frac{1}{2}$ oz. butter
8 bananas
1 large orange
1 lemon
4 oz. rolled oats
2 oz. dark soft brown sugar

SERVES 8

Use $\frac{1}{2}$ oz. butter to grease a $2\frac{1}{2}$-pt. shallow oven-proof serving dish. Peel the bananas and cut them into $\frac{1}{2}$-in. thick slices. Place in the dish in an even layer. Grate the rind from the orange and the lemon over the bananas. Combine rolled oats and sugar in a small basin and scatter over the bananas. Squeeze the juice from the fruit and pour over the topping. Press down gently. Divide 2 oz. butter into small pats and place evenly over the oats mixture. Bake un-covered at 375°F, 190°C (mark 5) for 40–45 minutes.

Melon and grapefruit jelly

4 level tsps. powdered gelatine
1-lb. 3-oz. can sweetened grapefruit juice
$2\frac{3}{4}$-lb. ripe honeydew melon
1 oz. stem ginger

SERVES 6

Soften the gelatine in a little of the fruit juice in a small bowl over a pan of hot water, then dissolve it in the bulk of the juice. Stir in the roughly chopped melon flesh and finely chopped ginger. When it begins to set, pour the jelly into a 2-pt. mould. Chill to set, then unmould and serve with pouring cream.

Blackcurrant brûlée

Crack through the sweet top crust to the sharp-tasting fruit below.

$\frac{1}{2}$ lb. stemmed blackcurrants
$\frac{1}{4}$ pt. water
3 oz. Demerara sugar
$1\frac{1}{2}$ level tsps. arrowroot
1 tbsp. water
$\frac{1}{4}$ pt. soured cream
soft light brown sugar
ground cinnamon
sponge fingers

SERVES 4

Place the blackcurrants and water in a saucepan. Cook gently until the fruit is almost tender, add the Demerara sugar, return to the boil and cook for a few minutes longer. Blend the arrowroot with 1 tbsp. water, stir it into the blackcurrants and gently boil, stirring, for 1–2 minutes. Cool and spoon into individual ovenproof dishes. Top with soured cream and cover with a layer of light soft brown sugar, to which is added a pinch of ground cinnamon. Flash under a hot grill until bubbling then chill. Serve with sponge fingers.

Blackcurrant galette

An open pie fashioned prettily with a lattice top. Bake in an oven-to-table flan dish.

8 oz. plain flour
4 oz. butter
2 oz. lard
2 level tbsps. caster sugar
1 small egg, beaten
2 oz. semolina
2 oz. caster sugar
$1\frac{1}{4}$ lb. blackcurrants, stalked

SERVES 8

Sift the flour into a bowl, grate the fat straight from the refrigerator into the flour and rub it in lightly. Add 2 tbsps. caster sugar and mix to a firm dough with cold water. Roll out the pastry and line a greased 9-in. fluted ovenproof flan dish. Trim off the excess pastry, prick the base with a fork and brush with a little beaten egg. Chill in the refrigerator. Mix together the semolina and caster sugar and layer it up with the blackcurrants in the pastry-lined dish. Roll out the pastry trimmings, cut them into strips with a pastry wheel and use to lattice the flan dish. Brush with beaten egg and bake at 425°F, 220°C (mark 7) for 30–40 minutes.

Blackcurrant cream slice

¼ pt. double cream
2 tbsps. milk
32 boudoir biscuits
14¼-oz. can blackcurrant pie filling

SERVES 6

Whip the cream with the milk until it just holds its shape. Arrange 8 biscuits side by side on a flat serving plate, sugar side up. Spread with a thin layer of cream and some of the pie filling. Repeat, layering to use all the biscuits and finish the top with a border of piped cream with pie filling down the centre. Chill for 5–6 hours.

Redcurrant Griestorte

We have not forgotten the flour in the 'Swiss roll'; instead semolina holds its light texture.

3 large eggs, separated
4 oz. caster sugar
juice and grated rind of ½ lemon
2 oz. semolina
1 level tbsp. ground almonds
6 fl. oz. double cream
1 tbsp. milk
¼ lb. redcurrants
icing sugar

SERVES 6

Grease and line a Swiss roll tin 8 in. by 12 in. with non-stick paper to extend above the sides. Grease the paper, sprinkle with caster sugar and a dusting of flour. Whisk the egg yolks with 4 oz. sugar until thick and pale. Whisk in the lemon juice. Stir in the rind, semolina and almonds mixed together. Whisk the egg whites until stiff and fold the egg yolk mixture through the whites. Turn the mixture into the tin, level the surface and bake at 350°F, 180°C (mark 4) for about 30 minutes, until it is puffed and pale gold. Turn the Griestorte carefully on to a sheet of non-stick paper dusted with caster sugar. Trim the long edges and roll it up loosely with the paper inside. Cool on a wire rack. To finish, whisk the cream with the milk until it just holds its shape. Unroll the Griestorte – don't worry if it cracks a little – spread the cream over but not quite to the edges and sprinkle with currants, reserving a few on the stem for decoration. Roll up, pressing the roll lightly into shape. Dust with icing sugar and decorate. Eat the same day.

Rhubarb mousse

This mousse has a hint of surprise – marmalade.

1 lb. rhubarb, prepared weight
4 oz. sugar
¼ pt. water
5 level tbsps. ginger marmalade
1 level tbsp. powdered gelatine
3 tbsps. water
1 egg white
¼ pt. double cream
1 tbsp. milk

SERVES 6

Cut the rhubarb into 1-in. lengths. Put the rhubarb, sugar, water and 4 tbsps. marmalade in a saucepan and cook until the rhubarb is tender. Purée it in a blender or put it through a sieve. Dissolve the gelatine in the water in a small bowl over a pan of hot water. Stir this into the rhubarb. When it is on the point of setting, fold in the stiffly beaten egg white. Divide between 6 stemmed glasses and chill. Whip the cream with the milk until it just holds its shape, fold in the remaining tbsp. marmalade and use to top the mousse.

✳ Frosted gooseberry plate pie

A tasty way to use the fruit in season.

8 oz. self-raising flour
pinch of salt
2 oz. lard
2 oz. margarine
1 oz. caster sugar
1 egg, separated
water
1 lb. gooseberries
3 oz. granulated sugar
2 level tbsps. flour
grated rind of 1 orange
2 oz. icing sugar

SERVES 6

Combine the flour and salt in a bowl. Rub in

the fats and add the sugar. Blend the egg yolk with 4 tbsps. water, stir it into the flour with more water to give a manageable dough. Divide the pastry in half and roll out to line an 8-in. pie plate, preferably metal. Top and tail the gooseberries and in so doing cut a small slice from the end. Pile the gooseberries over the pastry. Mix the sugar, flour and orange rind and sprinkle them over the fruit. Roll out the remaining pastry and use for a lid. Make a slit in the lid. Bake in the oven at 400°F, 200°C (mark 6) for about 45 minutes. Brush with frosting and return it to the oven for 5 minutes. Serve warm or cold.

For frosting: Blend the egg white and icing sugar together.

Gooseberry ice cream flan

Cornflakes make this flan crust really crunchy. Warm gooseberry sauce marries well with the ice cream filling.

For crunch crust
4 oz. cornflakes
2 oz. butter
2 oz. Demerara or light soft brown sugar

For filling
2 oz. caster or granulated sugar
½ pt. water
½ lb. gooseberries, topped and tailed
juice of 1 orange
1 level tbsp. cornflour
17-fl. oz. block Cornish ice cream

SERVES 6

Roughly crush the cornflakes. Melt the butter, stir in the sugar and heat, without boiling, until the sugar has dissolved. Stir in the cornflakes and heat gently for about 3 minutes. Spoon the cornflake mixture into a 9-in. fluted porcelain flan dish. Press it into the sides and base to form a shell and chill.

In a saucepan, dissolve the sugar in the water over a low heat. Add the gooseberries, halved if

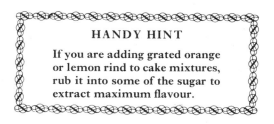

HANDY HINT

If you are adding grated orange or lemon rind to cake mixtures, rub it into some of the sugar to extract maximum flavour.

large, and simmer until just tender. Blend the juice from the orange into the cornflour. Stir in a little gooseberry juice and return to the pan, bring to the boil and simmer for 1–2 minutes. To serve, scoop the ice cream with a tablespoon and pack it into the chilled crust. If a home freezer or a freezing compartment of a refrigerator is available, the pie can be kept here until required. Spoon warm sauce over just before serving. Serve in wedges.

Gooseberry fool

Has a full, sharp fruit flavour that goes well after the week-end roast.

1 lb. gooseberries
2 tbsps. water
4 oz. sugar
¼ pt. custard and ¼ pt. double cream (or ½ pt. double cream)
green colouring
grated chocolate for decoration

SERVES 4

Top and tail the gooseberries. Cook them with the water and sugar until the fruit is soft and well reduced, then sieve it. Make a custard with ¼ pt. milk, 3 level tsps. custard powder and 3 level tsps. sugar; stir occasionally while cooling. Whip the cream. Fold the custard and then the cream into the gooseberry purée. Add a few drops of colouring and chill. Divide the fool between 4 sundae glasses and decorate with grated chocolate.

Ice cream fiesta

A quick dessert. Keep trifle sponges in the cupboard, ice cream in the freezer and change the fruit according to season.

2 trifle sponge cakes
sherry
1 level tsp. arrowroot
4 tbsps. rose-hip syrup
4 tbsps. water
¼ lb. strawberries, hulled and sliced
2 individual blocks plain dairy ice cream
chopped nuts or whipped cream for decoration

SERVES 2

Split the trifle sponge cakes in half. Place the bottom halves on individual plates and moisten with sherry. Combine the arrowroot, rose-hip syrup and water in a small pan and bring to the boil, stirring. Allow to cool and when lukewarm, fold in the strawberries. Sandwich the sponges with blocks of ice cream and spoon the strawberry sauce over. Decorate with chopped nuts or whipped cream and serve at once.

Berries with brandy

Simple but special.

1 lb. small strawberries (or raspberries)
3 tbsps. thin acacia honey
3 tbsps. brandy

SERVES 4–6

Hull the berries and place them in a bowl. Combine the honey and brandy and blend well together. Pour over the berries and turn gently so as to coat all the fruit well. Chill for about 2 hours, stirring occasionally. Serve the fruit with lightly whipped double cream.
Note: For youngsters, substitute orange juice for brandy.

Ice creams

You really need a freezer to make your own ice creams successfully, though it is possible to make small quantities in the freezing compartment of a refrigerator set at lowest. Turn ice cream mixture into a rigid container, preferably polythene, to give at least 1 in. depth or more. If using the ice cube compartment of a refrigerator, beat the mixture at the slushy stage and return to the refrigerator to freeze until firm. When using a home freezer freeze in the storage container.

Rum and raisin ice cream

A little exotic in flavour, this ice cream is a popular choice for dinner parties.

4 oz. seedless raisins
4 tbsps. rum
4 eggs
4 oz. icing sugar
$\frac{1}{2}$ pt. double cream

SERVES 6–8

Soak the raisins in rum for about 30 minutes. Separate the eggs and whisk the yolks and sugar together until thick and fluffy. Whip the cream until thick and fold into the egg mixture. Add the rum-soaked raisins. Whisk the egg whites until stiff and fold into the raisin mixture, then pour it into a polythene container. Freeze for about 1 hour, then stir the mixture to redistribute

the raisins. Seal the container, label and return it to the freezer till solid.

Strawberry liqueur ice cream

$\frac{1}{2}$ pt. double or whipping cream
1 lb. strawberries or raspberries
$\frac{1}{2}$ tsp. vanilla essence
1 tbsp. Maraschino
2 oz. icing sugar

SERVES 6–8

Whip the cream until it just holds its shape. Pass the berries through a fine nylon sieve. Combine all the ingredients together in a bowl. Turn the mixture into a rigid container, cover, seal, label and freeze. Store for up to 3 months. (Makes about $1\frac{1}{2}$ pt.)

Lemon ice cream

$\frac{1}{2}$ pt. double cream
2 eggs
grated rind and juice of 2 lemons
8–10 oz. caster sugar
$\frac{1}{2}$ pt. milk

SERVES 8–10

Beat together the cream and eggs, using a rotary whisk, until smooth and thick but not firm. Add the rind, juice and milk and mix thoroughly. Pour the mixture into a rigid container, seal, label and freeze. Store for up to 3 months. Makes about 2 pt.

Apricot ice cream

1 lb. ripe apricots
water
6 oz. sugar
5 egg yolks
½ pt. double cream

SERVES 12–15

Halve and stone the apricots, cook them until soft in the minimum of water, then sieve. Dissolve the sugar in ¼ pt. water, bring to the boil and boil to a syrupy consistency, or 217°F. Beat the egg yolks in a deep bowl and while still beating pour in the slightly cooled syrup; whisk until thick and frothy. When the egg mixture is cold, whip the cream until it holds its shape and fold into the egg mixture with the fruit purée. Turn the cream into a rigid container, cover, seal, label and freeze. Store for up to 3 months. Makes about 3 pt.

Grapefruit sorbet

6 oz. sugar
¾ pt. water
6½-fl. oz. can frozen grapefruit juice
2 egg whites
mint sprigs

SERVES 6

Dissolve the sugar in the water. When dissolved, bring the syrup to the boil and boil, uncovered, for 10 minutes. Turn the frozen juice into a bowl and pour on the sugar syrup. When cold, pour into a 1-pt. capacity rigid container and freeze to a slushy consistency. Whisk the egg whites until thick and foamy but not dry. Fold them into the grapefruit slush and return the mixture to the freezer and freeze until firm. Seal and label. Store for up to 3 months. Just before required, spoon the sorbet into chilled glasses, decorate with mint sprigs and serve with fan wafers.

Pineapple sorbet

1-lb. 4-oz. can pineapple
water
8 oz. sugar
2 tbsps. lemon juice
juice 1 orange
2 egg whites

SERVES 8–10

Drain the pineapple and make the juice up to 1 pt. with water. In a saucepan, dissolve the sugar in the pineapple juice, bring to the boil and boil rapidly in the open pan for 5 minutes. Cool. In an electric blender purée the drained pineapple and combine it with the syrup, lemon and orange juices. Freeze to a slush. Whisk the egg whites until stiff and fold into the half-set mixture. Turn the sorbet into a rigid container, cover, seal, label and freeze. Store for up to 3 months. Makes about 2 pt.

Summer cakes

✳ Strawberry split cake

A straight forward butter sponge for the family and friends.

4 oz. butter or block margarine
4 oz. caster sugar
2 large eggs
4 oz. self-raising flour
strawberry jam
butter cream, made with 2 oz. butter and 4 oz. sifted icing sugar
icing sugar to dredge

Grease and line an 8-in. double sandwich tin. Cream together the butter and sugar until light and fluffy. Add the eggs one at a time, beating well. Add the flour gradually, beating lightly after each addition. Turn the mixture into the prepared tin, spread it evenly and bake in the centre of the oven at 350°F, 180°C (mark 4) for about 30 minutes. Turn the sponge out on to a wire rack to cool. Split the cake and sandwich together with the jam and the butter cream. Thickly dredge the top of the cake with icing sugar and score diagonal lines across the surface, using a knife.

Little cheese cakes

Similar to curd tarts, these have a light filling glazed with a lemon icing.

8 oz. shortcrust pastry (8 oz. flour, etc.)
$\frac{1}{4}$ pt. soured cream
2 eggs, separated
3 oz. caster sugar
juice and finely grated rind of 1 lemon
8 oz. plain cottage cheese
1 level tbsp. flour
icing sugar

MAKES 24

Roll out the pastry and use it to line 24 $2\frac{1}{2}$-in. diameter (top measurement) patty tins, using a 3-in. plain cutter. In an electric blender goblet, blend the soured cream, egg yolks, caster sugar, 1 tsp. lemon juice and the finely grated rind, cottage cheese and flour until smooth. Stiffly whisk the egg whites and fold the blended ingredients through. Divide the mixture between the pastry shells and bake in the oven at 375°F, 190°C (mark 5) for about 20 minutes. Cool on a wire rack. Make up a little glacé icing with icing sugar and some lemon juice and brush some over the surface of each cheese cake.

✳ Fruit and almond slice

A moist nut and fruit topping on a short buttery base – best eaten fresh.

For the base
3 oz. plain flour
1 oz. caster sugar
2 oz. butter
1 oz. currants
12 glacé cherries, halved

For the topping
2 oz. butter
2 oz. caster sugar
1 egg
2 oz. ground almonds
1–2 drops almond essence

MAKES 12

Line the base of a shallow 7–$7\frac{1}{2}$-in. square baking tin with greased greaseproof paper. Sift the flour into a bowl, add the sugar and work in the butter. When the mixture binds together, press into an even layer over the base of the tin. Scatter the currants and halved cherries on top.
　　Cream the butter and sugar together until

light and fluffy. Add the beaten egg by degrees, beating very thoroughly. Stir in the ground almonds and essence. Spread the topping over the currants and cherries and bake at 375°F, 190°C (mark 5) for about 40 minutes, until just set and golden brown. Cool on a wire rack. Cut in fingers when cold.

✳ Date and raisin teabread

A teabread in the freezer is a valuable asset – if you make large loaves and there are only two in the family, then halve the baked loaf and store the other half in the freezer.

4 oz. butter or margarine
8 oz. plain flour
4 oz. stoned dates, chopped
2 oz. shelled walnut halves, chopped
4 oz. seedless raisins
4 oz. Demerara sugar
1 level tsp. baking powder
1 level tsp. bicarbonate of soda
$\frac{1}{4}$ pt. milk (approx.)

Grease and line a $9\frac{3}{4}$-in. by $5\frac{3}{4}$-in. (top measurement) loaf tin. Rub the fat into the flour to resemble fine breadcrumbs. Stir in the dates, walnuts, raisins and sugar. Mix the baking powder, bicarbonate of soda and milk in a measure and pour into the centre of the dry ingredients, then mix well together. Turn the mixture into the prepared tin and bake in the centre of the oven at 350°F, 180°C (mark 4) for about 1 hour, until well risen and a skewer comes out clean. Cool on a wire rack. Serve sliced and buttered.

✳ Coffee whirls

Serve plain or chocolate-filled at coffee time.

6 oz. butter
2 oz. icing sugar, sifted
2 level tsps. instant coffee granules
6 oz. plain flour
icing sugar or melted chocolate, optional

MAKES ABOUT 12

Cream the butter and sugar until soft and light. Beat in the coffee granules. Gradually work in the flour, then turn the mixture into a forcing bag fitted with a small vegetable star nozzle. Pipe little whirls of mixture on to greased baking sheets, leaving a small hole in the centre of each. Leave in a cool place, preferably the refrigerator, for at least 1 hour. Bake in the oven at 325°F, 170°C (mark 3) for about 25 minutes. Cool on a wire rack. Serve plain, dusted with icing sugar, or sandwich in pairs with melted chocolate.

✳ Buttermilk cherry loaf cake

Is there buttermilk left over? Here is an easy-to-put-together mixture for everyday occasions.

8 oz. self-raising flour
1½ level tsps. baking powder
¼ level tsp. mixed spice
¼ level tsp. ground ginger
4 oz. butter or margarine
4 oz. soft dark brown sugar
6 oz. glacé cherries, halved
½ tbsp. black treacle
1 egg, beaten
¼ pt. buttermilk

Grease and line a 9-in. by 4½-in. (top measurement) loaf tin. Sift the flour, baking powder and spices into a bowl. Rub in the fat and stir in the sugar and cherries. Mix together the treacle, egg and buttermilk and stir into the dry ingredients. Turn the mixture into the tin, level the surface and bake in the centre of the oven at 350°F, 180°C (mark 4) for 1–1¼ hours. Turn out and cool on a wire rack.

Lemon glazed meltaways

Short textured buttery cookies with a real lemon tang. Meltaways are best eaten within a day or two.

8 oz. butter
2 oz. icing sugar, sifted
grated rind of 1 lemon
8 oz. plain flour
apricot jam, sieved
icing sugar and lemon juice to glaze tops

MAKES 36–42

Grease 2–3 baking sheets. Cream the butter until soft, add the sifted icing sugar and beat well. Stir in the lemon rind and flour. When the mixture is well blended, put it into a nylon forcing bag fitted with a large star vegetable nozzle. Pipe about 20 rosettes and 20 shell shapes on the baking sheets and chill for 30 minutes. Bake in the centre of the oven or just below at 325°F, 170°C (mark 3) for about 25 minutes, or until slightly coloured; remove from the oven. Brush each cookie with a little apricot jam, then with a soft icing made by blending about 2 level tbsps. icing sugar to a coating consistency with lemon juice. Return to the oven for 5 minutes; remove and cool on a wire rack.

Almond bars

These are good picnic fare; the baked mixture travels best in the tin ready for cutting *in situ*.

4 oz. butter or margarine
9 oz. plain flour
3 oz. caster sugar
¼ level tsp. almond essence
4 level tbsps. apricot jam
2 tbsps. water
2 pieces stem ginger, chopped
½ lb. ready-made marzipan
2 oz. shelled walnut halves, coarsely chopped
icing sugar

Line a tin measuring 11¼ in. by 7 in. by 1¼ in. with greaseproof paper. In a bowl rub the butter into the flour and add the sugar and essence. Work to a dough then press into the base of the tin, using the knuckles. Heat together the jam, water and ginger and spread over the dough. Coarsely grate the marzipan over the jam and sprinkle with chopped walnuts. Bake in the oven at 300°F, 150°C (mark 2) for 45 minutes. When cold, dredge with icing sugar and cut into bars.

CHAPTER THREE

AUTUMN

As the leaves turn and the days mellow it's the time to gather in the last of the fruit and nut crops – plums, damsons, greengages are at their juiciest for eating and preserving. September is a good time for storing away pickles and chutneys. English apples and dessert pears arrive now in abundance and peaches are likely to be lower in price. It's the season for native Whitstable and Colchester oysters and the first scallops. As Autumn draws out look for tiny sprats and skate if you like them. October 1st brings the opening of pheasant shooting, game is now in full swing, with hare good value too. Juicy fresh figs come about now from the Mediterranean and there are grapes too.

If you are celebrating Hallowe'en, throw a party for the young folk that won't throw your budget. Start with a fruit cooler, then serve a bean pot with frankfurters and later in the evening perhaps a tray of stuffed baked apples, oozing with syrup straight from the oven, and a bowl of thick cream. A more sophisticated menu for parents and friends is on page 92.

Fireworks and glowing bonfires in the cold night air mean it's time to eat traditional parkin – a firm, mealy type of gingerbread. But they are also a reminder that you should be making Christmas cakes, puddings and mincemeat now to give them time to mellow. So when money and time are precious it's worth remembering valuable main meal meat buys, heart, kidney, liver and tripe. All these are ideal for stick-'em-in-the-oven dishes or quick grills. Cook these cuts immediately, or keep them in the fridge for no more than a day, loosely wrapped in foil so that air can get to the meat.

There is a wonderful choice of fresh vegetables at this time of year, all with plenty of flavour when cunningly cooked. Swedes are great for mashing with butter and serve crisply cooked cabbage with a generous grating of nutmeg. Spoon soured cream, gently warmed and lightly flavoured with finely chopped onion, over lightly cooked Brussels sprouts and when sautéeing potatoes include a dusting of paprika. Savour foil-wrapped whole baked onions to partner the roast. Carrots are even more tasty with a squeeze of lemon juice or a dash of curry and young parsnips become a delicious treat when roasted during the week. Add a few butter-fried flaked almonds with broccoli to make it crunchy.

Take the opportunity in Autumn to re-stock on those cereals which need regular replenishment – semolina for the quickest of creamy milk puddings or savoury

Italian gnocchi; rolled oats, the base for Swiss Muesli, syrup flapjacks and Christmas cookies; pudding rice for long slow delicious rice puddings (put mixed dried fruits on the list too to make a wonderful compote accompaniment). And don't forget rice flour for traditional shortbread – this is good too for thickening Autumn warmers like home-made broth.

For the freezer
Buy freshly killed game, hang it well and prepare for the table to appreciate when out of season. Freeze down apples, puréed and sliced, plums and damsons, but don't overload with only one thing – apples also store well out of the freezer. Look for turkey bargains as advance Christmas buys. It's worth putting in a little fresh coconut for curries, and also horseradish. Aubergines, courgettes and peppers should be down in price so it's a good time to make ratatouille.

Autumn fruits
Chinese gooseberries, clementines (arrive November), cranberries, dates, lychees (September is the end of season), loquats, mandarins (arrive November), mangoes (September), nectarines (October), chestnuts (arrive October), blueberries, quinces (October), satsumas, tangerines (arrive November), coconuts, uglis (arrive November), figs, bilberries (September is the end of season), damsons, greengages (September is the end of season), mulberries (September is the end of season), blackberries, plums, pomegranates, raspberries (September is the end of the season), papaws.

Autumn vegetables
Aubergines, broccoli, Brussels sprouts, Brussels tops, calabrese (September), celeriac, celery, chicory, corn on the cob (season ends October), courgettes, chillies (November), endive (season ends October), fennel, French beans, globe and Jerusalem artichokes, horseradish, kohlrabi (arrives November), kale (arrives November), leeks, parsnips, pumpkin, radishes, salsify, savoys (arrive November), shallots, spinach, spring greens (arrive November), vegetable marrow, turnips, swedes, sweet potatoes.

Autumn poultry/game
Duck (September only), goose, hare, mallard, partridge, pheasant (starts October 1st), rabbit, snipe, teal (September 1st–January 31st), venison, wild goose, woodcock, grouse, wild duck, plover, ptarmigan, widgeon (October–February), wood pigeon, black game.

Autumn menus

(Dishes marked * are included in the recipes on pages 93 to 121)

Harvest supper for 6
*Eggs indienne

*Hot pork and orange one-crust pie
Scalloped potatoes
Dressed broccoli spears
Chicory and cucumber salad

*Fluffy Jamaican creams

Family supper for 4
*Tuna-stuffed pancakes
Mixed salad

*Lemon shorties
Fresh fruit

Sunday lunch for 6
Tomato bouillon

*Rolled stuffed shoulder of lamb
Oven-browned potatoes
Buttered sprouts

*Apricot surprise

Mid-week menu for 4
*Liver and bacon pudding
Carrot ring sauté
Whole baked tomatoes

*Lemon delight

Saturday evening menu for 6
Fresh grapefruit

*Steak and wine pie

Casseroled onions and celery
Buttered potatoes with parsley

*Ice cream with rum and mince-
meat sauce

Cut the cost menus

*Cod oriental
Fluffy rice
Leaf spinach

*Applescotch flan

*Lambs' liver with mustard farce
Creamed potatoes
Broccoli

*Ambrosia

Dinner menu for 4
Sherried melon balls

*Roast pheasant
Thin gravy
Bread sauce
Fried crumbs
Potato chips
Dressed watercress
*Braised celery

*Red wine jelly

Dinner menu for 6
*Potage St Germain
Croûtons

*Chicken suprême julienne
Duchesse potatoes
Stuffed tomatoes
Green beans

*Nut meringue with marinaded
peaches

Flat-warming party for 12
*Pineapple, banana and pepper
cocktail

*Biryani
*Pork with peas
Sliced onions and tomato
Yoghurt dressed cucumber
Tossed green salad

*Pears brûlée with orange cream
*Caramel bavarois with coffee
sauce

Lager, cider or iced water

*Sausage Kiev
Curried rice
Peanut and apple salad

*Pineapple whip

*Haricot lamb
Sautéed leeks
Parslied potatoes

*Apple snow

Dinner menu for 6
* Three-fish pâté
Melba toast

*Roast duckling with grapefruit
sauce
Duchesse potatoes
Sweetcorn
Broccoli

*Apple and blackberry compote
Pouring cream

Tête à tête
Smoked mackerel
Brown bread and butter

*Paupiettes of pork
Asparagus with butter
Sautéed mushrooms
Casseroled potatoes

*Lemon and grape creams
Cigarettes russes

Stilton
Watercress

Hallowe'en party for 12
Spiced tomato soup or melon
laced with sherry
Oven-warmed baps

*Frankfurters en chemise
*Barbecued chicken with noodles
Artichoke and tomato salad
Garlic cream dressing
Cos lettuce

*Glazed cherry flan
*Orange snow

Cheeseboard
Coffee

Autumn starters

✳ Potage St Germain

This filling soup can be prepared in advance. Re-heat just before serving.

3 oz. butter
3 oz. onion, skinned and chopped
¾ lb. leeks, trimmed and sliced
½ lb. spinach, coarse stems removed
1 lettuce, trimmed and washed
1 pkt. thick pea soup mix
salt and freshly ground black pepper
1½ pt. stock

SERVES 6

Melt 2 oz. butter in a large saucepan, add the onion and leeks, cover and sauté for 5 minutes. Add the spinach and lettuce and cook for a further 10 minutes. Sprinkle the soup mix over the vegetables. Stir in, pour over the stock, cover and simmer for 20 minutes. Adjust the seasoning and purée in an electric blender. Re-heat and stir in the remaining 1 oz. butter just before serving.

✳ Pumpkin and leek soup

Easy to make, but extraordinarily good!

1½ oz. butter
1 lb. pumpkin, prepared weight, cut into cubes
2 leeks, washed and sliced
½ lb. tomatoes, sliced
1¼ pt. stock
salt and freshly ground black pepper
2 tbsps. chopped parsley

SERVES 6

Melt 1 oz. butter in a 4–5-pt. saucepan and add the pumpkin, leeks and tomatoes. Cook, covered, for about 10 minutes, shaking the pan occasion-

ally. Add the stock, adjust seasoning and cook for a further 15 minutes. Put through a sieve or purée in an electric blender. Return the soup to the pan, add the remaining butter and reheat. Just before serving, add the parsley.

✳ Three-fish pâté

An ideal starter to mellow the mood of the evening. There is no need to use top quality salmon.

7½-oz. can salmon
7-oz. can tuna
4 oz. peeled prawns
6 oz. fresh white breadcrumbs
4 oz. butter, melted
grated rind and juice of 2 lemons
3 tsps. anchovy essence
½ pt. single cream
salt and freshly ground black pepper

SERVES 6

Flake the contents of the can of salmon, adding the juices together with the contents of the can of tuna. Roughly chop the prawns. In a bowl, combine breadcrumbs, butter and lemon rind and juice. Add to the flaked fish with the prawns. Stir in the anchovy essence and cream and adjust seasoning to taste. Divide between 8 ¼-pt. individual soufflé dishes, level off the mixture and chill. Serve with fingers of freshly made toast.

✳ Bacon and liver pâté

For this substantial pâté in a pastry crust use off-cuts from thrifty cuts of bacon – they are fine for mincing.

½ lb. streaky or back bacon, rinded
4 oz. chicken livers
1 medium sized onion, skinned
1 level tbsp. flour
2–4 tbsps. milk
1 large egg, beaten
2 tbsps. sherry (optional)
salt and pepper
grated nutmeg
6 thin cut streaky rashers, rinded
1 egg, beaten, for glazing
7½-oz. pkt. frozen puff pastry, thawed

SERVES 6

HANDY HINT

When using vegetables in soups, sweat your vegetables in butter, not really frying them and certainly not browning them. Sliced thinly, they absorb more butter and cook more quickly and evenly.

Mince the ½ lb. bacon twice, then again with the livers and onion. Mix these in a bowl with the flour, milk (use the larger amount of milk if sherry is not included), egg, sherry and seasonings. Mix well. Line a loaf tin, 7¾ in. by 4 in. (top measurement) with streaky rashers. Turn the minced mixture into the tin, level the top and bake uncovered at 350°F, 180°C (mark 4) for 30 minutes. Cool in the tin for 10 minutes then turn it out and brush with egg.

Roll out the pastry thinly and enclose the pâté completely, sealing the edges with egg. Decorate with pastry trimmings, brush with egg, place on a baking sheet and bake at 400°F, 200°C (mark 6) for about 30 minutes until golden.

Piperade

Piperade is a delicious starter for 3 or serves 2 as a light lunch or supper dish with a tossed salad.

6½-oz. can red peppers (pimientos)
¼ lb. tomatoes
2 oz. butter
1 small onion, skinned and finely chopped
2 small cloves garlic, skinned and crushed
salt and freshly ground black pepper
4 eggs
2 tbsps. milk

SERVES 2–3

Drain the peppers and shred them finely. Skin the tomatoes, cut them into halves, discard the seeds and roughly chop the flesh. Melt the butter in a medium size pan and when frothy add the onion and garlic; cook for 1–2 minutes, then add the peppers and simmer for 4 minutes. Finally add the tomatoes. Season well and leave to simmer while you beat the eggs, milk and seasoning with a fork.

When the vegetables in the pan are well reduced, pour in the beaten eggs. Cook for 3–4 minutes, stirring continuously. When a soft-scrambled egg is obtained, turn on to a hot

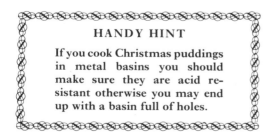

HANDY HINT

If you cook Christmas puddings in metal basins you should make sure they are acid resistant otherwise you may end up with a basin full of holes.

serving plate and surround with freshly fried croûtons.

Note: To make the croûtons, blend 3 oz. butter with ½ crushed clove of garlic, spread over 3 slices of bread and toast until melted and golden. Do the same to the other side, then cut into small squares.

Eggs indienne

3 oz. butter
6 oz. onion, skinned and very finely chopped
1 tsp. dried celery flakes
1½ level tsps. curry powder
9 tbsps. thick mayonnaise
3 tbsps. milk
2 eating apples, peeled, cored and finely chopped
few drops Tabasco sauce
salt and freshly ground black pepper
6 hard-boiled eggs
watercress for garnish

SERVES 6

Melt the butter in a saucepan and add the onion and celery flakes. Sauté until really tender, then stir in the curry powder and cook for 2 minutes. Cool and chop again until the mixture is pulpy. Combine the mayonnaise and milk in a basin, stir in the curried onion and eating apple. Season to taste with Tabasco, salt and pepper. Store covered. To serve, halve the eggs, place on individual plates and mask with the curry mayonnaise. Garnish with watercress.

Pineapple, banana and pepper cocktail

Enjoyed by many Good Housekeeping readers as an appetiser with a difference.

8 tbsps. salad oil
4 tbsps. wine vinegar
1 level tsp. French mustard
1 level tsp. caster sugar
½ level tsp. salt
freshly ground black pepper
2 cloves garlic, skinned and crushed
8 oz. green pepper, seeded and finely chopped
1-lb. 13-oz. can pineapple chunks, drained
6 medium bananas, peeled

SERVES 12

Shake together in a small screw-topped container the first seven ingredients. Marinade the chopped peppers in the dressing. Halve the pineapple cubes, if large, slice the bananas and toss all the ingredients together. Marinade for up to 1½ hours. Serve in stemmed glasses.

Pasta hors d'oeuvre

4 oz. pasta shells
1 egg yolk
¼ pt. corn oil
1 tbsp. vinegar
pinch sugar
¼ level tsp. dry mustard
salt and freshly ground black pepper
1 tbsp. top of the milk
2 oz. onion, skinned and finely chopped
1 level tsp. tomato paste
4 oz. cooked ham, sliced
4 oz. pressed tongue, sliced
6 oz. crisp green apples, cored and finely diced
chopped parsley

SERVES 6

Cook the macaroni shells until tender in salted water, as directed on the packet. Drain and rinse under cold running water. Make ¼ pt. mayonnaise using the egg yolk, oil, vinegar, sugar, mustard, salt and pepper. Blend in the top of the milk, onion and tomato paste. Slice the ham and tongue into strips, dice the apple and toss the macaroni, meats and apple together. Fork through the mayonnaise. Serve on individual plates garnished liberally with chopped parsley.

Sardine quiche

4 oz. shortcrust pastry (4 oz. flour, etc.)
½ lb. onions, skinned and thinly sliced
1 oz. butter
salt and freshly ground black pepper
4½-oz. can sardines in olive oil
2 large eggs
milk
lemon wedges

SERVES 4

Line an 8½-in. loose-bottomed, French fluted flan tin with the thinly rolled pastry. Cook the onions in the melted butter until soft but not brown, season and cool. Drain the sardines and discard their tails. Place the onions in the flan base, piled up a little under each sardine – these are positioned as the spokes of a wheel. Beat the eggs, season and make up to ½ pt. with milk. Carefully spoon the egg custard mixture round the sardines.

Bake in the oven at 400°F, 200°C (mark 6) for 20 minutes. Reduce the heat to 325°F, 170°C (mark 3) and cook further for about 20 minutes. Serve hot or cold with lemon wedges.

Mexican bean appetiser

(*see picture page 96*)

Serve this at impromptu lunches; keep a can of these unusual mealy beans in the store cupboard.

15-oz. can red kidney beans
4 sticks celery, chopped
1 oz. gherkins, chopped
2 level tbsps. finely chopped onion
4 tbsps. oil
2 tbsps. malt vinegar
½ level tsp. French mustard
¼ level tsp. caster sugar
salt and freshly ground black pepper
2 eggs, hard-boiled
1 Cos lettuce heart
a few celery leaves, optional

SERVES 6

Drain the kidney beans well and combine in a bowl with the chopped celery, chopped gherkins and onion.

Place the oil, vinegar, mustard, sugar, salt and pepper in a tightly lidded container, shake well, pour over the bean mixture and fold through. Slice the eggs lengthwise. Arrange 2 lettuce leaves on each plate, pile the bean mixture on to the base of these, spooning over any remaining dressing. Place 3 slices of hard-boiled egg on each and add a few celery leaves either side.

Autumn supper dishes

Cheese soup

A spur of the moment soup – rich and creamy – is a likely favourite at a round-the-fire supper.

1 large potato, peeled and finely diced
1 large onion, skinned and finely chopped
2 oz. diced carrot
2 oz. diced celery
½ pt. water
⅔ pt. white stock
¼ lb. Canadian Cheddar cheese, grated
¼ pt. single cream
salt and freshly ground black pepper
2 tbsps. chopped parsley

SERVES 4

Simmer the vegetables in a saucepan with the water for 15–20 minutes. Add the stock, cheese and cream. Adjust seasoning. Heat through, but do not boil. Stir in the parsley and serve at once.

Pizza rapide

Go Italian with a quick scone pizza, its pan-fried base topped with soft melting cheese, shreds of pink ham, onion, tomato and black olives.

4 oz. self-raising flour
½ level tsp. salt
5 tbsps. oil
3–4 tbsps. water
4 oz. onion, skinned and chopped
2 medium sized tomatoes, skinned and sliced
¼ level tsp. dried herbs
1 oz. butter
4 oz. canned ham cut into thin shreds
3 oz. mature Cheddar cheese, finely diced
8–10 black olives
chopped parsley

SERVES 2

Mix the flour and salt with 1 tbsp. oil and enough water to give a soft dough. Roll out into a 7-in. round and fry on both sides in the remaining oil in a large frying pan. Meanwhile make the topping by frying the onion, tomatoes and herbs slowly in the butter until the onion is transparent. Spread a third of the onion/tomato mixture on the base of the pizza and top with thin shreds of ham. Then add alternate

Mexican bean appetiser (*see page 95*)

layers of cheese and the remaining onion mixture. Dot with olives and place under a pre-heated grill for about 5 minutes. Serve immediately, scattered with chopped parsley.

Marrow and bacon au gratin

A simple, well flavoured oven-to-table supper dish.

2½ lb. marrow
4 oz. butter
3 oz. flour
1¼ pt. milk
salt and freshly ground black pepper
6 oz. onion, skinned and thinly sliced
2 cloves garlic, skinned and crushed
4 bacon chops, trimmed and diced
4 oz. mushrooms, wiped and diced
4 oz. Cheddar cheese, grated

SERVES 4

Peel the marrow, discard the seeds and cut it into large chunks. Cook in fast boiling salted water until tender but not soft. Drain. Melt 3 oz. butter in a saucepan, stir in the flour and cook over a low heat to a pale biscuit colour. Gradually stir in the milk, beating between additions. Bring to the boil, bubble for 2–3 minutes and season. Sauté the onion and garlic in the remaining butter until soft but not coloured. Add the bacon, continue to cook for about 10 minutes then toss in the mushrooms. Mix well and turn into a shallow dish. Fold the marrow into the well seasoned sauce and spoon it over the sauté mixture. Top with cheese. Grill until bubbling and brown.

Marrow soufflé

With a creamy base and cheese topping ideal for a light supper.

1 lb. marrow
2 oz. butter or margarine
1 oz. flour
½ pt. milk
salt and freshly ground black pepper
2 level tsps. dried summer savory
3 eggs, separated
4 oz. Cheddar cheese, grated

SERVES 2–3

Peel the marrow, cut it into thin slices and discard the seeds. Cook in boiling salted water until tender but still firm. Drain and roughly chop. Melt the fat and stir in the flour, then gradually stir in the milk and seasonings. Bring to the boil, stirring, and cook for 1–2 minutes. Pour half the sauce over the marrow, add the savory and spoon it into a greased 7-in. soufflé dish. To the remaining sauce add the beaten egg yolks and cheese. Adjust the seasoning and fold in the stiffly whisked egg whites. Spoon over the marrow. Bake in the oven at 375°F, 190°C (mark 5) for about 30 minutes.

Galette lyonnaise

Creamed potatoes and onion with a crisp golden crust will partner most meat and poultry dishes; galette lyonnaise is particularly delicious with sausages and cheers up cold meat.

1 lb. onions, skinned and chopped
1 lb. potatoes, boiled and creamed with butter, milk and seasoning
3 oz. butter
nutmeg

SERVES 4

Sauté the onion in 2 oz. butter until tender. Stir the onion into the mashed potato, add a little grated nutmeg and check the seasoning. Turn the mixture into a shallow ovenproof dish, smooth over the top, dot with the remainder of the butter and brown in the oven at 375°F, 190°C (mark 5) for about 30 minutes.

Haddock and sweet pepper sauté (*see below*)

Haddock and sweet pepper sauté

(*see picture above*)

12 oz. thick haddock fillet
seasoned flour
2 rashers streaky bacon, rinded
1 oz. butter
4-oz. can pimiento
½ pkt. instant potato (3 oz.)
knob of butter
milk
1 oz. Cheddar cheese, grated
2 tbsps. cream

For salad
1 head chicory
7-oz. can sweet corn kernels, drained
chives
lemon French dressing or mayonnaise

SERVES 2

Skin the fish, cut it into largish pieces and dredge with flour. Scissor-snip the bacon into small pieces.

Lightly fry the bacon, add the butter and, when melted and bubbling, add the fish. Turn occasionally to brown lightly, taking care not to break up fish more than is necessary. Drain the pimiento and slice the caps thinly. Add to the fish and heat through.

Meanwhile make up the potato as directed on the packet, using butter and milk to give a piping consistency. Beat in the cheese and when it is melted, pipe potato round two large, deep scallop shells. Brown under a hot grill. Pile the fish mixture in the centre. Spoon 1 tbsp. cream over each. Flash under the grill to reheat.

Salad accompaniments: Separate the chicory leaves and slice the small ones and arrange on flat scallop shells. Add the finely sliced chicory to corn; marinade in lemon dressing or mayonnaise. Spoon into the leaves and garnish with snipped chives.

✳ Tuna-stuffed pancakes

6½-oz. can savoury tuna, drained
2 oz. margarine
4 level tbsps. plain flour
½ pt. milk
1 level tsp. French mustard
1 tbsp. lemon juice
salt and freshly ground black pepper
2 oz. mature Cheddar cheese
½ pt. pancake batter (½ pt. milk, 1 large egg,
    4 oz. flour)
chopped parsley

SERVES 4

Flake the tuna. Melt the margarine in a saucepan and stir in the flour; cook for a few minutes then, off the heat, gradually beat in the milk. Bring to the boil, stirring, and add the mustard, lemon juice, seasoning, cheese and tuna. Adjust seasoning and keep warm. Make eight 7-in. pancakes in the usual way. Fold these into quarters, open out to give a pocket and fill with the tuna mixture. Arrange the pancakes in a shallow ovenproof dish. Brush with a little more margarine and cook in the oven at 325°F, 170°C (mark 3) for about ½ hour. Garnish with parsley.

Cauliflower fondue

A twosome lunch as a change from something on toast.

3 eggs
½ lb. cauliflower florets
2 tbsps. milk
½ level tsp. cornflour
few drops Worcestershire sauce
pinch of salt and pepper
4 oz. Cheddar cheese, grated
1 tbsp. chopped parsley
fingers of freshly made toast

SERVES 2

Hard-boil one of the eggs. Cook the even-sized florets of cauliflower in salted water for about 10 minutes – they should be tender but still crisp. Drain. While the cauliflower is cooking, combine the milk, cornflour, Worcestershire sauce and seasoning in the top of a double boiler. (If care is taken a small pan can be used over a low heat.) Heat until the cornflour thickens then add the cheese. When the cheese melts, stir in the remaining two eggs, previously beaten, and continue to stir until the sauce thickens. Arrange the cauliflower in two individual pre-heated pottery dishes and spoon the sauce over. Garnish with chopped hard-boiled egg mixed with parsley. Serve at once with toast fingers.

Nut cutlets

More than a snack. Nuts are wholesome, something different and under a crisp crumb coat they taste decidedly 'meaty'.

½ oz. butter or margarine
½ oz. flour
¼ pt. milk or stock
2 oz. onion, skinned and finely chopped
2 oz. mushrooms, chopped
2 oz. fresh breadcrumbs
4 oz. shelled nuts
¼ level tsp. vegetable extract
salt, pepper and lemon juice to taste
good pinch *fines herbes*
beaten egg and brown crumbs
oil for frying

SERVES 2

Melt the butter, stir in the flour and cook for 2 minutes. Add the milk, beat and cook for a further two minutes. Stir in the onion, mushrooms and breadcrumbs. Very finely chop or roughly grind the nuts – a mixture of half peanuts and half brazils is pleasant – and add to the pan with the seasonings. Shape into eight 'corks'. Coat the cutlets in egg and crumbs and shallow fry until well browned, turning once or twice. Serve really hot.

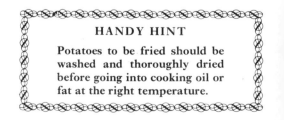

HANDY HINT

Potatoes to be fried should be washed and thoroughly dried before going into cooking oil or fat at the right temperature.

Kipper rarebit

Full-flavoured and bubbling hot on toast, kipper rarebit goes down well with a glass of ale. Coleslaw is the perfect partner.

2 fresh kippers or 10-oz. pkt. frozen kipper fillets
5 oz. Cheddar cheese, grated
½ oz. butter
3 tbsps. beer/brown ale
1 level tsp. made mustard
pinch of cayenne pepper
salt and freshly ground black pepper
4 slices buttered toast, freshly made

SERVES 2

Grill fresh kippers, then remove the fillets. If using frozen fillets, cook according to directions and drain. Skin and flake the fish. Place the cheese, butter, beer, mustard and seasoning into a small pan and heat gently, stirring well until the mixture is smooth. Add the finely flaked kipper and cook for 1-2 minutes, stirring until blended. Do not boil. Remove the crusts from the toast and top liberally with the kipper mixture, right to the edges. Place under a hot grill until bubbling and golden. Serve at once.

Autumn vegetables

Orange cabbage slaw

This is an all the year choice but best kept for the winter; use salted peanuts when pecans are not available.

1 egg yolk
salt and pepper
pinch of sugar
½ level tsp. French mustard
¼ pt. oil
1 tsp. lemon juice
1 tbsp. garlic vinegar
grated rind of ½ orange
1 tbsp. orange juice
10 oz. prepared white cabbage
2 oz. onion, skinned and grated
8 oz. celery, finely chopped
2 oz. shelled pecan nuts, coarsely chopped
3 large oranges

SERVES 4

Place the egg yolk with a little salt, pepper, sugar and the mustard in a small but deep basin. Whisk very thoroughly then add the oil drop by drop, beating hard all the time, adding more as it thickens, until creamy. Stir in the lemon juice, vinegar, orange rind and juice. Finely shred the cabbage. Combine it with the onion, celery and coarsely chopped nuts and fold the mayonnaise through the slaw mixture. Peel the oranges, free of all white pith, cut them into segments and place half of them in the base of a serving dish. Pile up the slaw mixture and top with the remaining segments. Chill for a short time before serving to infuse the orange flavour.

Potato dauphinois

Ring the changes on the potato theme. Garlic is optional but certainly enhances the flavour.

butter
1 clove garlic, skinned and crushed
1 lb. old potatoes, peeled and thinly sliced
salt and freshly ground black pepper
grated nutmeg
Lancashire cheese, grated
½ pt. milk
1 egg, beaten

SERVES 4

Butter an ovenproof dish, not too deep, and add the clove of garlic. Layer the potatoes in overlapping rows in the dish with a seasoning of salt, pepper, nutmeg and a little cheese between the layers. Warm the milk and combine it with the egg. Pour evenly over the potatoes and dot with knobs of butter. Grate more cheese over and cook in the oven at 375°F, 190°C (mark 5) for about 45 minutes.

Braised celery

2 heads celery
1 oz. butter
8 oz. onions, skinned and chopped
4 rashers bacon, rinded and snipped into small pieces
½ pt. stock or water
salt and freshly ground black pepper

SERVES 4

Trim the celery, discarding any very coarse stalks. Chop it into even lengths and blanch in boiling salted water for 10 minutes. Melt the butter, add the onion and fry until evenly brown. In a casserole combine the drained celery, onion, bacon and the stock. Adjust seasoning, cover and cook in the oven at 375°F, 190°C (mark 5) for about 1¼ hours, until the celery is fork-tender.

Stuffed aubergines

2 aubergines
2 tbsps. chopped ham
1 tsp. chopped onion
1 tsp. chopped parsley
grated lemon rind
2 mushrooms, chopped
salt and pepper
1 egg, beaten
breadcrumbs
1 oz. butter

SERVES 4

Wipe the aubergines and cut them in half lengthwise. Scoop out the seeds and pulp and chop it. Put the ham, onion, parsley, lemon rind and mushrooms into a basin with the pulp, season well and bind with beaten egg. Pile the mixture into the aubergine skins.

Sprinkle with breadcrumbs, place small pieces of butter on top and bake at 350°F, 180°C (mark 4) for 30–40 minutes.

Glazed turnips

An interesting way to cheer up this not-too-popular vegetable – choose even-sized turnips, avoiding the large ones.

1 lb. small turnips
1 medium sized onion, skinned and finely chopped
2 oz. streaky bacon, rinded and snipped into small pieces
1 tbsp. oil
sprig of parsley
small clove garlic, skinned
2–3 peppercorns
2 level tbsps. tomato paste
½ pt. stock
salt and pepper
chopped parsley

SERVES 4

Peel the turnips and cook them in boiling salted water for 15 minutes. Fry the onion and bacon in the oil until beginning to brown, add the parsley sprig, garlic clove, peppercorns, tomato paste and stock. Cover and simmer for 10 minutes then discard the parsley, garlic and peppercorns. Drain the turnips, add them to the onion mixture, adjust the seasoning and simmer for about 20 minutes. Garnish with parsley and serve with croûtons of fried bread. *Note:* If you wish tie the parsley, garlic and peppercorns in muslin.

Autumn main course dishes

✳ Liver and bacon pudding

When you are feeling especially budget conscious use ox liver and increase the cooking time.

8 oz. lean streaky bacon, rinded
8 oz. onion, skinned and chopped
1 lb. lambs' liver, chopped
2 level tbsps. flour
1 level tbsp. tomato paste
5 tbsps. stock or water
salt and freshly ground black pepper
12 oz. self-raising flour
½ level tsp. salt
1½ level tsps. dried mixed herbs
3 oz. butter or margarine
7 fl. oz. milk, approx.

SERVES 6

Scissor-snip the bacon into a large frying pan. Cook over a gentle heat until the fat runs then add the onion and liver and continue cooking until the onion is transparent. Stir in the flour, tomato paste and stock. Season, bring to the boil, reduce the heat and cook gently for a few minutes. Cool. Sift the flour and salt together into a basin. Add the herbs and rub the fat into the flour until the mixture resembles fine breadcrumbs. Stir in enough milk to form a fairly soft dough. Roll out the pastry about ¼-in. thick and using a 2-in. cutter, stamp out about 30 rounds to line a 3-pt. greased ovenproof pudding basin. Slightly overlap each round. Spoon the liver mixture into the centre. Roll out the pastry trimmings for a lid. Bake in the oven at 425°F, 220°C (mark 7) for 30 minutes. Reduce the heat to 375°F, 190°C (mark 5) and bake for a further

Hallowe'en party (*see page 92*)

30 minutes. Unmould and serve with a tomato sauce,

⚹ Rich casserole of hearts

4 lambs' hearts
1 oz. butter or margarine
4 oz. streaky bacon, rinded and roughly
 chopped
4 oz. shallots, skinned
1 oz. flour
1 pt. rich stock
salt and pepper
bouquet garni

For stuffing balls
4 oz. fresh white breadcrumbs
2 oz. shredded suet
grated rind of 1 orange
2 tbsps. chopped parsley
1 egg, beaten

SERVES 4

Wash the hearts, cut them open, remove any tubes and gristle and wash again. Cut into ½-in. slices. Melt the butter or margarine and fry the slices of heart until slightly browned then put them into an ovenproof casserole. Fry the bacon and shallots until coloured and add these to the casserole. Add the flour to the residue in the pan and blend together, gradually pour in the stock, bring to the boil, stirring, and cook for 2–3 minutes. Adjust the seasoning, pour into the casserole, add a bouquet garni, cover and cook at 325°F, 170°C (mark 3) for about 2½ hours. Remove any excess surface fat.

Combine the ingredients for the stuffing in a

HANDY HINT

If you have forgotten the 'tokens' in Christmas puddings it is not too late – wrap them in grease-proof paper and push into slits in the cold pudding. When the pudding is re-cooked the slits will close up.

bowl. Season to taste and shape into 10 medium-sized balls. Add to the casserole and continue to cook for a further 30 minutes. Before serving, skim the surface to remove any traces of fat and remove the bouquet garni.

Lambs' liver with mustard farce

Mustard and herbs impart the flavour appeal and the liver is sliced a little thicker than usual so that it doesn't cook too quickly.

6 $\frac{1}{4}$–$\frac{1}{2}$-in. slices of lambs' liver
salt and pepper
2 oz. flour
3 oz. margarine
1 tbsp. corn oil
3 level tbsps. French mustard
1 tbsp. chopped shallot
3 tbsps. chopped parsley
$\frac{1}{2}$ clove garlic, skinned and crushed
3 oz. fresh white breadcrumbs

SERVES 3

The liver should be free of any gristle. Season with salt and pepper and coat in flour. Melt 1 oz. margarine with the oil and sauté the liver quickly on each side until firm. Beat the mustard with the shallot, parsley and garlic and gradually add the pan juices, season and spread the liver slices with the mixture, then coat them with crumbs patting them well in. Arrange the slices in a grill pan and grill until golden on each side – baste with some more margarine as needed. Serve immediately.

*Barbecued spare ribs

2 tbsps. oil
6 oz. onion, skinned and chopped
1 clove garlic, skinned and crushed
2 level tbsps. tomato paste
4 tbsps. malt vinegar
$\frac{1}{4}$ level tsp. dried thyme
$\frac{1}{4}$ level tsp. chilli powder
3 level tbsps. honey
1 beef cube
$\frac{1}{4}$ pt. hot water
2 lb. spare ribs, American cut

SERVES 4

Heat the oil in a saucepan, add the onion and sauté until tender; add the garlic, tomato paste, vinegar, thyme, chilli powder, honey and beef cube dissolved in hot water. Bubble the sauce gently for 10 minutes. Place the spare ribs in a roasting pan just big enough to take them in a single layer. Brush them with a little sauce then roast at 375°F, 190°C (mark 5) for $\frac{1}{2}$ hour. Pour off the fat, spoon the remaining sauce over the ribs and cook for about 1 hour more.

Sausage Kiev

2 oz. butter
$\frac{1}{2}$ level tsp. tomato paste
1 level tsp. dried *fines herbes*
1 clove garlic, skinned and crushed
1 lb. pork sausage meat
1 egg, beaten
dried white breadcrumbs or sage and onion
    stuffing mix
1 pkt. curried rice
parsley for garnish

For salad
2–4 spring onions
1 green eating apple
2 oz. salted peanuts
1 tbsp. thin honey
1 tbsp. lemon juice

SERVES 3–4

Beat the butter to soften it then beat in the tomato paste, herbs and garlic. Put the dish in the ice-cream compartment of the refrigerator for the butter to harden. Meanwhile, divide the sausage meat into 6 and shape it into flat cakes on a floured surface. Place a piece of the chilled butter in the centre of each and quickly shape them up into balls. Brush with beaten egg and toss in breadcrumbs or stuffing mix. Deep-fat fry at 350°F, 180°C for about 10 minutes until golden and cooked through. Serve on a bed of curry rice, cooked according to the directions on the packet. Garnish with parsley.

Salad accompaniments: Trim the spring onions (use chives when onions are not in season) and slice thinly. Core and dice the apple. Toss together the onion, apple, peanuts, honey and lemon juice.

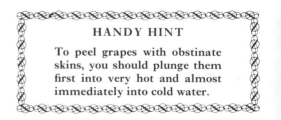

HANDY HINT

To peel grapes with obstinate skins, you should plunge them first into very hot and almost immediately into cold water.

✳ Sweet-sour pork balls

1 lb. pork, minced
1 clove garlic, skinned and crushed
1½ oz. flour
2 oz. fresh white breadcrumbs
salt and pepper
1 egg yolk
1 oz. lard

For sauce

3 oz. sugar
4 tbsps. cider vinegar
3 tbsps. soy sauce
1½ level tbsps. cornflour
½ pt. water
1 green pepper, blanched and cut in thin
strips
½ lb. tomatoes, skinned and quartered
11-oz. can crushed pineapple

SERVES 4

Mix together the pork, garlic, ½ oz. flour, breadcrumbs, salt and pepper. Add the egg yolk and mix well. Form the mixture into 24 balls and toss these in the remaining 1 oz. flour. Heat the lard in a frying pan. Add the balls and fry gently for 20 minutes, turning them frequently until golden.

Meanwhile, put the sugar, vinegar and soy sauce in a saucepan. Blend the cornflour with the water and add to the ingredients in the pan. Bring the sauce to the boil, stirring, and simmer gently for 5 minutes then add the green pepper, tomatoes and pineapple. Simmer for a further 5 minutes. To serve, put the pork balls into a warmed casserole and pour the sauce over.

✳ Pork with peas

4 tbsps. soy sauce
3 level tbsps. cornflour
1 level tsp. salt
2 lb. pork fillet or tenderloin
2 tbsps. corn oil
1 level tsp. sugar
1 pt. chicken stock
1 lb. frozen peas

For garnish

2 oz. shelled walnut halves
1 tbsp. corn oil

SERVES 8

Combine together the soy sauce, cornflour and salt in a bowl. Cut the pork into fork-sized pieces, heat the oil and fry the pork until evenly browned. Add the sugar and stock and mix well. Bring to the boil, stirring, then cover the pan, reduce the heat and simmer until the meat is tender (about 30 minutes). Add the peas and cornflour mixture and cook for a further 10 minutes, stirring. Meanwhile fry the walnuts in the oil until they colour, and scatter them over the pork before serving. Border the pork with plain boiled rice.

Hot pork and orange one-crust pie

1½ lb. shoulder of pork
¾ lb. stewing veal
1 oz. seasoned flour
4 tbsps. oil
6 oz. onion, skinned and sliced
6 oz. carrot, pared and grated
salt and pepper
1 large orange
2 level tsps. cornflour
8 oz. shortcrust pastry (8 oz. flour, etc.)
milk

SERVES 6

Trim the meat, and remove any fat. Cut it into small cubes and toss them in seasoned flour. Keep any surplus flour. Using a large frying pan, heat 2 tbsps. oil and fry the meat a little at a time until sealed and beginning to brown. Remove the meat from the pan, add the rest of the oil and fry the vegetables for 1–2 minutes; do not allow them to colour. Combine the meat and vegetables in a 2½-pt. capacity oval shallow pie dish. Season well. Remove the rind from half an orange, free of all white pith. Cut it into narrow strips and fork through the meat and vegetables. Squeeze the juice from the whole orange and make up to ¾ pt. with water. Blend the surplus flour and cornflour to a smooth paste with some of the liquor, add the remaining liquor and pour it into a pan. Heat, stirring, to thicken and clear then pour it over the meat and vegetables and leave to cool. Top the pie dish with a pastry crust, knocking up and fluting the edges; make a hole in the centre and decorate it with pastry leaves made from the trimmings. Brush the pie with milk and bake at 400°F, 200°C (mark 6) for 30 minutes, then reduce the temperature to 325°F, 170°C (mark 3) for about a further 15 minutes.

✳ Paupiettes of pork

2 6-oz. pork escalopes
2 oz. butter
2 oz. lean streaky bacon, rinded and diced
4 oz. onion, skinned and chopped
2 oz. fresh white breadcrumbs
4 oz. pork sausage meat
¼ level tsp. dried thyme
salt and freshly ground black pepper
1 level tbsp. flour
1 tbsp. oil
3 tbsps. dry white wine
¼ level tsp. paprika
½ pt. chicken stock
1 tbsp. cream

SERVES 2

The escalopes are cut from the leg. Beat these between wetted greaseproof paper until fairly thin. Melt 1 oz. butter in a small pan, add the bacon and a quarter of the onion and sauté them until soft. Cool and combine them with the breadcrumbs, sausage meat and thyme. Season the mixture and spread over the escalopes. Roll each one up and tie with string then toss the rolls in flour. Heat the oil in a small pan and add 1 oz. butter. When the butter begins to colour, add the pork and fry until evenly browned. Transfer the rolls to a small casserole. Reheat the pan juices, add the remaining onion and sauté it until transparent. Stir in the excess flour, wine, pinch of thyme, paprika, stock (made from a cube) and cream. Bring it to the boil and pour over the meat. Cook covered in the oven at 400°F, 200°C (mark 6) for about 1¼ hours. Skim off the excess fat using absorbent paper and remove the string before serving.

✳ Boeuf bourguignonne

(*see picture opposite*)

2 lb. topside of beef
1½ oz. lard
4 oz. thick rashers streaky bacon, rinded
1 level tbsp. flour
¼ pt. red wine (Burgundy)
¼ pt. stock
pinch of dried thyme
½ bayleaf
1 clove garlic, skinned
salt and pepper
6–12 shallots, skinned
3 tbsps. brandy (optional)

SERVES 6

Trim the meat and cut it into large cubes. Melt 1 oz. lard in a frying pan and brown the meat on all sides, a few pieces at a time, then transfer it to a 3-pt. casserole. Dice the bacon, add it to the frying pan and fry until beginning to colour. Stir in the flour and continue to cook until brown, stirring occasionally. Gradually stir in the wine and stock and bring to the boil. Add the thyme, bayleaf, crushed garlic and seasoning to taste. Pour this over the meat, cover and cook in the oven at 325°F, 170°C (mark 3) for 2 hours. Melt ½ oz. lard in a small pan and brown the shallots. Drain them, ignite the brandy and add with the shallots to the casserole. Reduce the heat to 300°F, 150°C (mark 2) and cook for a further 30 minutes until the meat is tender. Discard the bayleaf before serving.

✳ Beef and chestnut casserole

3–3½ lb. chuck steak
2 oz. seasoned flour
2 oz. lard
1 medium sized onion, skinned and sliced
15-oz. can tomatoes
4-oz. can pimientos, drained and sliced
¼ pt. hot water
1 beef stock cube
¼ pt. red wine
salt and pepper
3 oz. sliced garlic sausage
10-oz. can whole chestnuts, drained
butter
chopped parsley

SERVES 6

Trim the fat from the steak and cut the meat into 2-in. pieces. Toss in seasoned flour and retain any excess flour. Melt the lard in a frying pan and fry the meat, browning a few pieces at a time. Place the meat, when ready, in a large casserole. Add the onion to the pan and fry it gently until it begins to brown. Stir in the excess flour, then gradually add the tomatoes and pimientos. Blend the water and stock cube and add with the wine to the frying pan; bring to the boil and check the seasoning.

Cut the sausage into strips, add it to the beef in the casserole and pour the pan contents over. Cover the casserole and cook in the oven at 325°F, 170°C (mark 3) for about 3 hours; transfer to a clean hot casserole. Sauté chestnuts in melted butter until browned. Add these to the casserole and garnish with parsley.

Boeuf bourguignonne (*see opposite*)

✳ Chilli beef beanpot

4 oz. white bread
2 lb. lean chuck steak, minced
½ lb. lean bacon, rinded and minced
1 lb. onion, skinned and finely chopped
1 level tsp. salt
¼ level tsp. pepper
2 oz. flour
4 tbsps. corn oil
2 oz. butter
2 level tsps. Rajah chilli powder
¼ level tsp. paprika pepper
2 2-lb. 3-oz. cans tomatoes
2 14-oz. cans red kidney beans

SERVES 12

Soak the bread in cold water for 5 minutes then
squeeze out the excess water. Blend the steak,
bacon, half the onion, bread, salt and pepper.
Then take 1 level tbsp. meat at a time and mould
it into a ball. Toss the meatballs in flour to coat,
then heat the oil and 1 oz. butter and fry the
meatballs until golden – about 10 minutes. Drain
them and fry the remainder of the onion. Add
1 oz. butter to the pan, blend in the chilli powder
and paprika and add the tomatoes and meatballs.
Cover and simmer for 1½ hours. Add the drained
kidney beans; cook for a further 15 minutes.

HANDY HINT

A curdled mayonnaise means
you have added the oil too
quickly, or the ingredients were
not all at room temperature. If
this happens, start with a fresh
basin and another egg yolk. Add
the curdled mixture very slowly,
drop by drop, to the fresh yolk,
whisking all the time (as slowly
as you should have done it first
time!). The mayonnaise should
now blend smoothly.

✳ Haricot lamb

The subtle flavouring of rosemary and tomato combine with lamb for a warming casserole.

2 lb. shoulder of lamb, boned
6 oz. haricot beans, soaked overnight
8 oz. onion, skinned and sliced
8 oz. tomatoes, skinned and sliced
2 level tbsps. tomato paste
¾ pt. white stock
1 tbsp. lemon juice
1–2 level tsps. dried rosemary
salt and freshly ground black pepper

SERVES 4

Dice the lamb. Place it in a large frying pan and fry it slowly in its own fat until evenly brown. Drain and place the meat in a large flameproof casserole and add the drained haricot beans. Sauté the sliced onions in the pan fat until transparent, drain them well and add to the meat. Cover the onions with the skinned and sliced tomatoes. Blend the tomato paste with the stock, add lemon juice, rosemary and seasoning. Pour into the casserole, bring to the boil, reduce the heat, cover and simmer for about 2 hours.

✳ Steak and wine pie

2¼ lb. lean chuck steak
½ lb. kidney
3 oz. plain flour
salt and pepper
3 tbsps. corn oil
3½ oz. butter
1 large onion, skinned and chopped
6 oz. mushrooms, sliced
2 cloves garlic, skinned and crushed (optional)
1 pt. beef stock
½ pt. red wine
13-oz. pkt. frozen puff pastry, thawed
beaten egg

SERVES 6

Trim the meat and cut it into 1-in. pieces. Prepare kidney and toss both in seasoned flour. Heat 3 tbsps. oil in a large frying pan, add 2 oz. butter and when it is on the point of turning brown add the meat and fry briskly until brown. Stir in the excess flour. Turn the meat into a large casserole. Melt the remaining butter, fry the onion for a few minutes then add the mushrooms and garlic and fry for a further few minutes. Pour the stock and wine into a pan, bring to the boil and pour over the meat. Cover and cook in the oven at 325°F, 170°C (mark 3) for about 2 hours until really tender. Remove the lid and bubble down the juices, if necessary. Cool the meat quickly, turn it into a 4-pt. pie dish, add a pie funnel and cover with rolled-out pastry. At this stage, if you wish, you may leave the pie in a cool place until ½ hour before it is needed. To bake, brush with beaten egg, place in the oven at 450°F, 230°C (mark 8) for about 20 minutes until the pastry is golden and the filling is bubbling.

Frankfurters en chemise

Serve straight from oven to table; you can have the dough pre-prepared and rising in the fridge and the filling ready made for the final bake. Make 2 for the party menu.

1 lb. strong plain flour
2 level tsps. salt
1 level tsp. mustard
4 oz. Cheddar cheese, finely grated
½ oz. fresh yeast
½ pt. water
12 frankfurters
1½ oz. butter
¾ lb. onions, skinned and sliced
2 tbsps. chopped parsley
salt and pepper
beaten egg
poppy seeds

SERVES 6

Mix together the first 4 ingredients. Blend the yeast and water and stir into the dry ingredients to give a pliable dough. Turn it on to a floured surface and knead for 10 minutes. Place the dough in a large, lightly oiled polythene bag and leave to rise until doubled in size. Knead the dough again and roll out to 12 in. by 14 in.; place on a large baking sheet. Lay 8 frankfurters in pairs either side of centre and top each pair with another one. Cover with filling (see below). Slash the sides of the dough at intervals and overlap the frankfurters in a plait. Join and seal with beaten egg. Glaze the surface with more egg and dust with poppy seeds. Return the loaf to the polythene bag and allow to rise for 45 minutes. Remove it from the bag, re-glaze and bake at 375°F, 190°C (mark 5) for about 45 minutes until cooked through.

Onion filling: Melt the butter and fry the onions (without browning) until soft; add parsley and seasoning.

Biryani

4½-lb. leg of lamb, boned
¼ pt. natural yoghurt
1 level tbsp. curry powder
1 level tsp. curry paste
1 level tsp. chilli powder
1 lb. onions, skinned and sliced
3 oz. butter
1 lb. potatoes, peeled and diced
½ lb. long grain rice
small sachet powdered saffron
¼ pt. warm milk
4 oz. plump sultanas
2 oz. flaked almonds, fried

SERVES 8

Make about 1 pt. of stock with the lamb bones. Cut the meat into 1-in. chunks and marinade it for about 1 hour in the yoghurt, curry powder, paste and chilli powder. Fry the onions in 1 oz. butter until golden. Remove them from the pan, add the remaining butter and, when it begins to brown, add the meat. Brown the meat quickly over a fierce heat, then transfer it to a large 8-pt. shallow casserole. Add stock to the pan, loosen the sediment and add the potato; simmer for 10 minutes. Rain the rice into a pan of boiling salted water, return to the boil, cover and cook for 10 minutes whilst infusing the saffron in warm milk. Drain the rice. Combine the stock, potatoes, rice, saffron, milk, 2 oz. sultanas and the onion. Season and place this on top of the lamb. Top the casserole with foil and cover with a lid. Cook at 325°F, 170°C (mark 3) for about 1 hour. Garnish with the remaining sultanas and fried almonds.

Side dishes:
Sliced onion and tomato: you need 2 lb. firm tomatoes and 1 medium sized onion, skinned and sliced wafer thin.
Yoghurt-dressed cucumber: thinly slice 2 large cucumbers, sprinkle with salt, leave for ½ hour then drain. Add 2 tbsps. chopped parsley to ½ pt.

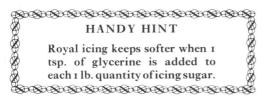
HANDY HINT
Royal icing keeps softer when 1 tsp. of glycerine is added to each 1 lb. quantity of icing sugar.

plain yoghurt. Pile the cucumber into side dishes and spoon the yoghurt over it.

Rolled stuffed shoulder of lamb

For a light soup to serve before the traditional roast, combine equal quantities of beef consommé and tomato juice – both from a can – and serve piping hot with a garnish of thinly sliced lemon.

6 oz. streaky bacon, rinded
1 oz. fresh white breadcrumbs
3 tbsps. chopped fresh mint
salt and freshly ground black pepper
beaten egg
4–4½ lb. shoulder of lamb, boned
1–2 tbsps. oil

SERVES 6

Finely scissor-snip the bacon and combine with the breadcrumbs, mint, salt and pepper. Add sufficient beaten egg to bind ingredients together. Spread out the lamb. Place the stuffing in the cavity where the bone has been removed, roll up the joint and secure with several bands of string. Weigh the joint and calculate cooking time by allowing 20 minutes per lb. plus 30 minutes. Lightly grease a roasting tin with oil. Place the joint in it and brush with the remaining oil. Cook near the top of the oven at 375°F, 190°C (mark 5).

✳ Moussaka
(*see picture page 109*)
3 aubergines (1½ lb. approx.)
flour
4 tbsps. oil
4 medium sized onions, skinned and thinly sliced
1 lb. lean beef or lamb, minced
4 firm tomatoes, peeled and thickly sliced
¼ pt. well seasoned stock
¼ pt. thick tomato purée
2 large eggs
¼ pt. single cream
salt and freshly ground black pepper

SERVES 4–6

Slice the aubergines and dust with flour. Fry the slices in 2 tbsps. oil and when beginning to colour, drain and arrange around a shallow 4½-pt. casserole. Add 1 tbsp. oil to the pan and when it is hot, fry the onions and meat until lightly browned. Place on top of the aubergines. Fry the tomatoes in 1 tbsp. oil and add to the dish. Pour in the stock and tomato purée. Bake, uncovered, in the oven at 350°F, 180°C (mark 4) for about 45 minutes then beat together the eggs and cream, season well and pour over the contents of the casserole. Return it to the oven and continue to cook for a further 15–20 minutes until the sauce is set and golden.

Barbecue chicken

Make 2 for our Hallowe'en party menu.

½ level tsp. each salt, caster sugar and ground ginger
freshly ground black pepper
6 chicken joints
1 oz. butter
2 tbsps. malt vinegar
2 tbsps. soy sauce
1 level tbsp. cornflour
1 tbsp. Worcestershire sauce
2 level tsps. caster sugar
8 level tbsps. tomato ketchup
2 bayleaves
2 cloves garlic, skinned and crushed
dash Tabasco sauce
12 oz. noddles
parsley

SERVES 6

Put the salt, caster sugar and ground ginger in a polythene bag and sprinkle in the pepper. Trim the chicken joints and toss in the bag to coat them evenly with the seasonings. Melt the butter and brown the joints in a large pan; fry them for 10 minutes. For the sauce, mix the vinegar, soy sauce, cornflour, Worcestershire sauce, caster sugar, tomato ketchup, bayleaves, crushed garlic and dash of Tabasco together. When the joints are brown, drain well, place in a casserole and pour the sauce over. Cover and bake at 350°F, 180°C (mark 4) for about 1 hour until the joints are tender. Skim off any surface fat. Cook the noodles until tender. Drain and

---

HANDY HINT

Dried onion and celery flakes are handy for flavouring stews, casseroles, soups, stocks and stuffings.

---

turn into a serving dish. Place the chicken and sauce on top and garnish with chopped parsley.

✳ Chicken cacciatore

4 chicken portions
1 level tbsp. flour
salt and pepper
6 tbsps. vegetable oil
1 small onion, skinned and chopped
2 medium carrots, pared and thinly sliced
1 clove garlic, skinned and crushed
1 bayleaf
pinch of dried oregano
1 lb. ripe tomatoes, skinned and sliced
3 tbsps. red or dry white wine
4 oz. short cut macaroni
chopped parsley

SERVES 4

Remove the chicken skin and chop each portion in two; dredge them with seasoned flour and fry in oil until evenly brown. Put aside. Pour off all but a thin covering of oil in pan then brown the onion and carrot. Add the garlic, bayleaf, oregano, tomatoes, wine and chicken. Bring to the boil, reduce the heat, cover and simmer until tender – about 1 hour. Serve garnished with freshly cooked macaroni and parsley.

Chicken suprême julienne

12 small fresh chicken breasts or 2 1-lb. pkts., frozen
2 oz. seasoned flour
2 tbsps. oil
2 oz. butter
4 oz. onion, skinned and finely chopped
2 level tsps. tomato paste
1 level tbsp. redcurrant jelly
¼ level tsp. dried oregano
4 tbsps. dry vermouth
1 pt. chicken stock
salt and freshly ground black pepper
2 oz. sliced cooked ham
2 oz. sliced pressed tongue
chopped parsley

SERVES 6

Thoroughly thaw frozen chicken. Coat the breasts in flour. Heat the oil and butter in a large frying pan or paella-type dish. When it is foaming, add the chicken and fry gently until golden on both sides. Remove, drain on absorbent paper then place in a large shallow casserole. Add the onion to the pan juices and

Moussaka (*see page 107*)

sauté until soft. Stir in the excess flour, tomato paste, jelly, oregano and vermouth. Pour in the stock, bring to the boil, stirring and adjust the seasoning. Pour over the chicken, cover and cook in the oven at 325°F, 170°C (mark 3) for about $1\frac{1}{4}$ hours. Meanwhile slice the ham and tongue into strips. Remove the chicken from the casserole, keep it warm and reduce the juices by half by rapid boiling. Add the ham and tongue and spoon over the chicken. Sprinkle with parsley.

Roast duckling with grapefruit sauce

2 $3\frac{1}{2}$-lb. ducklings, thawed if frozen
salt and freshly ground black pepper
2 level tbsps. plain flour
2 grapefruit
$6\frac{1}{4}$-fl. oz. can frozen concentrated unsweetened grapefruit juice
1 level tbsp. arrowroot

SERVES 6

Joint each duckling into 6. Trim off any excess fat, wipe and prick the flesh well. Season. Place the duckling on a wire rack in a roasting tin. Cook near the top of the oven at 350°F, 180°C (mark 4) for $1\frac{1}{4}$–$1\frac{1}{2}$ hours. Baste it with the pan juices twice during cooking. 20 minutes before the end of the cooking time sprinkle with flour and baste again. Remove all the peel and pith from the grapefruit, cut the flesh into segments; make the frozen fruit juice up to $\frac{3}{4}$ pt. with water. Blend a little with the arrowroot in small pan, add all the juice gradually and bring to the boil, stirring. Transfer the cooked duckling portions to a preheated serving dish. Arrange the fruit segments on top and return it to the oven for a few minutes. Drain the fat from the roasting tin, leaving the duckling juices. Add the grapefruit

HANDY HINT

Small onions will skin easily if you drop them first into boiling water, then in cold.

sauce, heat it then strain. Glaze the duckling with some of the sauce. Serve the rest separately.

Roast pheasant

This needs a light and refreshing starter to tickle the palate; try melon balls marinaded in sherry and stem ginger syrup.

1 brace of pheasants
butter
streaky bacon
flour

SERVES 4

Pluck, draw and truss the bird. Spread a knob of butter on each bird and cover each breast with strips of bacon. Roast in the centre of the oven at 450°F, 230°C (mark 8) for 10 minutes then reduce the heat to 400°F, 200°C (mark 6) and continue cooking for 30–40 minutes, according to the size of the bird, basting frequently with butter. About 15 minutes before the end of cooking, remove the bacon, dredge the breast of the bird with flour, baste well and finish cooking. Remove the trussing strings, put the pheasant on a hot dish and garnish with watercress. Serve with thin gravy, bread sauce and fried crumbs.

Haddock soufflé in pastry

6 oz. shortcrust pastry (6 oz. flour, etc.)
8 oz. smoked haddock fillets
water
lemon slices
bayleaf
2 oz. butter
2 oz. flour
$\frac{3}{4}$ pt. milk
2 tsps. lemon juice
salt and pepper
2 oz. Cheddar cheese, grated
3 eggs, separated
parsley and lemon wedges to garnish

SERVES 4–6

Make up the shortcrust pastry in the usual way and roll it out to fit a 9-in. plain flan ring placed on a baking sheet. Bake blind at 400°F, 200°C (mark 6) for about 20–25 minutes. Poach the haddock in water with a slice of lemon and a bayleaf. Drain, cool and flake. Make up $\frac{1}{2}$ pt. coating sauce with 1 oz. butter, 1 oz. flour and $\frac{1}{2}$ pt. milk. Season the sauce and cool it slightly. Combine the flaked haddock with the sauce,

add the lemon juice, adjust seasoning and spoon it into the flan case. To make a soufflé topping, melt 1 oz. butter, stir in 1 oz. flour and cook for 2–3 minutes; gradually stir in $\frac{1}{4}$ pt. milk and bring to the boil. Cool slightly and add the grated cheese. Add the egg yolks one at a time, beating well, then stiffly whisk the egg whites and fold these in. Spoon the soufflé mixture over the fish and bake in the centre of the oven at 400°F, 200°C (mark 6) for about 25–30 minutes, until risen and brown. Garnish with lemon wedges and parsley.

Waterzooi de poisson

A national dish from Belgium is a creamy fish stew with a luxury taste at modest expense. Soak up its succulent juices with crusty bread.

$1\frac{1}{2}$ lb. cod fillet
3 sticks celery, roughly chopped
1 oz. butter
1 level tsp. salt
freshly ground black pepper
3 egg yolks
2 fl. oz. double cream
2 level tsps. cornflour
chopped parsley
rye bread

SERVES 6

Remove any dark skin from the fish by making an incision in the flesh, holding the skin and firmly pulling away in one movement. Cut the fish into large pieces about $1\frac{1}{2}$-in. square. Place it in a saucepan, cover with cold water and add the celery, butter and seasoning. Poach gently for about 8–10 minutes until the flesh flakes easily when pierced with a fork. Carefully remove the fish using a draining spoon and place in a serving dish. Scatter the celery over. Cover and keep warm.

Strain the fish liquid then rapidly boil it down to about 1 pt. Remove it from the heat. Beat the egg yolks with the cream and cornflour until smooth. Stir in a little hot fish stock, then add this to the pan contents. Do not boil, but stir continuously until thickened. Cook for 2–3 minutes and adjust the seasoning if necessary. Pour the sauce over the fish, garnish with chopped parsley and serve rye bread alongside.

Cod oriental

Given a lift with a dressing of curry, fish on the menu is a good choice and full of protein.

1¼ lb. cod fillet, fresh or frozen
1 tbsp. lemon juice
flour
cooking oil
1 oz. margarine
2 oz. onion, skinned and chopped
1 level tbsp. curry powder
1 level tbsp. apple chutney
½ clove garlic
4 tbsps. water
¼ lb. tomatoes, peeled and chopped
salt and pepper

SERVES 3–4

Remove the skin from the cod and cut the fish into large pieces. Sprinkle lemon juice over and leave for 15 minutes. Lightly dredge with flour. Just cover the base of a medium sized frying pan with oil, heat it and quickly fry the cod until brown. Keep on one side. Wipe out the pan. Melt the margarine and fry the onion gently with the curry powder for 5 minutes. Add the chutney, garlic and water and simmer for about 5 minutes then stir in the tomatoes, bring to the boil and add the fish. Turn carefully in the curry mixture, check seasoning and reheat.

Autumn desserts

Apple snow

A light, old-fashioned favourite, perfect after roast game.

1 lb. cooking apples, peeled, cored and sliced
2 tbsps. water
2 tsps. lemon juice
1 oz. granulated sugar
sap green colouring (optional)
2 eggs, separated

SERVES 4

Place the apples, water, lemon juice and sugar in a saucepan and cook, covered, over a medium heat until the fruit is pulpy. Pass it through a nylon sieve. Combine the purée, a few drops of green colouring and the egg yolks in a basin and allow to cool. Stiffly whisk the egg whites and fold them into the apple purée until well blended. Turn into sundae dishes and chill before serving.

Spiced apple tart

Spice and apples make a firm friendship; apple purée, canned or bottled, can be used as an alternative, but the filling will be much smoother.

1½ lb. cooking apples
3 oz. sultanas, raisins or dates
¼ level tsp. mixed spice
sugar to sweeten
8 oz. rich shortcrust pastry (8 oz. flour, etc.)
icing sugar for dredging

SERVES 6

Peel and core the apples and cut them into eighths. Poach in very little water until almost soft. Lightly stir in the dried fruit and spice mixed with a little sugar. Use more sugar to sweeten to taste. Leave to cool whilst making the pastry.

Roll out two-thirds of the pastry and use it to line an 8-in. fluted flan ring, placed on a flat baking sheet. Fill the pastry case with apple mixture, cover with a pastry lid rolled from the rest of the pastry, damp the edges to seal and roll off any excess trimmings. Bake in the centre of the oven at 400°F, 200°C (mark 6) until browned (about 40–45 minutes). Remove the flan ring, lift the tart with a flat spatula on to a serving plate. Serve warm or cold, dredged with icing sugar.

Applescotch flan

8 oz. shortcrust pastry (8 oz. flour, etc.)
4 oz. golden syrup
1 large egg
1 lb. Bramley apples
1 oz. butter

SERVES 4–6

Roll out the pastry and use it to line a shallow tin 12 in. by 7½ in. Knock up the edges. Beat together the golden syrup and egg. Peel and core the apples and slice them thinly. Pour half the syrup mixture over the pastry base, arrange the apple slices on top and pour over the remainder of the syrup. Dot with tiny pieces of butter. Bake at 400°F, 200°C (mark 6) for about ¾ hour. If the pastry edge begins to overbrown, cover it with a strip of foil. Serve warm with whipped cream or ice cream.

Banana galette

4 oz. pâte sucrée (4 oz. flour, etc.)

For filling
1 lb. bananas
1 lemon
2 oz. butter
$\frac{1}{2}$ level tsp. ground cinnamon
1 oz. soft brown sugar
2 eggs, separated
2 oz. caster sugar

SERVES 4–6

Roll out the pastry and use it to line an $8\frac{1}{2}$-in. loose-bottomed, French fluted flan tin. Chill. Peel and slice the bananas, add the grated rind from half the lemon and the juice from the whole lemon and toss lightly. In a small pan, melt the butter, add the cinnamon and brown sugar and heat gently over a low heat for 5 minutes. Add the bananas and continue cooking for 3–4 minutes. Remove from the heat and add the beaten egg yolks; blend them in with a wooden spoon and spread over the flan case.

Cook the flan in the oven at 400°F, 200°C (mark 6) for about 15 minutes. Whisk the egg whites until stiff, add 1 oz. caster sugar and whisk until the meringue stands in peaks then fold in the remaining sugar. Pipe the meringue in a lattice over the filling. Return it to the oven for about 5 minutes and serve warm.

Ambrosia

11-oz. can mandarin orange segments
2 bananas
2 tbsps. long thread desiccated coconut

SERVES 3

Turn the oranges into a serving bowl and add the peeled and sliced bananas and the coconut. Chill well.

Fluffy Jamaican creams

$\frac{1}{2}$ oz. powdered gelatine
1 pt. freshly made black coffee
2 oz. soft brown sugar
4 tbsps. Tia Maria liqueur
$\frac{1}{4}$ pt. double cream
1 tbsp. milk
1 level tbsp. caster sugar
grated chocolate for decoration

SERVES 6

Sprinkle the gelatine over half the coffee in a small saucepan. Stir in the soft brown sugar. Dissolve gently over a low heat, do not boil. Off the heat, add the remaining coffee and liqueur. Allow to cool before dividing between 6 stemmed glasses. Put in a cool place to set. Whip the cream with the milk and sugar until it just holds its shape. Using a piping bag fitted with a large star vegetable nozzle, swirl cream over the set jelly and top with grated chocolate.

Apricot surprise

$15\frac{1}{2}$-oz. can apricot halves
3 eggs, separated
1 level tbsp. caster sugar
few drops vanilla essence
family block vanilla ice cream

SERVES 6

Chill a $2\frac{1}{2}$-pt. soufflé dish. Drain the apricots. Just before required for eating, put the egg yolks in a large deep basin with the sugar and vanilla and whisk until pale. Place the soufflé dish in a baking dish surrounded by ice cubes. Put the ice cream in the base and top with apricots. Fold the stiffly whisked (but not dry) egg whites into the yolks and pour over the fruit and ice cream. Place towards top of preheated oven at 450°F, 230°C (mark 8) for 7–8 minutes until golden brown on top. Serve at once.

Lemon shorties

Melt-in-the-mouth butter crust enclosing a delicious lemon filling, these are best eaten fresh on the day of making.

10 oz. plain flour
4 oz. caster sugar
6 oz. butter, softened
2 egg yolks

For filling
1 oz. butter
$\frac{1}{2}$ pt. single cream
1 oz. plain flour
2 oz. caster sugar
2 egg yolks
grated rind $\frac{1}{2}$ lemon
$\frac{1}{2}$ tsp. vanilla essence
icing sugar

MAKES ABOUT 12

Sift the flour on to a working surface, make a well in the centre and place in it the sugar, butter and egg yolks. Use the fingertips of one hand to work the flour into the other ingredients. Knead lightly. Chill for 30 minutes.

For the filling, heat the butter and half the cream in a small pan. Blend the flour and sugar and mix in the remaining cream. Add gradually to the mixture in the pan, beating well until smooth. Remove from heat and beat in the egg yolks, lemon rind and essence. Return to the heat and cook gently for 5 minutes then allow the lemon cream to go cold. Roll out the pastry on a floured surface. Cut 12 rounds with a 3-in. plain cutter and 12 rounds with a $2\frac{1}{2}$-in. fluted cutter. Line 12 deep patty tins with the plain rounds, divide the filling between the pastry cases and place the fluted lids in position. Press down lightly. Bake at 400°F, 200°C (mark 6) for 15–18 minutes until lightly browned. Allow to cool in the tin before turning out. Serve dusted with icing sugar.

Lemon delight

2 whole eggs
2 egg yolks
2 oz. caster sugar
1 pkt. (1 pt.) lemon jelly tablet
juice and grated rind of 1 lemon
$\frac{1}{4}$ pt. white wine
whipped cream (optional)
grated chocolate (optional)

SERVES 4

In a deep bowl whisk together the whole eggs, yolks and sugar over hot, not boiling, water until really thick, then allow to cool, whisking occasionally. In a small pan dissolve the jelly squares in $\frac{1}{4}$ pt. water over a very low heat, stirring. Pour into a measure, add the lemon juice, rind and wine, then make up to 1 pt. with water. Cool until on the point of setting then whisk into the cool egg mixture. Turn into a

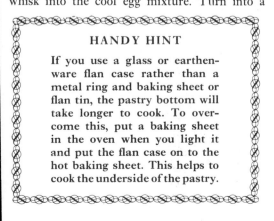

HANDY HINT

If you use a glass or earthenware flan case rather than a metal ring and baking sheet or flan tin, the pastry bottom will take longer to cook. To overcome this, put a baking sheet in the oven when you light it and put the flan case on to the hot baking sheet. This helps to cook the underside of the pastry.

serving dish and chill. Decorate if you wish with lightly whipped cream and grated chocolate.

Nut meringue with marinaded peaches

7 oz. icing sugar, sifted
3 egg whites
$4\frac{1}{2}$ oz. nibbed almonds
$\frac{1}{2}$ pt. double cream
4 tbsps. milk
15-oz. can white peaches
15-oz. can sliced or halved yellow peaches
2 level tsps. arrowroot
3 tbsps. brandy

SERVES 6

Line 2 baking sheets with non-stick paper. Mark 12 3-in. circles, well apart. Put the icing sugar and egg whites in a deep bowl, place over a saucepan of hot water and whisk steadily with a rotary whisk or electric hand-held mixer, until the mixture forms stiff peaks. Remove from the heat and stir in the nuts. Spoon discs of meringue within the circles. Cook in the oven at 300°F, 150°C (mark 2) for about 30 minutes until crisp on the outside and cream-coloured. Cool for a few minutes then use a palette knife to slide the meringues off the paper. Cool on a wire rack. Store in an airtight tin for a few days.

To serve, whip the cream and milk together until stiff enough to just hold its shape. Pipe a border of cream round each meringue disc and serve the compote separately.

Peach compote: Drain the juice from the white peaches and make up to $\frac{1}{2}$ pt. with juice from the yellow peaches. Thicken the juices with arrowroot by cooking in a pan and stirring until clear. Off the heat, add 3 tbsps. brandy. Finely slice or dice the fruit, pour over the juices and chill.

Red wine jelly

This full-flavoured wine jelly (best made on the day) cooly offsets the richness of game.

$\frac{1}{2}$ pt. Beaujolais
$\frac{3}{4}$ oz. powdered gelatine
1 oz. caster sugar
$\frac{1}{2}$ pt. fizzy lemonade
3 tsps. lemon juice
$\frac{1}{2}-\frac{3}{4}$ lb. black grapes
whipped cream

SERVES 4

Pour half the wine into a small pan, sprinkle the gelatine and sugar over and heat gently without boiling until the gelatine has dissolved. Off the heat add the remaining wine, lemonade and lemon juice. Pour into a 1-pt. plain ring mould and put in a cool place to set. To serve, unmould on to a serving place. Fill the centre with halved, pipped grapes and decorate with cream.

Rum and mincemeat sauce

For ice cream.

1 juicy eating apple
1 large banana
2 oz. butter
2 level tbsps. soft brown sugar
2 tbsps. lemon juice
1 oz. golden sultanas
6 tbsps. rum
$\frac{1}{4}$ lb. white grapes, halved and pipped

SERVES 6

Peel, core and finely chop the apple. Peel and roughly chop the banana. Melt the butter and add the apple and banana together with the sugar, lemon juice and sultanas; cook until the apple begins to soften. Add the rum and grapes, bubble a few minutes and serve over portions of vanilla dairy ice cream.
Note: Have the ice cream ready, scooped or sliced, in the ice compartment set at coldest. The sauce can be kept warm in the oven.

✳ Apple and blackberry compote

$2\frac{1}{2}$ lb. eating apples
$\frac{1}{2}$ lemon
3 oz. sugar
$\frac{3}{4}$ lb. blackberries
2 tbsps. Calvados liqueur

SERVES 6

Peel, core and thickly slice the apples. Poach them for about 7 minutes in $\frac{3}{4}$ pt. water with a sliver of lemon rind, until transparent. Drain the apples and set aside to cool. Add the sugar to the cooking liquid and reduce by half by boiling rapidly in an open pan for about 8–10 minutes. Pour over the apples. Place half the apples in the base of 6 individual dishes. Cover with half the blackberries. Fill up with layers of the remaining apples and blackberries. Add the Calvados to the remaining juice and spoon over the fruit. Chill well before serving with thick pouring cream.

Lemon and grape creams

1 level tsp. powdered gelatine
1 tbsp. water
6 fl. oz. mandarin and lemon yoghurt
7 tbsps. double cream

For topping
12 grapes
1 level tbsp. lemon curd
lemon juice

SERVES 2

Sprinkle the gelatine over the water in a small bowl or cup. Place the cup in a saucepan with a little water and heat until the gelatine has dissolved. Lightly whisk the yoghurt and stir in the gelatine. When it begins to show signs of setting, whisk the cream until it just holds its shape then fold in the yoghurt.

Divide between two stemmed glasses and chill in the refrigerator. Before serving halve the grapes and discard the pips. Blend the lemon curd with enough fresh lemon juice to give a thin coating consistency, pile the grapes over the lemon creams and spoon lemon glaze over. Serve with small biscuits and groups of sugared grapes.

Glazed cherry flan

To make a good-looking cherry flan you need a cherry stoner or a knife with a small, sharp point.

6 oz. plain flour
pinch salt
3 oz. butter, softened
3 oz. caster sugar
2 egg yolks
few drops almond essence
2 15-oz. cans red cherries
$\frac{1}{2}$ lb. redcurrant jelly
2 tbsps. lemon juice
8 oz. full-fat cream cheese
grated rind of 1 lemon
3 tbsps. single cream
1 oz. caster sugar

SERVES 8

Sift the flour and salt on to a board and make a well in the centre. Cut the butter into small flakes and put in the centre of the flour with the sugar, egg yolks and almond essence. Work with the fingertips, mixing in the flour. Continue working until all the flour is mixed in then place the pastry in a polythene bag and chill for $\frac{1}{2}$ hour. Roll out the pastry and use it to line a 10-in. French fluted flan tin. Prick the base and bake blind at 400°F, 200°C (mark 6) for about 15 minutes. Cool in the tin.

Drain the juice from the cans and measure off $\frac{1}{4}$ pt. Put this juice in a pan with the jelly and lemon juice and boil until well reduced. Stone the cherries, leaving them whole. Beat together the cheese, lemon rind, cream and sugar. Spread in a layer over flan base and arrange the cherries on top. Brush the fruit and pastry edge thickly with redcurrant glaze. To serve, remove the outside flan ring but leave the flan on the metal base for ease of cutting.

Pears brûlée with orange cream

2 large juicy oranges
water
3 oz. caster sugar
8 firm ripe eating pears
4 level tbsps. soft brown sugar
1 level tsp. arrowroot
2 tsps. cold water
2 oz. butter
$\frac{1}{2}$ pt. double cream

SERVES 8

Thinly pare the rind from 1 orange, free of all white pith, and cut it into very fine julienne strips. Squeeze out the juice from both oranges. Boil the orange rind strips in water until soft, then strain. In a large open pan, dissolve the sugar in 1 pt. water, bring to the boil and simmer to reduce. Peel the pears, halve and carefully remove the cores. Add the pears to the sugar syrup. Cover and simmer until tender – about 10 minutes. Drain. Place the drained pear halves, cut side down, in an ovenproof dish. Sprinkle with soft brown sugar and grill quickly until browning. Meanwhile add the orange juice to the syrup and reduce by boiling to $\frac{1}{2}$ pt. Reserve 3 tbsps. syrup, blend the arrowroot with 2 tsps. water, add to the syrup, boil until clear and stir in the butter. Pour over the pears, garnish with orange strips and serve slightly warm or cold with orange cream.

For the orange cream: Place the chilled cream and chilled, reserved orange syrup in a deep bowl. Whisk until the cream just holds its shape.

Orange snow

Fruity and frothy – a slip-down dessert for any occasion.

2 6$\frac{1}{4}$-fl. oz. cans frozen orange juice
water
4 thin-skinned oranges
4 level tsps. powdered gelatine
4 egg whites
2 oz. caster sugar
lemon slices

SERVES 8

To the contents of the cans, add 4 canfuls of water and stir until well blended. Prepare the orange segments free of peel, pith and membrane. Put 24 segments on one side for decoration and roughly cut up the remainder. Put 4 tbsps. water in a cup, sprinkle the gelatine over, place the cup in a pan with about $\frac{1}{2}$ in. hot water and leave the gelatine to dissolve. Add a little of the orange juice, then return it to the bulk, stirring. When the orange juice is beginning to set, whisk the egg whites until stiff, then whisk in the sugar. Fold the egg whites through the orange jelly and when evenly blended, divide between eight individual glasses. Chill. Serve decorated with reserved orange segments and half slices of lemon with the rind left on for contrast.

Grape pie

The subtle flavour of grapes in an unusual pie filling which thickens as it bakes. Try the same way with stoned cherries.

8 oz. rich shortcrust pastry (8 oz. flour, etc.)
1–1$\frac{1}{4}$ lb. white grapes
2 oz. sugar
2 level tbsps. flour
grated rind of 1 orange
$\frac{1}{2}$ oz. butter
caster sugar

SERVES 6

Roll out two-thirds of the pastry and use it to line an 8-in. fluted flan ring placed on a flat baking sheet. Roll out the remainder of the pastry to form a lid. Halve the grapes and remove the pips. Blend together the sugar, flour and orange rind. Stir into the prepared grapes. Spoon into the uncooked pastry case and dot with butter.

Damp the rim of the pastry lid, lift it into position and seal the edges. Make a slit in the centre of the lid. Bake towards the top of the oven at 425°F, 220°C (mark 7) for 10 minutes. Reduce the heat to 350°F, 180°C (mark 4) and lower the pie to the centre of the oven; continue cooking for a further 30–40 minutes. Dredge with caster sugar and serve warm or cold.

* Caramel bavarois

A sophisticated dessert; a rich coffee sauce partners the bavarois.

6 oz. caster sugar
4 tbsps. water
3 large eggs, separated
½ pt. milk
1½ level tbsps. powdered gelatine
3 tbsps. water
¼ pt. double cream
¼ pt. single cream
1 oz. flaked almonds for decoration

For coffee sauce
2 oz. butter
4 level tbsps. dark soft brown sugar
1 level tbsp. cornflour
2 level tbsps. instant coffee powder
½ pt. water

SERVES 6

Dissolve 4 oz. sugar in 4 tbsps. water in a small pan. Bring it to the boil and when a dark golden brown pour off into an oiled tin. Crush when cold. Whisk the egg yolks and the remaining 2 oz. sugar until thick. In a saucepan dissolve the caramel in warm milk, pour it on to the yolks and return to the pan and heat, stirring to a coating consistency – do not boil. Sprinkle the gelatine over the water; leave it to soften and when swollen stir it into the custard mixture until dissolved; cool until thickening. Whisk the creams together until a floppy consistency. Fold the whisked egg-whites into the cream and then fold the cream mixture into the egg custard. Pour into a 2½-pt. ring mould and chill. Unmould and decorate with flaked almonds; serve coffee sauce separately.

To make the coffee sauce, blend all the ingredients in a small pan. Heat gently until the butter has melted, then bring to the boil, stirring. Cook for 2–3 minutes and leave until cold.

Gingered pears with sabayon sauce

Sabayon sauce can partner other fruits.

4 large cooking pears
½ pt. water
4 oz. sugar
½ stick cinnamon
lemon peel
4 cloves
½ oz. root ginger

For sabayon sauce
2 oz. caster sugar
4 tbsps. water
2 egg yolks, beaten
rind of ½ lemon
2–3 tsps. lemon juice
1 tbsp. sherry
2 tbsps. double cream

SERVES 4

Peel the pears, halve and remove the cores. Poach in the water, sugar and flavourings until the flesh is transparent. Drain. Strain the liquor and reduce it to a glaze consistency. Pour over the pears and chill.

For the sauce, dissolve the sugar in the water, bring to the boil and boil to a 'thread' (i.e. when a little cool syrup forms a thread when pulled between the wet fingers). Pour slowly on to the egg yolks, whisking until thick and foamy. Add the lemon rind, juice and sherry. Lightly whisk the cream and gently fold into the egg mixture. Chill. Spoon sauce on to each halved pear for serving.

* Chocolate soufflé de luxe

(*see picture opposite*)

3 egg yolks
2 oz. caster sugar
2 oz. cooking chocolate
water
1 tbsp. coffee liqueur
2 level tsps. powdered gelatine
⅓ pt. double cream, whipped
4 egg whites
whipped cream and chocolate curls for decoration

SERVES 4–6

Prepare a 6-in. soufflé dish with a paper collar. Whisk the egg yolks and sugar over a pan of hot water until thick. Remove from the heat.

Chocolate soufflé de luxe (*see opposite*)

Melt the chocolate with 1 tbsp. water and coffee liqueur over a very low heat. Dissolve the gelatine in 1 tbsp. water in a cup over hot water and add it to the chocolate. Stir this into the whisked yolk mixture and when cool and beginning to set, quickly but lightly fold in the cream and lastly the stiffly beaten whites (these should be firm but not dry). Turn the mixture into the prepared dish and leave in the refrigerator until set. Before serving, carefully ease away the paper with a knife dipped in hot water. Decorate with whipped cream and chocolate curls.

Pineapple whip

1-pt. lemon jelly tablet
15-oz. can crushed pineapple
4-oz. can cream
glacé cherries and angelica for decoration

SERVES 4

Make the jelly tablet up to $\frac{1}{2}$ pt. with boiling water. Stir to dissolve. When it begins to set, turn into an electric blender, add the contents from the cans and blend until puréed. Turn into stemmed glasses. Leave until chilled and lightly set. Decorate with glacé cherries and angelica.

HANDY HINT

To keep a sauce warm without allowing a skin to form, place a circle of buttered or damp greaseproof paper over it in the pan. Sprinkle a sweet custard sauce with caster or icing sugar to prevent a skin forming.

Cinnamon and soured cream raisin pie

8 oz. digestive biscuits
4 oz. unsalted butter
2 standard eggs, separated
4 oz. cottage cheese, sieved
¼ pt. soured cream
½ tsp. vanilla essence
1 oz. caster sugar
1 level tsp. powdered cinnamon
½ level tsp. powdered nutmeg
4 oz. seedless raisins

SERVES 6

Evenly crush the biscuits into a fine crumb. Combine the crumbs with the melted butter and press the mixture against the sides and base of a 9-in. diameter ovenproof flan dish. Chill while making the filling. Put the egg yolks and remainder of the ingredients, except the egg whites, in a bowl and stir in well. Whisk the egg whites until stiff and fold into the filling, using a metal spoon in a figure of eight movement, until evenly incorporated. Pour into the biscuit crumb case. Bake in the oven at 350°F, 180°C (mark 4) for 35–40 minutes until set and lightly brown. Allow to go cold for the crumb to firm up, then dust with sieved icing sugar before serving on the day of making.

Mincemeat 1922

8 oz. dried apricots
1 orange
1 lemon
8 oz. stoned raisins
8 oz. currants
8 oz. sultanas
4 oz. mixed peel
1 lb. Demerara sugar
4 oz. nibbed almonds
8 oz. shredded suet
2 tbsps. marmalade
2 level tsps. mixed spice
½ level tsp. salt
4 fl. oz. rum
2 fl. oz. sherry

MAKES 4 1-LB. POTS

Soak the apricots overnight in water, pat dry and chop. Thinly grate the orange and lemon rind and squeeze the juices. Combine with the dried fruits, peel, sugar, nuts, suet, marmalade, spices and salt. Mix very thoroughly, cover and allow to stand for 24 hours, then add the rum and sherry. Pack into pots and cover as for jam. This mincemeat keeps for a year; if dry when opened, add more sherry or rum.

Christmas pudding 1922

You won't want to eat this yet but do make your puddings and mincemeat around about October so that you are ready for Christmas.

1 lb. stoned raisins
8 oz. currants
8 oz. sultanas
6 oz. mixed peel
2 large apples
1 lemon
8 oz. plain flour
12 oz. fresh white breadcrumbs
1 lb. shredded suet
1 lb. Demerara sugar
1 level tsp. salt
2 level tsps. mixed spice
6 eggs
8 oz. marmalade
2 tbsps. milk or stout
4 fl. oz. rum, brandy or sherry

MAKES 2 2½-PT. AND 1 1½-PT. PUDDINGS

Stone the raisins if necessary, chop coarsely; combine all the dried fruits and mixed peel. Peel and chop the apples and grate the lemon rind. Combine all the dry ingredients in a large basin. Beat the eggs, add with the marmalade and lemon juice to the dry ingredients. Moisten with about 2 tbsps. milk or stout. Blend all the ingredients thoroughly. Cover the basin and let the mixture stand for 24 hours before adding the spirit; then give a final stir. Pack into well greased pudding basins, cover with a double thickness of greased greaseproof paper with a pleat in it and then with foil. Place in a pan of boiling water, with water half-way up the basins and steam for 4–5 hours, topping up with more boiling water as needed. When the puddings are cooked, re-cover with greaseproof paper dipped in a little extra spirit and top with fresh foil. Store in a cool place until needed; steam for a further 2–3 hours before serving.

Autumn cakes

* Almond loaf cake

A rich and wholesome 'cut and come again' cake. Enjoy the last slices buttered.

2 oz. ground almonds
10 oz. Barbados sugar
a little beaten egg
8 oz. butter
4 eggs
8 oz. wholemeal plain flour
2 level tsps. baking powder
milk

Grease and line a 9-in. by 5-in. loaf tin (top measurements). Make a paste with the ground almonds, 2 oz. sugar and a little beaten egg. Cream together the butter and remaining sugar until soft and fluffy. Beat in the eggs one at a time. Sift the flour and baking powder together, fold into the creamed mixture, adding a little milk to give a soft dropping consistency and layer one third of the cake mixture in the tin. Place little pieces of almond paste over the cake mixture and continue to layer, finishing with creamed mixture. Bake on the centre shelf at 350°F, 180°C (mark 4) for about 1½ hours. Turn the cake out to cool on a wire rack.

⊀ Dark chocolate cake

Treacle is the hidden secret in this moist cake.

8 oz. butter
6 oz. light soft brown sugar
6 oz. black treacle
8 oz. self-raising flour
2 oz. cocoa powder
4 large eggs

For buttercream
2 oz. butter
3 oz. icing sugar
icing sugar for dusting

Grease and line two 8½-in. or 9-in. straight-sided sandwich tins. Cream the butter until soft, add the soft brown sugar and black treacle (or 3 oz. black treacle and 3 oz. golden syrup) and beat the mixture until light and fluffy. Sift together the flour and cocoa. Beat the eggs and gradually beat into the creamed mixture, adding 1 tbsp. of the measured flour. Lightly beat in the rest of the flour. Divide the mixture between the tins. Bake in the centre of the oven or just above at 350°F, 180°C (mark 4) for about 40 minutes. Turn out and cool on a wire rack. Sandwich with buttercream and dust the cake heavily with icing sugar.

* Honey butter sandwich

4 oz. block margarine or butter
4 oz. caster sugar
2 large eggs
4 oz. self-raising flour
½ level tsp. ground cinnamon

For honey butter frosting
3 oz. butter
6 oz. icing sugar, sifted
1 level tbsp. clear honey
1 tbsp. lemon juice
icing sugar for dusting

Grease and base-line two 7-in. straight-sided sandwich tins. Cream the fat and sugar, beat in the eggs one at a time and lightly beat in the flour and cinnamon sifted together. Divide the mixture equally between the prepared tins and bake in the centre of the oven at 350°F, 180°C (mark 4) for about 25 minutes until well risen and spongy to the touch. Turn out and cool on a wire rack. Meanwhile, cream the butter for the frosting and gradually beat in the icing sugar, with the honey and lemon juice.

Layer the sandwich cakes with half the filling, top with the remainder and swirl it with a knife. Dust with icing sugar.

* Parkin

Make a week before eating and, if you like, serve sliced and buttered. Don't worry if it sinks slightly.

8 oz. plain flour
2 level tsps. baking powder
2 level tsps. ground ginger
2 oz. butter or margarine
2 oz. lard
8 oz. medium oatmeal
4 oz. caster sugar
6 oz. golden syrup
6 oz. black treacle
4 tbsps. milk

Grease and line a tin measuring 10 in. by 8 in.

by $1\frac{1}{2}$ in. deep. Sift together the flour, baking powder and ginger. Rub in the fats. Add the oatmeal and sugar. Heat together the golden syrup and black treacle, make a well in the dry ingredients and stir in the syrup, treacle and milk. Mix until smooth then pour into the tin. Bake in the centre of the oven at 350°F, 180°C (mark 4) for 45–60 minutes until the mixture springs back when lightly pressed and has shrunk away from the sides of the tin. Turn out and cool on a rack. Wrap in foil.

Blackberry mace shortcake

Mace is traditionally used in shortcake mixtures, to give a nice golden colour and it also goes well with fruit, whether cherries, blackberries or strawberries.

6 oz. self-raising flour
2 oz. cornflour
$\frac{1}{4}$ level tsp. salt
$\frac{1}{2}$ level tsp. ground mace
3 oz. butter
3 oz. sugar
1 egg, beaten
1–2 tbsps. milk
$\frac{3}{4}$ lb. blackberries (sprinkled with sugar if necessary)
$\frac{1}{4}$ pt. double cream

Grease two 8-in. sandwich tins. Sift the flours, salt and mace. Rub in the butter until the mixture resembles fine breadcrumbs; add the sugar. Add the beaten egg a little at a time, until the mixture begins to bind and add milk if necessary to form a fairly stiff dough. Knead lightly and divide the mixture into two. Press the dough into the tins, making the tops as smooth as possible. Bake just above centre of the oven at 375°F, 190°C (mark 5) for 15–20 minutes. Remove and after 2 minutes turn out carefully on to a wire rack. Whisk the cream until stiff. Spread two-thirds of it on to one of the shortcakes. Arrange all but 7 of the blackberries on top of the cream and cover with the other shortcake. Spoon or pipe the remainder of the cream on the top and

---

HANDY HINT

Dishes set in a refrigerator need less gelatine than those set at room temperature – over-chilling can spoil the texture.

---

place a blackberry on the centre of each swirl of cream.

Chocolate pralines

No cooking, equally good for tea-time and with coffee, chocolate pralines can even turn into a dessert with ice cream.

$\frac{1}{2}$ lb. digestive biscuits
2 oz. caster sugar
2 heaped tbsps. golden syrup
4 oz. butter
3 level tbsps. cocoa
vanilla essence
1 oz. cooking chocolate
1 tbsp. water
4 oz. icing sugar, sifted
chocolate vermicelli

Break the biscuits into small pieces – not crumbs. Put the sugar, syrup and butter into a saucepan and stir over a low heat until the sugar is dissolved and the other ingredients melted. Bring to the boil, remove from the heat and add the cocoa and vanilla. Stir in the biscuits. Press this mixture into a shallow 7-in. by 11-in. greased tin.

Melt the chocolate with the water. Gradually add the icing sugar until mixture is thick enough to coat the back of a spoon. Pour it over the 'cake' and decorate with chocolate vermicelli. Leave to set, then cut into small squares or fingers.

✳ Walnut cookies

For enjoying with a mug of frothy coffee.

4 oz. block margarine or butter
4 oz. soft light brown sugar
6 oz. plain flour
$\frac{1}{2}$ level tsp. bicarbonate of soda
$\frac{1}{2}$ level tsp. cream of tartar
walnut halves
melted chocolate

MAKES ABOUT 14

Cream the fat and sugar together. Sift in the flour, bicarbonate of soda and the cream of tartar, work into the creamed mixture then shape into balls the size of a shelled walnut – about 28. Place well apart on a greased baking sheet, press a half walnut on every other cookie and bake at 350°F, 180°C (mark 4) for about 20 minutes until pale brown. Cool on a wire rack. Sandwich in pairs with melted chocolate, walnut cookie uppermost. Leave to set.

✳ Ginger snaps

Crisp, spicy, wafer thin, these can be cut to any shape.

8 oz. plain flour
$\frac{1}{2}$ level tsp. bicarbonate of soda
1 level tsp. ground ginger
4 oz. caster sugar
3 oz. butter
5 oz. golden syrup
nibbed almonds

MAKES ABOUT 50

Sift together the flour, soda and ginger. Add 4 oz. sugar. Warm the butter and syrup in a saucepan, stir in the dry ingredients and knead the mixture lightly until no longer sticky. Roll out thinly on a floured surface and stamp into star shapes. Place on greased baking sheets and press in a few nibbed almonds. Bake in the centre of the oven at 350°F, 180°C (mark 4) for 12–15 minutes. Cool on a wire rack.

Date and raisin crunch

A fruity sweetmeat to be cut up in wedges and foil-wrapped for the lunch box or served warm as a pudding.

2 oz. stoned dates
1 oz. seedless raisins
juice and grated rind of 1 orange
4 oz. rolled oats
$1\frac{1}{2}$ oz. plain flour
3 oz. block margarine
$1\frac{1}{2}$ oz. sugar

Scissor snip the dates into a small pan and add the raisins. Make the juice of the orange up to $\frac{1}{4}$ pt. with water, add to the pan and cook gently until the mixture is thick. Cool. In a bowl, mix the oats and flour, rub in the margarine and add the sugar and grated orange rind. Press half into a 7-in. sandwich tin. Spread the filling over and sprinkle the rest of the oat crumble on top. Press down lightly with a round bladed knife and bake in the oven at 375°F, 190°C (mark 5) for 40 minutes.

Good Housekeeping's favourite Christmas cake

8 oz. plain flour
$\frac{1}{2}$ level tsp. ground cinnamon
$\frac{1}{2}$ level tsp. ground mace
8 oz. butter
8 oz. dark, soft brown sugar
grated rind 1 lemon
4 large eggs, beaten
8 oz. currants
8 oz. stoned raisins, chopped
8 oz. sultanas
4 oz. small glacé cherries, halved
4 oz. mixed chopped peel
2 oz. nibbed almonds
1–2 tbsps. brandy

Grease and double-line an 8-in. round cake tin. Tie a band of brown paper firmly round the outside, or place the tin in another slightly larger tin and omit the brown paper.

Sift together the flour and spices. Beat the butter until creamy, add the sugar and cream until light and fluffy. Add the lemon rind. Gradually add the beaten eggs. Fold in the flour alternately with the fruit and nuts and finally stir in the brandy. Turn the mixture into the prepared tin and hollow the centre slightly. Bake below the oven centre at 300°F, 150°C (mark 1–2) for about $3\frac{3}{4}$ hours. Cool in tin for about 10 minutes when cooked, then turn out on to a wire rack to cool. To store, wrap in greaseproof paper and kitchen foil. If wished, 1–2 tbsps. brandy may be added during storage – prick the cake with a fine skewer and spoon the brandy over.

CHAPTER FOUR

WINTER

Winter is the time to seek the best food buys for meals that will be hot, heartening and nutritious for families coming in from the cold. It is the time for skilful cooking of economy cuts and for choosing meals that look after themselves in the pre-Christmas rush. Meat puddings – for economy choose mince and carrot – or ragouts such as beef cooked in a robust brown sauce, richly flavoured blanquette of rabbit; navarin of lamb with lots of vegetables or boiled salt beef and dumplings. Remember fish too; herrings and mackerel are nutritionally sound, or for a touch of the unusual but still with budget in mind, try mussels and scallops. Pop the last of the game into a casserole for long slow cooking and delicious tenderness. It's worth having an extra baking day to fill airtight containers with mountains of cookies that keep.

Cut shopping time and buy fresh meat for days ahead. Once home, unwrap and sit it on a piece of greaseproof paper on top of refrigerator shelf rungs – joints for up to 5 days, cuts for 3–4 days. The surface will darken but this doesn't matter. Take meat from the refrigerator at least half an hour before cooking; when very cold, the juices will be lost more rapidly during cooking. For a change from the Christmas poultry, try oven-baked spare rib of pork or salt beef with herby dumplings.

With a touch of frost root vegetables are still good value; try carrots, turnips and swedes mashed together with a little margarine or butter and plenty of freshly ground black pepper. Look out for Florence fennel – a perfect partner to fish – Jerusalem artichokes – make a memorable soup – and sweet potatoes. At the end of Winter enjoy young Cornish greens, but never cook them in too much water. For salads there is curly endive, celeriac, green-stemmed celery (eat the heart with cheese and braise the outer stems) and chicory, finely shredded (never buy heads with green tips to the spears – they could be bitter).

Fruit is limited – Conference pears could be a good buy as a change from apples for a crumble; blanch them after peeling then slice, sweeten with golden syrup and add a flavouring of grated lemon. Fresh grapefruit halves or sliced peeled oranges should appear regularly on the menu. Small Spanish Almeria grapes are delicious when added, with nuts, to a Winter cabbage slaw or to your favourite fresh fruit salad. Forced pale pink rhubarb is a post-Christmas choice to make a change. For the fruit bowl include the first clementines, tangerines and satsumas, and in case of a pre-holiday shortage pop some imported first-of-the-season's cranberries into the freezer. At the turn of the year plan a Seville marmalade session and include limes too.

For the freezer

Christmas comes early for the freezer owner. Cook ahead. The Christmas cook-in can be started about a month before, when nearly everything can go in: quiches, cooked rice, sliced bread or uncooked dough, breadcrumbs, extra butter, including butter balls, double cream, soft cheese like Camembert or Valmeuse, hard sauce and Cumberland rum butter, mince pies, tea breads, scones, sandwiches, cranberry relish or just cranberries bought when first in season, chestnuts peeled and par-cooked, rolls of cookie dough ready to slice and bake, freshly made sausages, pâtés, cheese biscuits and straws, choux cases and vol-au-vents, cream cheese dips, meats and poultry, dry stuffing mixes, gâteaux, grated cheese, sausage rolls, thick cheese and chutney or ham and cheese sandwiches to fry or toast straight from the freezer.

In the new year if there is no time to make marmalade, stow away the oranges in polythene bags. Before the season wanes freeze some sautéed leeks for vichyssoise. Old potatoes are coming to an end, so here is the last chance for cottage pie, duchesse potatoes and chips. Make pancakes well ahead for Shrove Tuesday and store them between sheets of greaseproof paper. Fresh stocks of new season's New Zealand lamb are in the shops ready for freezing and February is the time to freeze curly kale and winter broccoli.

Winter fruits

Apricots, Cape gooseberries (February only), Chinese gooseberries, clementines, cranberries, dates, cumquats (arrive February), lychees, mandarins, mangoes, nectarines, passion fruit, chestnuts (December is the end of season), coconuts (December is the end of season), peaches, plums, pomegranates, rhubarb (forced), satsumas, tangerines, papaws (limited), ortaniques (arrive February).

Winter vegetables

Aubergines, broccoli, Brussels sprouts, Brussels tops, celeriac, celery, chicory, chillies (December), courgettes, endive, fennel, French beans, globe and Jerusalem artichokes, horseradish, kale, kohlrabi, leeks, parsnips, new potatoes, radishes, salsify, savoys, seakale, shallots (January), spinach, Spring greens, sweet potato, turnip, swede.

Winter poultry and game

Goose, grouse (season ends December 10th), hare (season ends February 28th), partridge (season ends February 1st), pheasant (season ends in Scotland on December 1st, in England on January 31st), rabbit, snipe and teal, wild duck, venison, wild goose, woodcock, black game (season ends December 20th), plover, ptarmigan (season ends December 10th), widgeon, wood pigeon.

Winter menus

*(Dishes marked * are included in the recipes on pages 126 to 167)*

Children's tea party

*Chicken puffs
*Red sails
*Sausage kebabs
Crisps
*Lollipop cookies
*Alaska express
*Roundabout cake
Orange fizz

The young idea party for 12

*Fish chowder
Crisp breads or crackers
*Chicken curry
*Polynesian kaukau
*Sambals
Tossed green salad
*Baked bananas
Pineapple spears
Spicy fruit punch

Family dinner for 6

*Vegetable broth
Bread sticks
*Beef pies
Green salad bowl
Fresh fruit

Supper for 4

*Sausage, tomato and pasta bake
Hot French bread
Dressed green beans
Rhubarb fool

Guest dinner for 6

Pâté
*Lamb Italian style
Risotto
Asparagus tips
*Pineapple meringue

Cut the cost menus

*Beef and carrot pudding
Potato crisps
Brussels sprouts

*Pears Bristol

*Herring fillets with onion sauce
Baked tomatoes
Sauté potatoes

Grilled peach halves

Guest menu for 4 (1)

*Portuguese sardines
*Lamb and mushroom pudding
Brussels sprouts with buttered
   crumbs
Baby onions sweet and sour
*Banana sundae

Tray supper for 2

Chicken and leek soup
*Sardine scrunchies
Celery sticks
Orange slices
Hazelnut yoghurt

Family high tea for 4

*Beefburger decker
*Pineapple-banana crush
Blackcurrant shake

Cold buffet for 12 on Boxing Day

Leek broth, bread sticks
*Orange glazed baked gammon
*Cold turkey mayonnaise
Salads:
   *Tomato and celery
   *Rice, mushroom and walnut
   *Jellied beetroot and orange
   *Cabbage and carrot slaw
*Strawberry cream trifle

Dinner for 4

Chilled sherry and devilled
   walnuts
*Roast duckling with cranberry
   glaze
Parsley potatoes
Broccoli spears with lemon butter
Chicory side salad
*Grape brûlée
*Petits fours

*Venetian liver
Fluffy rice

*Golden apple Charlotte

*Somerset tripe
Mashed potatoes
Sliced carrots

Apricot crunch flan

Guest menu for 4 (2)

Cucumber sweet and sour
*Pork and cranberry curry
Buttery broccoli
Parsley rice
*Apricot liqueur croissants

Menu for Christmas Day for 6–8

*Avodaco cocktail
or
*Grapefruit and grape cocktail

Stuffed roast turkey
Giblet gravy
Bread sauce
Golden roast potatoes
*Cranberry and bacon balls
Brussels sprouts with almonds

*Cherry cream trifle
Cheese and celery
Coffee and *Rum truffles

Cheese and wine party for 25

*Blue cheese dip with dunks
*Cheese olives
Sardine pyramids
*Talmouse
*Pâté fleurons
Celery slices
*Savoury choux
Crisps
French bread and butter
Cheeseboard
Cheese and fruit cocktail wheel

Welcoming punch
Assorted wines

Cheese and wine party (*see page 147*)

Winter appetisers

Avocado cocktail

2 small grapefruit
4 tbsps. salad oil
2 tbsps. wine vinegar
salt and pepper
good pinch caster sugar
$\frac{1}{2}$ level tsp. French mustard
2 medium avocados, ripe
1 small lettuce, washed and well drained
$\frac{1}{2}$ pt. thick mayonnaise
6 oz. frozen shelled shrimps, thawed

SERVES 6–8

Peel the grapefruit with a sharp knife to remove outside pith and show the flesh. Segment close to the dividing membrane and catch the juice in a bowl. Fork together the next six ingredients. Halve the avocados, discard the stones and peel away tough outer skin. Cut most of the avocado flesh into small dice but reserve enough to cut into about 16 thin slices to garnish. Toss the avocado in the grapefruit juice. Shred the lettuce and toss it in the oil and vinegar. Drain well and arrange in the base of 6–8 medium sized glasses. Divide the diced avocado between the glasses and spoon over the mayonnaise. Garnish with alternate slices of grapefruit and avocado. Toss the shrimps in the remaining oil and vinegar and arrange them around the sides of the glasses.
Note: Prepare the cocktails up to 1 hour in advance.

Spiced cauliflower

An interesting appetiser to serve hot.

1 medium sized cauliflower
1 large egg
salt and pepper
browned breadcrumbs
deep oil for frying
chopped parsley to garnish

For vinegar sauce
6 tbsps. oil
6 tbsps. vinegar
$\frac{1}{2}$ level tsp. paprika pepper
2 small cloves garlic, skinned and crushed

SERVES 2–3

Trim the cauliflower and break it into florets;

blanch in boiling salted water for 5 minutes then drain well. Beat the egg lightly with the seasoning. Dip the florets into the egg, then into breadcrumbs, and coat thoroughly. Heat the oil to 375°F, 190°C and deep fry the coated florets for 5–7 minutes until golden brown. Drain on absorbent paper. Keep warm. Meanwhile, have ready the sauce ingredients in a small pan. Bring to the boil and pour over the crisp florets. Garnish with chopped parsley.

Grapefruit and grape cocktail

Allow half a grapefruit per person. Loosen the segments and raise each alternate one. Pile halved, skinned and pipped white grapes (6 per person) in the centre. Dress with sugar or French dressing.

＊Farmhouse pâté

A mild, smooth-textured pâté for all the family, good for open sandwiches.

$\frac{1}{2}$ lb. belly pork
$\frac{1}{2}$ lb. pig's liver
$\frac{1}{2}$ lb. pie veal
1 golden stock cube
salt and freshly ground black pepper
1 clove garlic, skinned and crushed
$\frac{1}{2}$ level tsp. dried sage
2 tbsps. red wine (optional)
12 rashers bacon, rinded and stretched

SERVES 6–8

Mince the pork, liver and veal. Crumble the

HANDY HINT

To dice an onion, first skin it keeping the root intact. Cut in half through the root. Holding the root end away from the knife and using a sharp, pointed knife, cut down in even slices about $\frac{1}{4}$–$\frac{1}{2}$ in. apart. Make a similar number of horizontal cuts, stopping short of the root. Holding the onion firmly, cut down at right angles to the previous cuts, the onion will then fall away in neat dice.

stock cube and stir it into the meat mixture. Add salt, pepper, garlic, sage and wine. Stir well to mix. Line an $8\frac{1}{2}$-in. by 5-in. by $2\frac{1}{2}$-in. loaf tin with 6 rashers of bacon. Spoon the pâté mixture into the tin and cover with the remaining bacon rashers. Bake at 325°F, 170°C (mark 3) for $1\frac{1}{2}$ hours in a baking dish containing 1 in. water. Remove from the oven and when almost cold, cover with greaseproof paper, top with a weight and leave in a cool place overnight.

*Sild pâté

4 oz. butter
3 oz. fresh white breadcrumbs
2 tbsps. lemon juice
1 level tsp. capers
1 level tsp. snipped parsley
$3\frac{3}{4}$-oz. can sild in oil
salt and freshly ground black pepper

SERVES 4–6

Melt 3 oz. butter in a small pan, add to the breadcrumbs in a bowl with the lemon juice, capers, snipped parsley and the sild. Beat well together and adjust the seasoning to taste. Spoon this mixture into a small soufflé dish. Melt the remaining butter and pour over the pâté. Chill until firm.

Dressed chicory spears

(*see picture page 128*)

$\frac{3}{4}$ lb. chicory heads
juice of 1 large lemon
1 egg yolk
salt and pepper
$\frac{1}{4}$ pt. salad oil
green and red pepper

SERVES 4

Cut the base off each head of chicory. Separate the leaves under cold running water and drain thoroughly. Toss in 2 tbsps. lemon juice. Beat the egg yolk with a pinch of salt and freshly ground pepper. Add the oil, a little at a time, whisking continually; a hand-mixer is very suitable. When thick, stir in the lemon juice, drained from the chicory. Adjust the thickness of the mayonnaise to a stiff pouring consistency at this point by the addition, if necessary, of a little warm water. Divide the chicory between 4 large goblets or balloon glasses. Just before serving, spoon over the dressing and sprinkle with finely chopped green and red pepper.

*Celery and carrot soup

2 heads of celery (about 2 lb.)
3 oz. butter
10 oz. onion, skinned and chopped
2 pt. lightly seasoned white stock
2 bayleaves
$\frac{1}{2}$ level tsp. *fines herbes*
1 level tsp. salt
freshly ground black pepper
1 oz. flour
$\frac{1}{2}$ pt. milk
$\frac{1}{2}$ lb. carrot, pared and grated

SERVES 12

Trim and wash the celery. Reserve a few young leaves. Cut the sticks into $\frac{1}{4}$-in. slices and place them in a large saucepan with 2 oz. butter. Sauté covered, for about 10 minutes, stirring frequently. Stir in the onion and sauté for 5 minutes more. Add the stock, bayleaves, herbs and seasonings. Bring to the boil. Reduce the heat to simmering point, cover the pan and cook for 1 hour. Remove the bayleaves and, using an electric blender, purée the contents of the pan. Melt the remaining butter, stir in the flour and cook the roux 1–2 minutes. Off the heat, gradually incorporate the milk until fully blended. Add the celery purée and carrot. Bring to boiling point, stirring, reduce the heat and cook for 5–7 minutes until the carrot is tender. Check seasoning. Garnish with the young celery leaves snipped over the top and serve accompanied by freshly fried croûtons, lightly tossed in celery seeds.

Almond soup

An interestingly different recipe from Spain.

2 tbsps. olive oil
4 oz. blanched almonds, finely chopped
1 level tbsp. chopped onion
$\frac{1}{2}$ level tsp. crushed garlic
1 tsp. chopped parsley
1 oz. fresh white breadcrumbs
2 pt. chicken stock
salt and freshly ground black pepper

Heat the olive oil and in it slowly cook the almonds, onion, garlic and parsley, stirring all the time. Do not brown. Stir in the breadcrumbs and cook for a further 3 minutes. Pour on the stock, season well and simmer for 15 minutes.

✳ Cream of artichoke soup

Here is a cut-the-cost soup that can make a reputation, one of the finest ways to serve artichokes.

2 lb. Jerusalem artichokes
2 slices of lemon
1½ pt. cold water
1 oz. butter
4 oz. onion, skinned and chopped
2 level tbsps. cornflour
¾ pt. milk
1½ tbsps. lemon juice
2 level tbsps. chopped parsley
1½ level tsps. salt
white pepper
4 tbsps. single cream
croûtons for garnish

MAKES ABOUT 2¼ pt.

Wash the artichokes well. Place them in a large saucepan with the lemon slices, cover with water and bring to the boil. Cook until tender (about 20 minutes), drain off the water and reserve 1 pt. Allow the artichokes to cool before peeling away the skins. Roughly mash the flesh. Melt the butter in a clean saucepan, add the onion and fry until soft but not coloured. Stir in the cornflour, reserved artichoke water and milk.

Dressed chicory spears (*see page 127*)

Stir in the artichokes. Bring the soup to the boil, stirring and cook for 2–3 minutes. Remove from the heat and purée in an electric blender. Return to the saucepan, stir in the lemon juice, parsley, seasoning and cream. Bring to serving temperature and garnish with croûtons.

✳ Vegetable broth

1½ oz. butter
8 oz. onion, skinned and chopped
8 oz. leeks, trimmed, finely sliced and washed
1 small red pepper, seeded and diced
1 small green pepper, seeded and diced
8 oz. carrots, pared and diced
2 pt. stock
½ pt. milk
1 bayleaf
salt and freshly ground black pepper
1 level tbsp. cornflour
chopped parsley

SERVES 6

Heat the butter in a large pan, add the onions, cover and fry until transparent. Add the leeks, peppers and carrots to the pan. Stir well. Cover and cook over a fairly high heat for 10 minutes. Gradually add the stock, milk and bayleaf. Cover and simmer for 15–20 minutes, then season to taste. Mix the cornflour with a little water to a smooth cream. Add a little of the hot liquor and then stir it into the soup. Bring to the boil, stirring all the time, and serve garnished with plenty of chopped parsley.

Fish chowder

¾ lb. salt pork or green back bacon
1½ oz. butter
1½ lb. cod fillet, skinned
1½ lb. potatoes, peeled and diced
¾ lb. onions, skinned and chopped
1 bayleaf
1½ pt. water
1 pt. milk
salt and pepper
2 tsps. lemon juice

SERVES 12

Rind the pork or bacon and cut it into ½-in. slices. Fry it in a large saucepan until the fat begins to run, add the butter and when melted, add the skinned cod cut into large cubes, discarding the bones. Stir in the potatoes, onion,

Young idea party for 12 (*see page 124*)

bayleaf and water. Cover, bring to the boil, reduce the heat and simmer for about $\frac{1}{2}$ hour until the potato is cooked. Add the milk and seasoning, including the lemon juice. Simmer a further 5 minutes and serve hot with crackers.

Portuguese sardines

Serve sardines in oil on lettuce leaves with a cucumber dressing.

8–12 sardines in oil, drained
$\frac{1}{2}$ lettuce
$\frac{1}{2}$ cucumber
1 thick slice of onion
1 small clove garlic, skinned
2 tbsps. soured cream
1 tsp. Worcestershire sauce
a good squeeze of lemon juice
salt and freshly ground black pepper

SERVES 4

Divide the sardines and lettuce between 4 in-

dividual plates. Finely chop the cucumber, onion and garlic. Put these in a piece of muslin and squeeze out the moisture. Turn into a basin and fold through the soured cream, mayonnaise, Worcestershire sauce, lemon juice and seasoning. Spoon the dressing over the sardines.

HANDY HINT

For deep fat frying, the temperature of the fat should be 350–375°F, 180–190°C. If you do not have a frying thermometer, the only way to test the temperature is to drop a cube of bread into the fat. At 350–375°F it should brown in 1 minute. Remember that with oil it will be too late when a haze is seen, the temperature will be much too high.

Winter main course dishes

*Chicken curry

5-lb. oven-ready chicken
1 onion, skinned
1 bayleaf
1½ level tbsps. salt
6 peppercorns
4 oz. desiccated coconut
2¼ pt. milk
3 oz. butter
1 lb. onions, skinned and thinly sliced
2 level tbsps. curry powder
2 cloves garlic, skinned and crushed
½ oz. green ginger, peeled and sliced
3 level tbsps. cornflour

SERVES 8

Place the chicken in a saucepan just large enough to take the bird, add 1 whole onion, the bayleaf, salt and peppercorns. Pour on enough water to come half-way up the bird. Bring to the boil, reduce heat to simmering, cover and cook until the bird is tender – about 1½ hours. Lift the chicken from the pan and carve the flesh discarding skin and bones. Cut the flesh into fork-size pieces. Soak the coconut in the milk for 15 minutes. In a large flameproof casserole or saucepan, melt the butter and fry the sliced onions until golden. Stir in the curry powder and cook for 5 minutes more. Add the garlic, ginger, milk with the coconut and chicken meat. Cover and simmer gently for about 20 minutes. Blend the cornflour to a paste with a little water, add it to the curry and boil, stirring until the mixture thickens. Simmer for 10 minutes then adjust seasoning and serve with plain boiled rice.

Honey glazed chicken with banana

3-lb. oven-ready chicken
oil
4 tbsps. clear honey
3 level tsps. French mustard
2 tbsps. Worcestershire sauce
freshly ground black pepper
2 firm bananas

SERVES 4

Using a sharp knife, cut the chicken in half through the breast bone. Preheat electric rotary spit; for oven cooking lightly oil a roasting pan and preheat the oven to 400°F, 200°C (mark 6). Combine the honey, mustard, Worcestershire sauce and pepper. Thread the chicken halves on the bar of the spit lengthwise, position under the grill and cook on full heat for 5 minutes. Reduce the heat as directed in the manufacturers' instructions and brush the chicken with glaze – cook for a further 30–35 minutes. If you are using the oven, place the chicken halves skin side up in the pan, brush with glaze and cook in the preheated oven for about 40 minutes. Reglaze in both instances regularly during cooking until a rich brown crust forms over the skin. Pour any juices from the chicken, free of excess fat, into a pan, add the sliced banana and heat just to warm the banana. Spoon over the chicken to serve.

*Chicken puffs

The day before, prepare and bake. Just before needed, reheat the puffs in the oven at 350°F, 180°C (mark 4) for about 15 minutes.

1 lb. cooked chicken meat
2 oz. butter or margarine
4 oz. onion, skinned and finely chopped
2 oz. flour
½ pt. milk
lemon juice
salt and pepper
13-oz. pkt. frozen puff pastry, thawed
beaten egg to glaze

MAKES 24

Discard the skin from the chicken, remove the chicken flesh and cut it into ½-in. pieces. Melt the fat in a saucepan, add the onion and sauté it until soft but not coloured. Stir in the flour and cook for 2 minutes. Off the heat, add the milk, stirring; bring to the boil, still stirring, reduce the heat and cook for 3 minutes. Add the chicken, lemon juice and seasoning to taste. Turn into a bowl, cover it closely with damp greaseproof paper and leave to cool. Roll out the pastry very thinly, then cut out 24 4-in. rounds. Brush the edge of each with egg. Put a teaspoonful of the chicken mixture in the centre, fold the pastry over, seal and glaze with egg. Cook on a baking sheet at 400°F, 200°C (mark 6) for about 20 minutes until puffed and golden. Serve warm rather than hot.

Escalope of chicken

A tasty quickie for two; crisps and leaf spinach make suitable accompaniments.

2 chicken breasts, boned
1½ oz. fresh white breadcrumbs
1 level tbsp. grated Parmesan cheese
pinch of dried *fines herbes*
freshly ground black pepper
½ beaten egg
oil and butter for frying
½ lemon

SERVES 2

Place the chicken breasts on a board and beat them out with a rolling pin. Combine the breadcrumbs (made from a day-old loaf) cheese, herbs and pepper. On a plate, dip the chicken in the egg to coat evenly; any stray piece of flesh can be included. Drain off the egg, lifting the chicken on a slatted spatula. Coat in crumbs and pat these on well. In an easy-clean frying pan, heat some oil and a knob of butter to cover the base well. Fry the escalope of chicken until brown on one side, turn and brown the second side (7–10 minutes altogether). Cut two slices of lemon and twist for garnish. Squeeze the remainder of the juice over the chicken and serve at once, garnished with lemon twists.

Roast duckling with cranberry glaze

2 3½-lb. ducklings (thawed, if frozen)
⅓ pt. water
salt
flour for dredging
2 level tbsps. cornflour
2 tbsps. lemon juice
4 tbsps. red wine
14-oz. jar whole cranberry sauce
watercress sprigs for garnish

SERVES 4

Place the giblets and measured water in a pan, cover and simmer for about 1 hour. Prick the skin of the birds with fine skewer and rub salt well in. Place on a rack in a roasting tin and cook in the oven at 400°F, 200°C (mark 6) for 20 minutes per lb. or according to producer's directions. Baste for a dark crisp skin. 15 minutes before the cooking time is up, baste, dredge the ducklings with flour and return to the oven at 425°F, 220°C (mark 7). Meanwhile, blend the cornflour, lemon juice and wine together and stir in the strained giblet stock. Heat the cranberry sauce until softened, add the cornflour and bring to the boil, stirring. Simmer for 3–4 minutes. Pour off one-third and strain into a clean pan (do not push the berries through the sieve). Pour the remainder without straining into a sauce boat; keep warm. Cut the ducklings into two lengthwise and arrange them on a warm serving dish. Keep warm. Spoon all the fat from the pan juices and add the juices to the strained sauce; boil rapidly for a rich glaze. Pour evenly over the duckling and garnish.

Cold turkey mayonnaise

1½–2 lb. carved turkey breast and ¾ lb. dark
meat or 2 3½-lb. chickens, roasted
10 oz. quick-cook macaroni
salt
¾ pt. thick mayonnaise
1 oz. onion, skinned and finely chopped
4 level tsps. Lea & Perrins concentrated
curry sauce
dash of Tabasco sauce
grated rind of ½ lemon
3 tsps. lemon juice
¼ level tsp. *fines herbes*
freshly ground black pepper
4 tbsps. chopped parsley

SERVES 8–10

Carve the breast of turkey or chicken into thin slices; roughly dice the dark meat; keep it covered. Cook the macaroni in boiling salted water as directed, drain it well and cool. Combine the mayonnaise, onion, curry sauce, Tabasco, lemon rind and juice, herbs and pepper. Measure off ¼ pt. and combine with the diced meat. Fold the remainder of the mayonnaise through the macaroni. Arrange it over the base of a large flat serving platter and scatter 3 tbsps. parsley over. Overlap the breast meat round the edge and fill the centre with dark meat. Garnish with the remaining parsley.

HANDY HINT

Before serving ice cream, chill the serving dishes and dip scoops or spoons in cold water. It makes the job easier.

Turkey and bacon hash

1 lb. cooked turkey flesh
1 lb. lean streaky bacon
4 oz. onion, skinned and chopped
2 level tbsps. flour
$\frac{3}{4}$ pt. turkey stock
1 tbsp. Worcestershire sauce
1 lb. firm tomatoes, skinned and seeded
salt and freshly ground black pepper
$\frac{1}{2}$ oz. butter
chopped parsley

SERVES 6

Dice the turkey flesh finely. Rind and dice the bacon and fry it in a pan until crisp and brown. Remove the bacon, add the onion and cook until tender. Stir in the flour and cook for a few minutes. Stir the stock into the roux and bubble for 1–2 minutes more, stirring. Add the Worcestershire sauce and meats. Roughly dice the tomato flesh and stir half into the turkey and bacon. Season to taste, but be cautious as the bacon might be salty. Reheat. Melt the butter and lightly sauté the remaining tomato. Garnish the hash with parsley and tomato.

* Lamb Italian style

3 lb. chump ends of lamb, trimmed
salt and freshly ground black pepper
$1\frac{1}{2}$ oz. butter or margarine
3 medium sized onions, skinned and chopped
3 carrots, pared and sliced
3 stalks celery, chopped
$\frac{1}{3}$ pt. dry white wine
$1\frac{1}{2}$ level tbsps. flour
$\frac{3}{4}$ pt. stock
1 lb. tomatoes, skinned
pinch dried rosemary

For garnish
3 tbsps. chopped parsley
1 clove garlic, skinned and chopped
grated rind of 1 lemon

SERVES 6

Season the meat with salt and pepper. Melt the butter or margarine in a frying pan and slowly brown the lamb all over. Set it aside on kitchen paper to drain. Fry the vegetables in the reheated pan fat until pale golden brown. Remove and put them to drain on kitchen paper. Put the drained meat and vegetables in a saucepan or flameproof casserole, add the wine, cover and

simmer for 20 minutes. Skim the surface fat if necessary. Blend the flour with a little stock to a smooth cream. Add the remaining stock and pour it over the meat. Halve the tomatoes and discard the seeds; add the flesh to the pan with the rosemary. Bring to the boil, cover and simmer for a further $1\frac{1}{2}$ hours or until the meat is fork tender. Skim the surface fat again and garnish with a mixture of chopped parsley, garlic and lemon rind.

Daube d'agneau

Lamb slowly cooked with a robust red wine – and it is even better heated up the next day.

3 lb. leg of lamb
1 pt. red wine
4 oz. onion, skinned and chopped
3 medium carrots, pared and diced
1 level tsp. salt
$\frac{1}{4}$ level tsp. black pepper
5 sprigs of parsley
2 sprigs of thyme
1 bayleaf
3 fl. oz. olive oil
$\frac{1}{2}$ lb. salt pork
1 pig's foot, split
2 cloves garlic, skinned and crushed
4 firm red tomatoes, skinned and quartered

SERVES 6–8

Place the lamb in a heavy gauge polythene bag, or place it in one thin bag inside another. Place in a large bowl. Cover the meat with the wine, onion, carrot, seasoning and herbs. Pour over the olive oil and marinade overnight, turning it twice. Scrub the rind of the salt pork. Place it in a pan with the pig's foot, cover with water and bring to the boil. Pour off the water and stand in fresh cold water overnight. Next day, place the lamb and marinade in a deep casserole. Cut the rind off the pork and scissor-snip it into small squares. Cut the flesh into narrow strips. Add with the pig's foot, garlic and the tomatoes to the lamb. Cover tightly and cook in oven at 300°F, 150°C (mark 2) for about $3\frac{1}{2}$ hours. Baste the joint occasionally. Skim the

HANDY HINT

Most average-sized lemons give 3 tbsps. juice; oranges give about 4–5 tbsps.

surface fat from the juices, remove the lamb and keep warm. Strain the diced vegetables and salt pork and spoon them round the joint. Discard the pig's foot and reduce the pan juices by a quarter by fast boiling and pour over the meat.

✳ Lamb and mushroom pudding

½ oz. flour, seasoned with salt and ½ level tsp. paprika pepper
1 lb. boned leg of lamb, cubed
4 oz. mushrooms, wiped and quartered
1 level tbsp. tomato paste
4 tbsps. stock or water
6 oz. self-raising flour
pinch of salt
3 oz. shredded suet
water

SERVES 4

Toss the lamb in the seasoned flour and add the mushrooms. Dissolve the tomato paste in stock. Sift together the self-raising flour and salt, add the suet and mix to a soft pliable dough with water. Knead lightly on a floured surface, roll out and use two-thirds to line a 2-pt. pudding basin. Turn the meat mixture into the lined basin and pour over the stock. Damp the edges of the pastry, top with a pastry circle and seal well. Cover the pudding with greased greaseproof paper and kitchen foil and steam for 3½ hours.

Veal casserole

3 lb. pie veal
2 tbsps. oil
2 oz. butter
1 lb. lean streaky bacon
8 oz. onion, skinned and chopped
2 level tbsps. flour
1 pt. stock
2 level tbsps. tomato paste
½ level tsp. dried thyme
10 black olives, stoned and chopped
lemon juice
salt and freshly ground black pepper

SERVES 10

Cut the trimmed veal into even-sized pieces. Heat the oil in a large heavy-based frying pan. Add the butter and when it is on the point of turning brown, add the veal a third at a time, reheating the fat between each addition; fry

until evenly browned. Remove from the pan and transfer it to a 4-pt. casserole. Cook the bacon and onion in the frying pan for 5 minutes, stir in the flour and cook for 1 minute. Stir in the stock, tomato paste, thyme, olives and lemon juice to taste. Pour over the veal, adjust the seasoning and cook covered in the oven at 325°F, 170°C (mark 3) for about 1¾ hours.

Polynesian kaukau

2 lb. pie veal
1 onion, skinned
salt
1 bayleaf
boiling water
12 oz. long grain rice
saffron
¾ lb. white grapes, halved and pipped
small head of celery, finely sliced
¼ lb. shelled mixed nuts, coarsely chopped
lettuce

For dressing
¼ pt. corn oil
3 fl. oz. tarragon vinegar
1 level tsp. salt
freshly ground black pepper
½ level tsp. French mustard
½ level tsp. sugar

SERVES 8

Remove any fat from the veal and cut the meat into 1-in. cubes. Place it in a pan with the onion, salt and bayleaf. Just cover with boiling water, add a lid and simmer until the meat is tender – about 1 hour. Drain the veal, discard the onion and bayleaf but reserve the stock. Make the stock up to 1½ pt. with water, add a pinch of saffron and use this to cook the rice. Leave to cool. Toss together the veal, rice, grapes, celery and nuts in a large bowl. Shake together the dressing ingredients, which should be well seasoned. Pour the dressing over the mixture

HANDY HINT

To prevent dark rings forming round the yolks of hard-boiled eggs, cool the eggs quickly by cracking the shells and holding under cold running water until completely cold. Do not over-cook in the first place.

in the bowl and leave in a cool place for at least 1 hour. Serve with a border of lettuce.

Saltimbocca alla romana

(see picture page 136)

Italy's delicacy: veal with prosciutto, cooked in Marsala.

8 thin slices of veal
lemon juice
freshly ground black pepper
8 fresh sage or basil leaves or a pinch of
    powdered marjoram
8 thin slices prosciutto
butter
2 tbsps. Marsala
½-in. squares day-old bread, fried

SERVES 4

Ask the butcher to flatten the veal to about 4-in. by 5-in. pieces or do it yourself between sheets of waxed paper using a flat mallet or chopper. Season each piece with lemon juice and freshly ground pepper. Place a leaf of sage, basil or a little marjoram in the centre of each, cover with a slice of prosciutto cut to fit. Roll up and fix firmly with a wooden cocktail stick. Melt enough butter to cover the base of a frying pan and gently fry the veal rolls until golden brown. Do not overheat the butter. Add the Marsala, bring to simmering point, cover the pan and simmer gently until the rolls are tender. Serve with the juices poured over and surround with beans, peas and fried croûtons.
Note: Saltimbocca means literally 'jumps into the mouth'. Prosciutto is a special smoked Italian ham.

Beef Strogonoff

(see picture page 144)

1½ lb. fillet of beef
½ lb. onion, skinned
½ lb. button mushrooms
2 oz. butter
salt and freshly ground black pepper
¼–½ pt. soured cream

SERVES 4

Trim the beef and cut it into thin strips about 2 in. long and ¼ in. wide. Slice the onions thinly. Wipe the mushrooms, trim the stems and slice the caps thinly. Heat 1 oz. butter in a frying pan, add the onions and fry slowly until soft and lightly coloured. Add the mushrooms and fry

for a few more minutes. Remove the onions and mushrooms and keep them warm. Add the rest of the butter to the pan and, when hot, quickly fry the steak for about 4 minutes, turning it occasionally. Return the onions and mushrooms to the pan, season well with salt and freshly ground pepper and shake over the heat for 1 minute. Add soured cream, stir and cook over a high heat for 1 minute. Serve at once.

✳Beef and carrot pudding

A good corner-filler for cold days.

6 oz. self-raising flour
3 oz. shredded suet
salt and pepper
water

For filling
½ lb. onion, skinned and chopped
2 oz. dripping
1 lb. minced beef
½ lb. carrots, peeled and grated
2 tbsps. ready-made brown sauce
2 level tsps. mixed dried herbs
2 level tbsps. flour
½ pt. beef stock (made with a cube)

SERVES 4

In a bowl mix together the flour, suet and seasoning. Add just enough water to give a soft but manageable dough. Roll out two-thirds of the pastry and use it to line a 2½-pt. pudding basin. Fry the onion in dripping until it begins to colour. Add the meat and carrots and fry for a further 5 minutes, stirring. Stir in the brown sauce, herbs, flour and stock. Turn the mixture into the pastry-lined basin, and cover with a lid made from rolling out the remaining pastry. Damp and pinch the edges together. Cover with greased greaseproof paper and kitchen foil, twisting the edges to firmly close the rim. Place the basin in a saucepan and boiling water to come half-way up. Simmer for about 2½ hours. Serve from the basin.

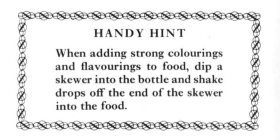

HANDY HINT

When adding strong colourings and flavourings to food, dip a skewer into the bottle and shake drops off the end of the skewer into the food.

* Chilli con carne

1 tbsp. corn oil
1½ lb. minced lean beef
6 oz. onion, skinned and chopped
1 level tbsp. flour
2 level tbsps. tomato paste
2 level tsps. chilli seasoning
¼ level tsp. garlic granules
¼ level tsp. cayenne pepper
14-oz. can tomatoes
salt and freshly ground black pepper
15-oz. can red kidney beans, drained
10 oz. long grain rice
3½-oz. can sweet red peppers

SERVES 6

Heat the oil in a large saucepan and quickly brown the beef. Add the onion and cook for a little longer. Sprinkle the flour over and mix well with the meat, add tomato paste, chilli seasoning, garlic granules, cayenne, tomatoes, salt and pepper and mix well. Bring to the boil, reduce the heat, cover and simmer for 40 minutes; add the kidney beans after 30 minutes. Cook the rice in boiling salted water, drain it and make a border around the edge of a large shallow serving dish. Drain the peppers, and cut them into thin strips and roll up into 15 small pinwheels. Chop the trimmings and add to the meat mixture. Pile it into the centre of the rice border and garnish with pinwheels in groups of three.
Note: Use chilli seasoning, not chilli powder, for this recipe.

Steak au poivre

½ oz. whole black peppercorns
2 rump steaks (about 6–8 oz. each)
2 oz. butter
1 tbsp. oil
1–2 tbsps. brandy (optional)
2–3 tbsps. single cream (optional)
salt and freshly ground black pepper

SERVES 2

Crush the peppercorns between sheets of paper with a rolling pin, or by using a pestle and mortar, working until of a fine texture, or use ready-crushed peppercorns. Coat each side of the steak with crushed peppercorns, pressing them in with the back of a spoon. Heat the butter and oil in a large frying pan. Add the steaks. When moisture beads appear on the surface, turn the steaks. Cook for 6–10 minutes then keep them warm on a serving plate. Either serve at this stage, or if wished add the brandy to the pan juices, flame, remove from heat and stir in the cream. Heat gently, adjust seasoning then pour over steaks

* West African beef curry

(*see picture page 141*)

4 lb. chuck steak
2 oz. flour
¼ level tsp. paprika pepper
¼ level tsp. cayenne pepper
¼ level tsp. chilli powder
corn oil
1 lb. onions, skinned and chopped
2 level tbsps. desiccated coconut
4 level tbsps. curry powder
2 level tbsps. curry paste
clove of garlic, skinned and crushed
few drops Tabasco sauce
2 pt. stock

SERVES 8

Trim and cut the steak into serving-size pieces. Toss in flour seasoned with paprika, cayenne and chilli powder; use just enough flour to coat the steak thoroughly. Heat 3 tbsps. oil in a large saucepan, fry the onions until evenly browned, add the coconut, curry powder, curry paste, garlic, Tabasco and stock and bring to the boil. In a large frying pan, heat enough oil to just cover the base, fry the meat a little at a time until sealed and brown. Drain and add it to the curry sauce. Cover and simmer until the meat is tender, about 2 hours.

*Les carbonades flamandes

This is the most famous of all Belgian meat dishes. Carbonade was the original name for meat cooked over charcoal; nowadays it is used for certain versions of beef stew. The Flemish

HANDY HINT

When buying chicory, be careful to pick the whitest you can find. If there are traces of green at the tips, this indicates the chicory has been exposed to the light and will be excessively bitter.

Saltimbocca alla romana *(see page 134)*

(flamande) recipe calls for a potent local dark beer. The cheesy toast topping is our extra.

2 lb. stewing steak
salt and black pepper
3 oz. lean bacon
2 oz. margarine
1½ oz. plain flour
½ pt. brown ale or stout
½ pt. stock
2–3 tbsps. vinegar
1 clove garlic, skinned
bouquet garni
1 small French loaf
1½ oz. Cheddar cheese, grated
chopped parsley

SERVES 4–6

Cube the meat and season it well. Rind and chop the bacon. Heat the margarine in a heavy-based pan and fry the meat for 5 minutes. Add the bacon and continue cooking for a few minutes. Remove the meat and bacon from the pan and place them in a 3-pt. flameproof casserole. Stir the flour into the juices in the pan and brown lightly; gradually add the beer, stock and vinegar, stirring until the mixture thickens.

Add the crushed garlic. Pour the sauce over the meat and add the bouquet garni; cover and simmer for 2 hours. Cut about 10–12 slices of bread, toast them on both sides and top with grated cheese; flash under a hot grill and put the toasted cheese on top of the carbonades. Sprinkle with chopped parsley.

Old English steak pudding

(see picture opposite)

12 oz. self-raising flour
6 oz. shredded suet
salt and freshly ground black pepper
about 12 tbsps. water
2 oz. flour
pinch of nutmeg
1½ lb. chuck steak, cubed
8 oz. kidney, cored and chopped
4 oz. small mushrooms, wiped and quartered
3½-oz. can smoked oysters, drained (optional)
¼ pt. boiling stock
¼ pt. red wine

SERVES 6–8

Sift the self-raising flour into a basin, add the suet, season well, stir in the water and mix to a soft but manageable dough. Knead lightly on a floured surface, roll out two-thirds and use it to line a $3\frac{1}{2}$-pt. basin in the usual way. Mix the 2 oz. flour with the nutmeg and season well. Toss the steak and kidney in the flour. Add the mushrooms and oysters. Mix well. Place the meat mixture in the basin. Pour over the boiling stock and wine. Place a pastry lid on top. Cover with greased greaseproof paper and foil, pleated across the centre, and secure with string. Place the pudding in a large saucepan. Pour in enough boiling water to come two-thirds of the way up the basin, cover with a lid and gently boil for $4\frac{1}{2}$–5 hours. From time to time replenish with boiling water. After the cooking time, remove from the water. Lift the paper off the pudding and, if you wish, place in a preheated oven at 400°F, 200°C (mark 6) for about 20 minutes to dry the pastry lid to a pale golden brown. Serve with a napkin around the basin.

✳ Beef pies

The filling for these meaty pies can be made a day ahead and refrigerated, then they can be given their crusts at re-heating time.

$3\frac{1}{2}$ lb. stewing steak
2 tbsps. red wine vinegar
10-fl. oz. bottle pale ale
1 clove garlic, skinned and crushed (optional)
2 tbsps. oil
6 oz. onion, skinned and sliced
4 level tbsps. flour
5-oz. can tomato paste
salt and freshly ground pepper
13-oz. pkt. frozen puff pastry, thawed
beaten egg
paprika pepper
parsley

MAKES 6

Trim the meat and cut it into 1–$1\frac{1}{2}$-in. pieces. Marinade in vinegar, ale and crushed garlic overnight. Fry the onions in oil until transparent. Drain the meat, reserve the marinade and dredge the meat with flour. Fry in reheated oil to seal the surface then add the onions, tomato paste and seasoning. Pour the marinade over and bring to the boil, stirring. Cook for 2–3 minutes then turn into a casserole and cook at 300°F, 150°C (mark 2) for about 2 hours. Cool. Roll out the pastry to 14 in. by 18 in. Cut in half widthways,

brush with egg, sprinkle with paprika and roll up from the long side. Cut at an angle into $\frac{1}{4}$-in. slices. Divide the meat between 6 $\frac{3}{4}$- 1-pt. ovenproof dishes. Spoon over 1–2 tbsps. of the juices. Arrange the pastry slices around the edge, overlapping, and brush with egg. Bake just above oven centre at 400°F, 200°C (mark 6) for about 30 minutes. Garnish with parsley. Reheat the meat juices to serve separately.

✳ Buffet patties

These are best served warm from the oven at party time – tender crisp pastry with a really meaty filling.

$\frac{1}{2}$ oz. butter or margarine
4 oz. onion, skinned and chopped
1 lb. minced lean beef
4 oz. carrot, pared and grated
1 beef stock cube
1 level tbsp. flour
$\frac{1}{4}$ pt. water
salt and pepper
1 lb. shortcrust pastry (1 lb. flour, etc.)
beaten egg to glaze

MAKES 24

Melt the butter or margarine and fry the onion until soft. Add the beef and continue to cook for 10 minutes, stirring. Add the carrot, crumbled stock cube, flour and water, bring just to the boil, adjust seasoning and reduce the heat. Cover and cook gently for 20 minutes. Cool quickly. Roll out about half the pastry and use it to line 24 $2\frac{1}{2}$-in. diameter (top measurement) patty tins, using a 3-in. plain cutter. Divide the filling between the tins and, with a plain smaller cutter, cut lids. Damp the rims, cover with

Old English steak pudding (*see page 136*)

pastry lids and seal. Make a slit in each one, brush with egg and bake just above the oven centre at 400°F, 200°C (mark 6) for about 25 minutes. Garnish with parsley sprigs.

✳ Queue de boeuf aux olives noires

Traditional French oxtail stew garnished with black olives.

2 oxtails
cold water
2–3 tbsps. olive oil
6 tbsps. brandy, warmed
⅓ pt. dry white wine
stock or water
bouquet garni comprising bayleaves, thyme, parsley, orange peel and clove of garlic, crushed
½ lb. black olives, stoned
12–16 oz. long grain rice

SERVES 6–8

The day before required, ask the butcher to chop the oxtails into serving-size pieces. Place in a bowl, cover with cold water and leave for 2 hours. Drain and dry the oxtail on kitchen paper. Heat the oil in a frying pan or, better still, a flameproof casserole. Seal a few pieces of meat at a time. If a frying pan is used, transfer the contents to a heat-proof casserole. Ignite the brandy and pour it over the oxtail. When the flames have died down, add the wine and let it bubble rapidly for a few minutes. Add just sufficient stock or water to cover. Add the bouquet garni. Cover and cook in the oven at 300°F, 150°C (mark 1–2) for 3 hours. Pour the liquor off into a bowl. Remove the bouquet garni and keep the liquor and meat separately in the refrigerator overnight. Next day, remove the fat from the liquor. Bring the rest to the boil and add the oxtail then the olives; cover and cook on top of the cooker for another 1–1½ hours, until the meat comes easily away from the bones. Thicken juices with a little beurre manie. Serve with a separate dish of boiled

rice. Ideally oxtail is best eaten in an open soup-type plate to catch all the juices.

Lasagne
(*see picture page 140*)

2 14-oz. cans tomatoes, drained
1 level tbsp. tomato paste
1 level tsp. dried marjoram
salt and freshly ground black pepper
1 lb. minced beef
4 oz. lasagne
1 oz. butter
1 oz. flour
½ pt. milk
3 oz. Canadian Cheddar cheese, grated
oil for glazing
8 oz. Mozzarella cheese, sliced

SERVES 4

Combine the canned tomatoes, tomato paste, marjoram, salt and pepper. Simmer in an open pan for 30 minutes. Add the mince and simmer for a further 25 minutes to reduce. Cook the lasagne for 10–15 minutes in a large pan of fast boiling, salted water, then drain it. Melt 1 oz. butter in a small saucepan, stir in the flour and gradually add the milk. Stirring constantly, bring to the boil, remove from the heat, add cheese and season. Cover the base of a 9-in. fluted flan case 1½ in. deep with strips of pasta. Add alternate layers of meat and cheese sauce. Finish the final layer with strips of lasagne placed diagonally across, with the sauces between. Lightly oil the lasagne to prevent it drying and bake at 375°F, 190°C (mark 5) for about 30 minutes. Take from the oven, add the Mozzarella between the lasagne and return to the oven at 425°F, 220°C (mark 7) until golden and bubbling.

Gammon steaks with gingered apricots

½ level tsp. dry mustard
1 level tsp. ground ginger
4 level tsps. brown sugar
2 tsps. Worcestershire sauce
2 tbsps. lemon juice
2 gammon steaks
1 small green pepper, seeded
8-oz. can apricot halves, drained
2 pieces stem ginger, chopped

SERVES 2

HANDY HINT

When chopping glacé fruits and candied peel, use a wet knife to prevent sticking, shaking off the excess water first.

Combine together the mustard, ground ginger, sugar, sauce and lemon juice. Brush over both sides of the gammon. Arrange the gammon steaks side by side in a lightly oiled shallow ovenproof dish and pour over any remaining marinade. Cook uncovered in the oven at 375°F, 190°C (mark 5) for about 30 minutes. Baste with the juices in the dish after 20 minutes. Meanwhile, slice or chop the pepper, blanch in boiling water for 30 minutes and drain. Arrange quartered apricots down the centre of the dish with the chopped ginger and pepper. Return to the oven for 15 minutes to reheat. Serve with boiled rice or creamed potatoes and sliced green beans.

Pork and cranberry curry

$1\frac{1}{4}$ lb. pork fillet
1 oz. butter
2 tbsps. oil
6 oz. onion, skinned and chopped
1 small clove garlic, skinned and crushed
1 level tbsp. flour
4 level tsps. curry powder
2 level tbsps. tomato paste
juice of 1 lemon
8-oz. can cranberry sauce
$\frac{1}{2}$ pt. water
3 cloves
1 bayleaf

SERVES 4

Slice the fillet into $\frac{1}{4}$-in. rounds. Heat the butter and oil in a wide pan and sauté the meat until beginning to brown. Drain from the fat and transfer to a casserole. Fry the onion in the pan juices for 5 minutes then, off the heat, stir in the garlic, flour, curry powder, tomato paste, lemon juice, cranberry sauce, water, cloves and bayleaf. Bring to the boil, stirring, pour over the pork, cover and cook at 325°F, 170°C (mark 3) for about 1 hour.

Orange-glazed baked gammon

12–14 lb. gammon, soaked overnight

For glaze
6 oz. clear honey
4 oz. soft brown sugar
4 tbsps. orange juice
cloves
pineapple rings
parsley sprigs

SERVES 25–30

Calculate the cooking time by allowing 15 minutes per lb. and 15 minutes over. Place the gammon in a large preserving pan and cover completely with cold water. Bring to the boil and remove any scum. Reduce the heat, cover and simmer (water just bubbling all the time) for half the cooking time. To make the glaze, combine the honey, sugar and orange juice in a small pan. Bring to the boil, stirring, and remove from the heat. Remove the gammon from the cooking liquor and carefully peel away the rind while it is still hot. Heat the oven to 350°F, 180°C (mark 4). Place the gammon in a baking tin and, using a sharp knife, score the fat into 1-in. wide diamonds. Press a clove into each centre. Brush the fat all over with glaze and bake in the oven for the remaining cooking time. Coat with fresh glaze every 20–30 minutes. When it is cooked, place the glazed gammon on a plate and leave until cold. To serve, garnish with interlocking slices of pineapple round the base, with parsley sprigs in between.

Nasi goreng

A Dutch national favourite, spicy pork curry from Indonesia.

4 oz. onion, skinned and chopped
1 clove garlic, skinned and crushed
2 oz. butter
8 oz. long grain rice
$\frac{1}{2}$ level tsp. coriander powder
$\frac{1}{2}$ level tsp. caraway seeds
$\frac{1}{2}$ level tsp. chilli seasoning
1 level tsp. curry powder
1 tbsp. soy sauce
1 lb. cooked pork, diced
$\frac{1}{2}$ lb. frozen peas, freshly cooked
1 egg
2 tbsps. water
salt and pepper
tomato wedges

SERVES 4

Fry the onion and garlic in the butter until soft. Meanwhile boil the rice until cooked but still firm; drain and rinse it under cold water. Stir the spices and soy sauce into the onion, cook for 1–2 minutes then stir in the meat and heat thoroughly; add the cooked rice, blending all the ingredients. When the meat and rice are thoroughly heated, add the peas. Break one egg into a bowl, whisk lightly, add 2 tbsps. water and salt and pepper. Lightly grease the base of a frying pan and pour in the omelette mixture.

When it is set, turn it out on to a warm, greased baking sheet and cut into strips. Turn the nasi goreng into a serving dish and decorate the top with a lattice of omelette. Garnish with tomato wedges.

Spicy pepper casserole

2 tbsps. oil
2 onions, skinned and sliced
1 red pepper, seeded and sliced
1 green pepper, seeded and sliced
1½ lb. shoulder pork, trimmed (or you could use chuck steak or lamb)
2 level tbsps. flour
salt and pepper
1 level tsp. paprika pepper
1 pt. stock
1 level tbsp. tomato paste
¼ pt. natural yoghurt

SERVES 4

Heat the oil in a large saucepan and gently fry the onion until soft. Transfer to casserole, fry the peppers and add to the dish. Cut the meat into 1-in. cubes and toss in flour seasoned with salt, pepper and paprika. Brown in the reheated oil, add stock and tomato paste and bring carefully to the boil, stirring. Add to the casserole, cover and cook at 350°F, 180°C (mark 4) in the oven centre for about 1½ hours. Just before serving add the yoghurt.

Lasagne (*see page 138*)

Habas a la catalana

Robust meaty smoked sausage combines well with broad beans to make a hearty Spanish supper dish. Serve in small individual bowls so that you can enjoy every drop of the juice.

1 lb. smoked garlic sausage
½ oz. lard
4 oz. salt pork, finely diced
6 tbsps. finely chopped spring onions
6 tbsps. dry white wine
6 tbsps. water
2 tsps. chopped fresh mint
1 bayleaf
½ level tsp. salt
freshly ground black pepper
1½ lb. shelled broad beans, cooked
2 tbsps. finely chopped parsley

SERVES 4–6

Cut the sausage into ¾-in. thick slices, then cut into quarters. Melt the lard in a flameproof casserole. Add the salt pork and cook until crisp and golden brown. Drain on kitchen paper. Add the spring onions to the fat in the pan and cook for about 5 minutes until the onions are soft but not brown. Pour in the wine and water, add the quartered sausage slices, diced pork, mint, bayleaf, salt and pepper. Bring to the boil over high heat, reduce to low, then cover and simmer for about 20 minutes. Add the beans and parsley then simmer, uncovered and stirring frequently, for about 10 minutes more.

Venetian liver

Liver: it's nutritionally sound, a good buy and can taste delicious. Serve it in this cunning disguise and you'll win customers for a once-a-fortnight repeat.

2 oz. dripping
2 large onions (½ lb.), skinned and chopped
¾ lb. lambs' liver
2 tbsps. chopped parsley
juice of 1 lemon
salt and freshly ground black pepper
¼ pt. soured cream

SERVES 4

Melt the dripping in a large frying pan, add the onions and cook until tender without browning. Cut the liver into thin strips about 2½ in. long; add to the pan. Keep it over a moderate heat until the liver is cooked through – about 10

West African beef curry (*see page 135*)

minutes. Stir in the parsley and lemon juice (don't throw the rind away – it's handy for adding zest to milk puddings and simple cakes). Adjust the seasoning with salt and pepper and reheat. Serve topped with soured cream, along with boiled rice or pasta and crisply cooked sprouts.

Somerset tripe

Rich and creamy, this is a dish to serve with well-seasoned mashed potatoes and carrots.

2 lb. prepared tripe
1 large onion, skinned and chopped
6 tbsps. oil
1 bayleaf
$\frac{1}{4}$ pt. dry cider
$6\frac{1}{2}$-oz. can tomatoes
1 clove of garlic, skinned and crushed
pinch of dried rosemary and grated nutmeg
1 tbsp. chopped parsley
3 level tsps. beef extract
$\frac{1}{4}$ pt. water
salt and freshly ground black pepper
extra chopped parsley to garnish

SERVES 4

Cut the tripe into fine strips. Fry the chopped onion in oil until golden, then add the bayleaf and cider. Cover the pan and cook slowly until the cider is well reduced. Add the tripe, tomatoes, crushed garlic, rosemary, nutmeg, parsley and beef extract dissolved in water. Season, cover and cook gently for 1 hour. Remove the tripe from the juices, using a draining spoon. Reduce the juices by fast boiling to $\frac{1}{2}$ pint. Return the tripe and reheat. Serve with more chopped parsley.

✳ Casserole of venison

$1\frac{1}{2}$ lb. shoulder of venison
6 level tbsps. seasoned flour
2 oz. dripping or lard
2 onions, skinned and chopped
2 carrots, pared and sliced
$\frac{1}{2}$ pt. unseasoned stock
$\frac{1}{4}$ pt. red wine
salt and pepper
bouquet garni
2 tsps. malt vinegar

SERVES 4

Cut the venison into $\frac{1}{2}$-in. cubes and toss in the seasoned flour. Heat the fat in a frying pan and fry the venison for about 8–10 minutes until evenly browned; remove it from the pan, draining well, and put in a casserole. Fry the onion and carrot in the reheated pan drippings for about 5 minutes until golden. Drain well and add to the casserole. Stir any excess flour into the pan and cook slowly until browned. Off the heat, gradually add the stock and wine and bring to the boil. Pour over the venison, adjust seasoning and add the bouquet garni and vinegar. Cover the casserole and cook in the oven at 325°F, 170°C (mark 3) for $2–2\frac{1}{2}$ hours until the venison is fork tender. Discard the bouquet garni before serving.

Pheasant Burgundy

Prepare the bird as for roasting.

1 tender pheasant
3 shallots or 1 small onion, skinned
1 tbsp. oil
2 oz. butter
6 small onions
2 level tsps. sugar
$\frac{1}{2}$ pt. red Burgundy
2 oz. button mushrooms
1 level tbsp. flour
salt and pepper

SERVES 4

Chop the shallots finely and put inside the pheasant with its liver. Heat the oil and 1 oz. butter in a heavy pan and sauté the pheasant gently until brown all over. Meanwhile, skin the onions, leave whole and boil them in salted water until just tender. Drain. Melt $\frac{1}{2}$ oz. butter in a separate pan, add 2 level tsps. sugar, stir, add the onions and cook slowly until colouring. Put the pheasant in a casserole with the onions. Add the wine and mushroom stalks to the juices in the pheasant pan and reduce by about half. Melt an additional $\frac{1}{2}$ oz. butter in the onion pan, sauté the mushroom caps and add them to the casserole. Work the flour into the juices and when bubbling, gradually stir in the liquor from the other pan. Add seasoning, simmer to thicken and strain over the pheasant. Cover and cook in the oven at 350°F, 180°C (mark 4) for about $\frac{1}{2}$ hour or until the pheasant is tender.

Plaki

Tomatoes and onion cooked with olive oil boost the flavour of white fish in this recipe from Greece.

$\frac{1}{2}$ lb. onions, skinned and finely chopped
olive oil
4 ripe tomatoes, skinned and sliced
chopped parsley
salt and pepper
2 lb. white fish, filleted
lemon juice
1 clove garlic, skinned and crushed
1 tomato and 1 lemon for garnish

SERVES 4–5

Fry the onions in a little oil until tender but not coloured, add the tomatoes and parsley and season. Arrange the fish in a lightly buttered ovenproof dish and sprinkle with lemon juice. Add the crushed garlic to the onion mixture and spoon over the fish. Bake at 425°F, 220°C (mark 7) for about 15 minutes. Garnish with slices of tomato and lemon.

Casserole of rabbit with juniper berries

The aromatic flavour of juniper berries is stronger than most herbs, so use them sparingly.

corn oil
$2\frac{1}{2}$ lb. rabbit pieces
4 level tbsps. flour
2 level tbsps. tomato paste
$\frac{1}{2}$ pt. rich brown stock
$\frac{1}{4}$ pt. red wine
1 level tsp. dried *fines herbes*
2 bayleaves
1 level tsp. salt
freshly ground black pepper
8 juniper berries
1 clove garlic, skinned and crushed
8 oz. back bacon rashers, rinded
4 slices white bread

SERVES 6

Heat 3 tbsps. oil and quickly brown the rabbit pieces. Place them in a large ovenproof casserole. Add the flour and tomato paste to the pan juice and cook for 1–2 minutes, stir in the stock and wine. Add the herbs and seasoning. Lightly crush the berries and add them to the pan with the garlic. Bring to the boil for 2 minutes, pour over rabbit, cover and cook in the centre of the oven at 325°F, 170°C (mark 3) for 2–2$\frac{1}{2}$ hours or until tender. Stretch the bacon with the back of a knife. Halve the rashers and make into rolls. Thread the rolls on skewers and grill until crisp, take them off the skewers and fold through the casserole 30 minutes before the end of the cooking time. Trim the crusts from the bread and cut it into triangles. Heat a little corn oil and fry the bread. Drain and arrange round the casserole.

Cod basque

1 red pepper, seeded
4 tomatoes, skinned
1 level tsp. caster sugar
1 level tsp. tomato paste
1 level tsp. paprika pepper
1 clove garlic, skinned and crushed
1 tbsp. red wine vinegar
2 tbsps. corn oil
salt and freshly ground black pepper
4 frozen cod steaks

SERVES 4

Finely slice the pepper and blanch it in boiling water for 2 minutes, then drain. Slice the tomatoes. Combine the sugar, tomato paste, paprika, crushed garlic, vinegar, oil, pepper and seasoning. Place the cod steaks in single layer in the base of a buttered shallow ovenproof dish. Layer the sliced tomato and pepper mixture on top. Cover with foil and bake in the oven at 425°F, 220°C (mark 7) for about 30 minutes.

HANDY HINT

Whole almonds are best bought with their skins on and blanched as you need them – this way they are juicier. If you have only blanched almonds in your store cupboard, soak them in hot water for 30 minutes to make them plump and juicy again.

Beef Strogonoff (*see page 134*)

Herring fillets with onion sauce

Fish in a crumb coat look nice and plump. Onion gives interest to the flavour.

6 oz. onions, skinned and thinly sliced
butter or margarine
2 level tbsps. flour
$\frac{1}{2}$ pt. milk
$\frac{1}{2}$ level tsp. sugar
$\frac{1}{2}$ level tsp. dry mustard
salt and pepper
2 tbsps. single cream
6 herrings, filleted
2 oz. fresh white breadcrumbs
snipped chives

SERVES 4

Sauté the onions in $1\frac{1}{2}$ oz. fat in a covered pan until soft but not coloured. Stir in the flour, cook for a few minutes then add the milk slowly, beating. Bring to the boil, stirring, and season with sugar, mustard, salt and pepper. Add the cream and cook for 2 minutes. Meanwhile, rub the herring fillets with salt, dip them in milk and coat in crumbs. Fry in a little hot butter or margarine until golden on both sides. Arrange the fillets overlapping on a dish, pour the sauce over and garnish with chives.

HANDY HINT

Don't cover the pan when cooking pasta. Feed long pasta into the boiling salted water; as it softens curl it into the pan.

Winter snacks

Crumpet pizzas

Quick when there's shopping to be done. Start with a mug of hot soup, and wind up with fruit from a well-stocked bowl.

½ oz. butter
2 oz. onion, skinned and chopped
3 tomatoes, skinned
1 level tsp. mixed dried herbs
4 crumpets
3 oz. mature Cheddar cheese
few sliced olives or anchovy fillets

SERVES 2–4

Melt the butter and fry the onion until soft. Chop the tomatoes and add to the onion with the herbs. Toast the crumpets until golden on one side only. Turn them over and cover with the tomato mixture; top with diced cheese and olives or anchovy. Continue to grill until golden brown and bubbling.

Leek and bacon crisp

This transforms leftover potatoes, burying them under a creamy sauce of delicate green leeks, topped with crisp bacon bits. Here's how to cook it from scratch.

1 lb. potatoes
1½ lb. leeks
6 oz. lean streaky bacon
1½ oz. butter or margarine
1½ oz. flour
¾ pt. milk
4 oz. cheese, grated
salt and pepper

SERVES 3–4

Peel the potatoes, cut into thick slices and cook in salted water till tender, not mushy, and drain well (or use leftovers). Discard two-thirds of the green part of the leeks, slice the rest finely and wash thoroughly. Cook in boiling salted water for about 5 minutes. Rind the bacon, scissor-snip and lightly fry it until the fat runs. Make a cheese sauce with the butter or margarine, flour, milk, cheese and seasoning; fold in the leeks. Place the potatoes in a large casserole dish – about 3-pt. capacity – cover with leek and cheese sauce and top with bacon. Place the dish on a baking sheet and reheat in the oven, uncovered, at 350°F, 180°C (mark 4) for 30 minutes.

Sausage, tomato and pasta bake

Slices of garlic sausage give a fine flavour to this mould, which you'll find just as delicious as it is thrifty.

6 oz. sliced garlic sausage
5 oz. pasta shapes
1 oz. butter or margarine
½ oz. flour
¼ pt. milk
2 oz. mature Cheddar cheese, grated
4 level tbsps. chopped parsley
pinch of mustard
salt and pepper
¾ lb. tomatoes

SERVES 4

Line a 2-pt. basin with 4 oz. sausage, overlapping the slices. Chop the remaining sausage. Cook the pasta in boiling salted water, then drain. Melt the butter, stir in the flour and cook for 1–2 minutes. Stir in the milk, bring to the boil and simmer for a few minutes more. Off the heat, fold in the cheese. Add the pasta, chopped sausage and parsley. Season. Skin and slice the tomatoes and layer half in the basin. Cover with half the pasta mixture. Repeat layering once. Cover the basin with kitchen foil and cook in the oven at 375°F, 190°C (mark 5) for 30 minutes. Unmould to serve.

Pasta in soured cream sauce

6 oz. butter
chopped parsley
1 lb. pasta cartwheel shapes
2 shallots, skinned and chopped
2 level tbsps. flour
¼ pt. chicken stock
¼ pt. dry white wine
¼ pt. soured cream
salt and freshly ground pepper
4 oz. button mushrooms, quartered
4 oz. Canadian Cheddar cheese, grated
1 lb. tomatoes, skinned, quartered and seeded
2 7-oz. cans tuna steak, drained

SERVES 6–8

Soften 3 oz. butter and beat in 1 tbsp. chopped parsley. Form it into a roll in greaseproof paper and chill. Cook the pasta in boiling salted water. For the sauce, melt 2 oz. butter and sauté the shallots; stir in the flour and cook for 1 minute. Gradually add the stock and wine, then bring to the boil, stirring. Reduce the heat and stir in the soured cream. Season to taste. Keep warm over a low heat. Quickly sauté the mushrooms in 1 oz. butter. Drain the pasta. Add to it the mushrooms, sauce, cheese and most of the tomatoes. Toss lightly. Put the flaked tuna in the base of a hot shallow ovenproof dish, and spoon over the sauce mixture. Slice the chilled butter and dot it over the top with the remaining tomatoes. Reheat at 375°F, 190°C (mark 5) for 10 minutes. Garnish with more chopped parsley.

Beefburger decker

1 bloomer loaf
3 pkts. of 4 frozen beefburgers
1 tbsp. oil
$\frac{1}{2}$ lb. onions, skinned and sliced
6 oz. Lancashire or Cheddar cheese, grated
1 level tsp. cornflour
2 tbsps. milk
$\frac{1}{2}$ lb. tomatoes, sliced
curled anchovy fillets for garnish

SERVES 4

Cut 8 slices from the loaf, cutting at an angle across the slashes to give elongated slices. Fry the beefburgers in a large frying pan or paella-type pan in the oil for about 10 minutes, turning half way through the cooking time. Remove from the pan and keep warm. Add the onions to the pan and fry until soft and just beginning to colour. Meanwhile blend the grated cheese, cornflour and milk together. Toast the bread until golden. Spread the cheese mixture over half the slices, grill until the cheese starts to melt, top with slices of tomato and return to the grill until golden. Butter the remaining slices of toast and top each with 3 beefburgers and the onions. Position the lids on top and garnish with curled anchovies.

Sausage kebabs

1 lb. pork chipolatas
1 lb. streaky bacon rashers
1 lb. Cheddar cheese
cocktail sticks

Twist each sausage in half and cut into two small sausages. Place them in a baking tin and cook in the oven at 400°F, 200°C (mark 6) for about 30 minutes. Meanwhile, rind the rashers and on a flat surface stretch each with the back of a knife. Cut them in half crosswise and form into rolls. Place the rolls in a tin and cook in the oven until beginning to colour. Cut cubes of cheese and spear them with cocktail sticks. Spear the sausages and bacon rolls on sticks. For the table, stick them all into a cabbage, large apples or a long French loaf. The sausages and bacon are best eaten just warm. Surround with potato crisps.

Sardine scrunchies

$4\frac{3}{8}$-oz. can sardines in olive oil
8-oz. can spaghetti with tomato and cheese
   sauce
4 oz. strong Cheddar cheese, grated
freshly ground pepper
1 small lemon
4 thick slices white bread from a large
   ready-sliced loaf
parsley sprigs

SERVES 2

Drain the sardines, turn them into a bowl and break them up with a fork. Add the contents of the can of spaghetti, together with half the cheese. Season with freshly ground pepper and add a squeeze of lemon juice. Toast one side of the bread, turn it over and spread the topping equally between the 4 slices. Sprinkle the remaining grated cheese over and grill until golden under a medium heat. Garnish with lemon slices and parsley.

Spanish omelette
(*see picture page 148*)

This should be in everybody's repertoire of snacks.

1 small onion, skinned and chopped
2 small potatoes, peeled and diced
1 tbsp. cooking oil
2 caps. canned pimiento
1 tomato
2 level tbsps. cooked peas
4 eggs
salt and freshly ground black pepper

SERVES 2

Fry the onion and potatoes in oil in an 8-in. pan for 3–4 minutes. Chop the pimiento, peel and chop the tomato and add to the pan with the peas and cook for a few minutes longer. Whisk the eggs, season well and pour into the pan over the vegetables. Stir once or twice and cook until the underneath is just set. While the top is still runny, put the omelette under the grill to brown it slightly. Loosen it with a palette knife and slide from the pan on to a hot dish.

✳Red sails

The scone base can be made a day ahead then refreshed in the oven and filled before required.

For scone base
2 oz. butter or margarine
8 oz. self-raising flour
pinch of salt
3 oz. Cheddar cheese, finely grated
1 large egg, beaten
4 tbsps. milk, approx.
egg to glaze

For filling
4 oz. cream cheese
1 stick of celery, finely chopped
1 large firm tomato, roughly chopped
salt and pepper

For garnish
celery 'masts'
tomatoes
parsley

MAKES ABOUT 24

Rub the fat into the sifted flour and salt until the mixture resembles fine breadcrumbs. Add the cheese, mix well, then add the egg whisked with half the milk. Add more milk to give a fairly soft but manageable dough. Turn out on to a lightly floured surface, knead and roll out to ½-in. thickness. Using a 3-in. fluted cutter stamp out rounds. With the same cutter, nip off an oval from each side of the round so that each cut meets in the centre. Lightly knead the trimmings, roll out and cut to give 24 'boats' altogether. Place them on a baking sheet. Brush the tops of the scone 'boats' with egg and bake in the oven at 425°F, 220°C (mark 7) for 10–15 minutes. Cool on a wire rack.

Beat the cream cheese to soften it then gently fold in the celery and tomato with seasoning to taste. Split the scones in half lengthwise and sandwich with the cheese mixture. Make a small hole in the centre of each 'boat'. Cut masts of celery about 3 in. long. Quarter the tomatoes, discard the seeds, make a slit at the pointed ends of the tomato quarters and carefully slide them on to the celery sticks. Press the sticks into the scones and add parsley sprigs.

Cheese and wine party

(*see picture page 125*)

While this can be a non-cooking easy-on-the-hostess affair, such items as home-made bread, dips and a few tit-bits add to the pleasure. Allow about 4 oz. cheese per person, excluding the little extras, and offer at least eight varieties, to include soft, semi-hard and veined cheeses. Crisp and juicy fruits not only add to the decor but complement the cheeses. Radishes, gherkins or onions go well with tangy Double Gloucester, and smoked Austrian or German Limburger cheese is pleasing with blackcurrant preserve. Some cheeses can be pre-cut into cubes with plenty of cocktail sticks alongside, but the Swiss cheese with holes and also Danish Havarti and Samsoe are better if cut in wafer-thin slices with a special cheese slice. The cheese-and-fruit cocktail wheel nibblers soon vanish. Reckon about 36 little pieces or cubes from each 1 lb. slab. Our partners: Double Gloucester speared with pineapple and Maraschino cherries; Caerphilly speared with melon and black grapes or white grapes alone; Port Salut speared with anchovy fillet; Samsoe/Havarti speared with halved walnuts and thick banana slices dipped in lemon juice; Danish Blue speared with strips of canned red pimiento or grapes. Ring the changes with some ends off other cheeses, but try to avoid the crumbly loose-textured varieties.

Have a good selection of breads, crispbreads and biscuits, allowing about 6 biscuits or crispbreads and the equivalent of 3 hunks of French bread per person. Breads to choose from – French, granary, rye, Pumpernickel, Dorset knobs, Scotch baps or homebaked. Biscuits – oatcakes, water biscuits, digestive, crackers and wheatmeal.

The Drinks – for a large party it would be rather complicated to serve as many regional wines as there are cheese, therefore compromise with two styles of white specially to suit the creamy cheeses. Choose the reds to suit the English selection and the continental 'blues', but it's largely a matter of personal preference.

Have flag-labels for the different cheeses, giving their names, country of origin and a word or two to describe their characters. It is always better for guests to know what they are trying without having to ask.

Spanish omelette (*see page 146*)

Blue cheese dip

3 3-oz. pkts. full-fat cream cheese
4 oz. Danish blue cheese
$\frac{1}{4}$ pt. soured cream
salt and pepper

Beat together the cream and blue cheeses and
when smooth gradually work in the soured
cream. Adjust seasoning to taste.

Pâté fleurons

$7\frac{1}{2}$-oz. pkt. frozen puff pastry, thawed
beaten egg
$4\frac{1}{4}$-oz. tube liver pâté
2 oz. butter

MAKES ABOUT 50

Roll out the pastry as directed. Using a $1\frac{1}{2}$-in.
fluted round cutter, stamp out as many rounds
as possible, brush them with beaten egg and
fold over into semi-circles. Place on a baking
tray. Allow to stand in a cool place for at least
30 minutes then brush again with beaten egg
before baking at 400°F, 200°C (mark 6) for
about 15 minutes. With a sharp knife, almost

cut through the pastry to allow steam to escape.
Leave to cool on a wire rack. Combine the pâté
with the butter. Beat well. Fill a piping bag,
fitted with a No. 8 star cake icing nozzle. Pipe
the pâté in a 'shell' down the centre of each.

Savoury choux

$1\frac{1}{2}$ oz. butter or margarine
$\frac{1}{4}$ pt. water
$2\frac{1}{2}$ oz. plain flour
2 eggs, beaten
4 oz. cream cheese
2 oz. softened butter
1 tsp. lemon juice
1 small clove garlic, skinned and crushed
aspic jelly (optional)

MAKES 24 CHOUX

Make a basic choux paste using the butter or
margarine, water, flour and eggs. Using a $\frac{1}{2}$-in.
plain vegetable nozzle, pipe out about 24
walnut-sized balls of paste on to a greased
baking sheet. Bake above the oven centre at
400°F, 200°C (mark 6) for 15–20 minutes until
golden and crisp. Cool on a wire rack. If wished,

store overnight and refresh next day before filling. For the filling: cream together the cheese, butter, lemon juice and crushed garlic. Make a hole in the base of each choux bun with a small plain vegetable nozzle and pipe filling into the buns. If wished, glaze the tops with half-set aspic.

Talmouse

7½-oz. pkt. smoked haddock fillets
¼ pt. white sauce
13-oz. pkt. frozen puff pastry, thawed
salt and freshly ground black pepper
1 egg, beaten

MAKES 10-12

Cook the smoked haddock fillets as directed. Allow them to cool, then discard skin and any bones and flake the flesh. Bind it with ¼ pt. white sauce and adjust the seasoning. Firmly roll out the pastry and, using a 3-in. plain cutter, stamp out as many rounds as possible, re-rolling as necessary. Brush the rim of each with beaten egg. Place a little fish in the centre of each round and shape the pastry into a tricorn. Brush with more beaten egg. Place them on a baking sheet and bake at 400°F, 200°C (mark 6) for about 20 minutes until golden. Serve hot.

Cheese olives

8 oz. full-fat cream cheese
15 stuffed olives
chopped walnuts

MAKES 30 HALVES

Cream the cheese until well blended. Take about a heaped teaspoonful and roll it around a stuffed olive to completely enclose. Lightly toss in chopped walnuts. Chill for about 1 hour. Before serving, cut in half with a sharp knife.

Winter side-dishes

✻ Cranberry and bacon balls

These are for our Christmas turkey menu.

6 oz. onion, skinned and finely chopped
4 oz. streaky bacon, rinded and chopped
1 oz. butter
4 oz. fresh cranberries
2 oz. shredded suet
1 level tsp. dried thyme
finely grated rind of 1 orange
6 oz. fresh white breadcrumbs
1 level tsp. salt
freshly ground black pepper
1 large egg, beaten
orange juice

MAKES 16-20

Fry the onion and bacon in the butter until tender. Add the cranberries and cook a little longer until the cranberries 'pop'. Cool a little then add the suet, thyme, orange rind and bread-crumbs. Fork through to blend evenly and adjust the seasoning. Stir in the egg and enough orange juice to moisten. Form the mixture into balls. Heat the lard or dripping to give a ¼-in. depth in a baking tin and cook the stuffing balls at 400°F, 200°C (mark 6) for about 20 minutes. Turn the balls half way through cooking time. *Note:* The balls can be prepared and shaped and kept in a cool place overnight. The dry mix can be frozen in a heavy-duty plastic bag for up to 4 weeks.

Sambals

Toasted coconut: Lightly grill ½ lb. long thread coconut until golden brown, turning often.

Sautéed cashews: Heat 1 oz. butter with 1 tbsp. corn oil, add 8 oz. cashew nuts and fry, stirring often, until golden brown. Drain on kitchen paper and whilst still hot sprinkle with salt. Serve plain or with quartered hard-boiled eggs.

Dressed peppers: Halve 3 medium green peppers and discard the seeds. Slice very

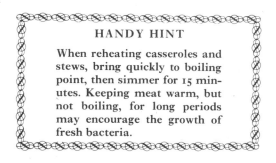

HANDY HINT

When reheating casseroles and stews, bring quickly to boiling point, then simmer for 15 minutes. Keeping meat warm, but not boiling, for long periods may encourage the growth of fresh bacteria.

finely. In a screw-top jar, shake 4 tbsps. salad oil, 2 tbsps. tarragon vinegar, ½ level tsp. salt, freshly ground black pepper, ½ level tsp. dry mustard and ½ level tsp. sugar. Pour over the peppers and leave to marinade for ½ hour.

Cucumber and yoghurt: Coarsely grate 1½ large cucumbers, do not remove the skins. Layer the cucumber in a bowl, sprinkling each layer with salt. Leave to stand for 15 minutes, then turn the cucumber into a nylon sieve and squeeze out all the juice. Fold 2 5-fl. oz. cartons natural yoghurt and 2 tbsps. chopped parsley through the cucumber and season with salt and freshly ground black pepper.

Almond salad: Fry 3 skinned and sliced onions and 3 seeded and chopped green peppers in 6 tbsps. corn oil until soft but not brown. Add 4 oz. blanched almonds, cut in slivers; 2 cloves garlic, skinned and crushed; 3 tbsps. soy sauce and the grated rind and juice of ½ lemon. Cook gently for about 5 minutes. Serve warm or cold.

Cranberry and orange ring

juice and rind of 1 orange
1 oz. powdered gelatine
7 fl. oz. red wine vinegar
¼ level tsp. salt
3 large oranges
2 15-oz. cans cranberry sauce
celery sticks for decoration

SERVES 8

Put the orange juice in a small basin. Sprinkle the gelatine over it and allow to soak for 1–2 minutes, then heat gently in a pan of hot water until the gelatine has dissolved. Remove from the heat. In a saucepan, gently heat the vinegar, salt and orange rind to infuse the flavour. Add the gelatine, remove from the heat and allow to cool. Peel the oranges, removing all pith, and cut into thin slices. Cut each slice into four and combine with the cranberry sauce. Gently fold in the liquid and pour into a 2½-pt. capacity plain ring mould. Chill until firm. When set,

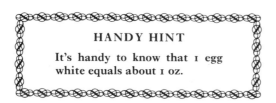

HANDY HINT

It's handy to know that 1 egg white equals about 1 oz.

gently ease around the edges with your fingers. Dip the mould into hot water, place a serving plate over the base and invert the mould. Decorate the centre with crisp celery.

Grape coleslaw

A crunchy bowl of cabbage salad with a lemon yoghurt dressing.

1 lb. white or pale green firm cabbage
½ lb. white grapes
¼ pt. natural yoghurt
½ clove garlic, skinned and crushed
2 level tsps. made mild mustard
1 tbsp. lemon juice
chives
salt and freshly ground black pepper

SERVES 6

Trim the cabbage, discard the stem, and shred it finely. Skin the grapes and remove the pips. In a large bowl, whisk together the yoghurt, garlic, mustard and lemon juice. Add plenty of scissor-snipped chives and seasoning. Add the cabbage and grapes, toss and lightly chill.

Leeks with tomato

A fresh way with leeks to retain their full flavour.

2 lb. leeks
3–4 tbsps. cooking oil
salt and pepper
2 tomatoes, skinned and chopped
1 clove of garlic, skinned and crushed
1 tbsp. chopped parsley
1 tsp. lemon juice

SERVES 4

Remove the coarse outer layers from the leeks and trim off most of the green part. Cut away the very thick bulbous part. Cut lengthwise down each leek almost to the base. Wash carefully to remove any grit. Heat the oil in a frying pan. Lay the leeks side by side in the pan and cook until the oil bubbles, then turn the leeks. Season, cover and cook gently for about 10 minutes. When tender (a fork should easily pierce the leeks), lift them from the pan and keep warm. Add the tomatoes, garlic and parsley to the pan. Cook quickly for 2–3 minutes, stirring, then add lemon juice. Check the seasoning and pour over the leeks.

Pan haggerty

Very good to cheer up the tail end of the cold roast.

1 oz. dripping
1 lb. potatoes, peeled and sliced
8 oz. onion, skinned and sliced
4 oz. Cheddar cheese, grated
salt and freshly ground black pepper

SERVES 4

In an 8-in. shallow frying pan, melt the dripping and gently swirl it around the edges. Layer alternately the potatoes, onions and grated cheese. Season well between each layer. Finish with grated cheese on top and overlap potatoes round the edge. Cover with a lid, then let the contents fry gently for about 30 minutes until the onions and potatoes are nearly cooked. Remove the lid and brown the top under a hot grill. Serve the haggerty straight from the pan.

* Ratatouille

½ lb. courgettes, trimmed
½ lb. aubergines, trimmed
salt
10 tbsps. olive oil
½ lb. onions, skinned and thinly sliced
2 green peppers, seeded and sliced
2 cloves garlic, skinned and crushed
ground black pepper
1 lb. firm ripe tomatoes, peeled
3 tbsps. chopped parsley

SERVES 6

Cut the courgettes and aubergines into ¼-in. slices. Sprinkle them with salt, leave to stand for ½–2 hours then dry on absorbent paper. Heat 4 tbsps. olive oil in a large, thick-based frying pan, add half the courgettes and aubergines in a single layer and sauté on both sides until golden. Remove from the pan and cook the remaining aubergines and courgettes in a further 4 tbsps. oil. Cook the onions and peppers in a further 2 tbsps. oil for about 10 minutes. Stir in the garlic and season. Quarter the tomatoes and add them to the onions; season further. Cook, covered, over a low heat for 5 minutes. Place one-third of the tomato mixture in a flameproof casserole, sprinkle over 1 tbsp. parsley. Arrange half the aubergines and courgettes on top, then half the remaining tomatoes and parsley. Finish with the remaining aubergines, courgettes, tomatoes

and parsley. Cover and bake at 325°F, 170°C (mark 3) for about 1 hour.

Cauliflower niçoise

(*see picture page 157*)

1 medium sized cauliflower
salt
1 oz. butter
1 small onion, skinned and finely sliced
½ lb. firm tomatoes, peeled, seeded and roughly chopped
1 small clove garlic, skinned and crushed
freshly ground black pepper
1 tbsp. chopped parsley

SERVES 4

Divide the cauliflower head into florets and cook these in boiling salted water for about 10 minutes. Drain thoroughly. Meanwhile have ready the niçoise mixture. Melt the butter and fry the onion until soft. Lightly stir in the tomato and crushed garlic. Heat through and season with black pepper. Arrange the cauliflower in a serving dish. Top with the tomato mixture and plenty of parsley.

Cauliflower, date and banana salad

(*see picture page 152*)

A side-salad in a light mayonnaise garnished with endive; this would be delicious with cold roast chicken and ham.

1 egg yolk
¼ level tsp. salt
freshly ground black pepper
¼ level tsp. dry mustard
¼ pt. salad oil
1 level tsp. caster sugar
1 tbsp. distilled vinegar
1 lemon
12 oz. prepared cauliflower florets
2 bananas
2 oz. whole dates, stoned and scissor-snipped
3 oz. sprigged endive

SERVES 4

For the lemon mayonnaise, whisk the egg yolk and seasoning together very thoroughly in a small but deep basin. Gradually beat in the salad oil, a little at a time, until all is incorporated, then add sugar, vinegar, the grated rind from half the lemon and 1 tbsp. of the juice. Blanch

Cauliflower, date and banana salad (*see page 151*)

the small cauliflower florets in boiling water for 3 minutes, drain and plunge them at once into cold water. Pat dry before using. Peel the bananas and cut into $\frac{1}{4}$-in. slices. Toss in the juice from half the lemon. Add two-thirds of the slices to the cauliflower, mash the rest and add to the mayonnaise. Lightly combine the cauliflower, mayonnaise and dates. Cover 4 small sides plates with prepared endive. Divide the cauliflower mayonnaise equally and spoon into the centres of the endive. Chill for about $\frac{1}{2}$ hour before serving.

Aubergines with parsley

(*see picture page 157*)

4 aubergines ($1\frac{1}{2}$ lb.)
salt
flour (optional)
4–5 tbsps. cooking oil
2 oz. butter
1 small clove garlic, skinned and crushed
2 tbsps. chopped parsley
freshly ground black pepper

SERVES 4

Wipe the aubergines with a damp cloth, discard the stem and calyx. Peel, if wished. Cut into $\frac{1}{2}$-in. slices and arrange in a wide dish before sprinkling with salt. Leave for $\frac{1}{2}$–1 hour then drain thoroughly, wipe well and dip, if wished, in flour. Heat half the oil and butter. When hot, fry the aubergines a few slices at a time until brown and tender. Drain and keep hot in a

serving dish. Add the remaining oil and butter to the pan as required. When all the sliced aubergine is cooked, pour off all but 1 tbsp. pan drippings, add the crushed garlic and parsley. Spoon this over the aubergines, add freshly ground pepper and serve as an accompaniment.

Scalloped potatoes

$1\frac{1}{2}$ lb. old potatoes, peeled
1 medium sized onion, skinned and sliced
3 oz. butter
salt and pepper
dusting of powdered herbs (optional)
$\frac{1}{4}$ pt. milk
chopped parsley for garnish

SERVES 4

Cut the potatoes into thin slices. Fry the thinly sliced onion in a little of the butter until soft but not coloured. In an ovenproof dish, layer up the onion, potatoes, seasoning, herbs and small pieces of butter. Pour the milk over, cover with foil and cook in the oven at 400°F, 200°C (mark 6) for 50–60 minutes until the potatoes are skewer-tender. Serve from the dish with a light dusting of chopped parsley.

Pommes Anna

$3\frac{1}{2}$ lb. even-sized old potatoes, peeled
8 oz. butter
salt and pepper

SERVES 6

Slice the potatoes thinly and evenly. A special mandolin slicer is ideal for this job, otherwise use the plain slicer on a grater, or a very sharp knife. Liberally butter a 6-in. cake tin. Cover the base with neatly overlapping slices of potato, layer up the rest of the potatoes, overlapping the slices for each layer in the reverse direction. Season each layer with salt and pepper and pack down well. Cover with browned butter poured over the last layer. Cover with a circle or square of greaseproof paper and weight down with a slightly smaller tin and a weight. Cook in the oven at 425°F, 220°C (mark 7) for 45 minutes–1 hour, removing the covering for the last 20

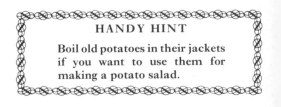

HANDY HINT

Boil old potatoes in their jackets if you want to use them for making a potato salad.

minutes to brown the top potato layer. A fine skewer used to pierce the centre will indicate when the potatoes are done. To serve, ease the potatoes from the edge of the tin with a palette knife. Invert the tin over a warm plate, then turn back on to a warm serving plate.

Rice salad, Greek style

(*see picture below*)

2 lb. long grain rice
$\frac{1}{4}$ pt. French dressing
$\frac{1}{2}$ lb. onions, skinned and finely chopped
1 green pepper, seeded and chopped
1 red pepper, seeded and chopped
4 sticks celery, chopped
14-oz. can pimientos, drained
black olives, stoned
chopped parsley

SERVES 25

Cook the rice as directed on the packet. Meanwhile make up a well-seasoned dressing. Drain the rice and while it is still hot pour the dressing over it and mix well. Add the onion, green and red peppers, celery and all but two of the pimientos, chopped. Brush two $2\frac{1}{2}$-pt. plain ring moulds with oil then make a pattern in the base using the remainder of the sliced pimientos, black olives and parsley. Carefully spoon the rice mixture into the ring moulds. Cool, then turn out on to flat plates.

Fried rice

$\frac{1}{2}$ lb. long grain rice
6 oz. butter or margarine
2 small onions, skinned and sliced
2 oz. stoned raisins
2 oz. blanched and toasted almonds
1 bayleaf
salt and pepper
$\frac{3}{4}$ pt. hot stock or water
1 rounded tbsp. diced green pepper, celery or cooked peas

SERVES 6

Rice salad, Greek style (*see above*)

Wash and drain the rice. Melt half the fat in a 3-pt. saucepan, add the sliced onions and fry slowly until brown. Stir in the rice and remainder of the fat. Cook stirring frequently until the rice has absorbed most of the fat. Add the raisins, almonds, bayleaf and seasoning. Just cover with hot stock or water, cover the pan and simmer until rice is tender and the liquid absorbed. Fold in the pepper, celery or peas. Serve very hot.

Tomato and celery salad

In a lidded container shake together 4 tbsps. salad oil, 2 tbsps. vinegar, $\frac{1}{2}$ level tsp. Dijon mustard, $\frac{1}{2}$ level tsp. caster sugar, $\frac{1}{2}$ level tsp. celery seeds, and salt and pepper to taste. Skin and slice $1\frac{1}{2}$ lb. tomatoes, slice $\frac{1}{2}$ large head of celery. Arrange in rows and spoon the dressing over $\frac{1}{2}$ hour before serving.

Cabbage and carrot slaw

Finely chop 10 oz. white cabbage and 2 oz. onion; combine with 8 oz. carrot, grated, and 2 tbsps. chopped parsley. Fold in 6 fl. oz. thick mayonnaise. Season with pepper. Combine 1 oz. aspic crystals with 3 tbsps. hot water and when dissolved fold into the mayonnaise mixture.

Turn into a $1\frac{1}{2}$-pt. mould. Chill until set; unmould.

Rice, mushroom and walnut salad

Shake together $\frac{1}{4}$ pt. corn oil, 2 fl. oz. tarragon vinegar, 1 level tsp. Dijon mustard, $\frac{1}{4}$ level tsp. salt, freshly ground black pepper, 2 tbsps. chopped parsley, a little sugar and 1 tsp. Worcestershire sauce. Trim 6–8 oz. button mushrooms, wipe them and marinade in dressing for 3–4 hours or overnight. Cook 8 oz. long grain rice in boiling salted water until tender. Drain well and while warm, fork mushrooms, dressing and 3 oz. shelled walnut halves through the rice. Chill.

Jellied beetroot and orange

Place $1\frac{1}{2}$ orange jelly tablets in a saucepan, add $\frac{1}{2}$ pt. water and stir over a *low* heat to dissolve. Off the heat, add the juice from an 11-oz. can mandarins and 2 fl. oz. cider vinegar. Pour in $\frac{1}{4}$ pt. cold water. When the jelly is on the point of setting, fold in scissor-snipped mandarins and $\frac{3}{4}$ lb. diced cooked beetroot. Turn into a 2-pt. square mould. Chill until set; unmould when required.

Winter desserts

Tarte de quetsches

Local plums are used to make a delicious seasonal open tart, a speciality of Luxembourg.

$5\frac{1}{2}$ oz. flour
$1\frac{1}{2}$ oz. caster sugar
3 egg yolks
4 oz. unsalted butter, softened
$1\frac{1}{2}$ level tsps. grated lemon rind
2 oz. ground almonds
2 oz. fresh breadcrumbs
$1\frac{1}{2}$ lb. small firm plums, stoned and halved
6 oz. redcurrant jelly

SERVES 8–10

Sift the flour and sugar into a basin. Incorporate the egg yolks and beat in the butter, a little at a time. Sprinkle over this the lemon rind and

knead to a smooth, pliable dough, then gather into a ball, wrap in greaseproof paper and chill for 30 minutes. Line a 10-in. loose-bottomed French fluted flan ring with the pastry; chill for about 30 minutes until quite firm. Combine the almonds and breadcrumbs and sprinkle over the base of the flan. Lay plum halves on top in concentric circles. Bake at 375°F, 190°C (mark

HANDY HINT

Remove the syrup from glacé cherries before using them in a cake. Halve cherries, place them in a sieve and rinse under cold running water. Dry them thoroughly on kitchen paper before using.

5) for about 45–60 minutes until the plums are tender and the pastry cooked. Heat the jelly in a saucepan then allow it to cool before glazing over the fruit, using a pastry brush. Leave the tart to cool before serving, but do not refrigerate.

Baked apple flambé

6 large cooking apples
4 oz. soft brown sugar
4 oz. butter
1 lemon
6 oz. glacé cherries, halved
1 tbsp. brandy

SERVES 6

Wipe and core the apples. Make a cut in the skin around the middle of each apple. Place them in an ovenproof dish and fill each centre with a little of the sugar and a small knob of butter taken from 1 oz. Bake in the centre of the oven at 350°F, 180°C (mark 4) for about 30–35 minutes, basting occasionally. Meanwhile melt the remaining butter and sugar in a pan. Boil gently for about 4 minutes until a rich caramel sauce is obtained. Remove the rind of the lemon free of any white pith, cut into very fine shreds. Add the lemon juice and rind, halved cherries and brandy to the pan. Blend thoroughly and simmer for 1–2 minutes. Fill each baked apple with the mixture and serve at once.

Loukomades

Yeast fritters from Greece are served warm with honey and lemon syrup on them.

For the syrup
8 oz. caster sugar
6 oz. clear honey
4 tbsps. lemon juice
thinly pared rind of 1 lemon
6 tbsps. water

For the fritters
¾ oz. fresh yeast
8 fl. oz. lukewarm water
12 oz. plain flour
½ level tsp. salt
6 tbsps. lukewarm milk
1 egg, beaten
oil for deep frying
chopped walnuts

MAKES ABOUT 14

Put the sugar, honey, lemon juice, rind and water in a heavy saucepan and heat gently, stirring, until the sugar dissolves. Increase the heat and boil, until sugar reaches 220°F, 110°C. Remove the rind and leave the syrup to cool. Blend the fresh yeast with a little of the lukewarm water. Whisk well with a fork and leave to stand in a warm place for 15–20 minutes. Sift the flour and salt into a large bowl, make a well in the centre and pour in the yeast, milk and rest of the water. Add the beaten egg and stir well with a spoon. Beat vigorously until the batter is smooth and just thick enough to hold its shape. Cover with oiled polythene and leave to rise for about 45 minutes until double its size. Heat the oil to 375°F, 190°C. Dip a tablespoon in cold water and use to scoop a level spoonful of batter into the oil. Cook the fritters for 3–4 minutes then drain on absorbent kitchen paper and keep warm. When all the fritters are cooked, pour the syrup over them and sprinkle with chopped walnuts.

Tarte tatin

The combination of dessert apples with a butter caramel glaze and French pastry base is truly delicious.

6 oz. plain flour
4 oz. butter or margarine
2 level tsps. caster sugar
1½ oz. ground almonds
1 egg yolk
1 tbsp. water
1 oz. butter
2 oz. caster sugar
2 lb. juicy dessert apples

SERVES 8

Sift the flour into a bowl, rub in 4 oz. butter or margarine and add 2 tsps. sugar and the almonds. Blend the yolk with water and stir it into the flour. Knead the dough lightly. Melt 1 oz. butter in a 9-in. round shallow, flameproof dish. Add 2 oz. sugar and caramelise over a gentle heat until golden. Remove the dish from the heat. Peel and halve the apples, remove the cores and slice thickly. Pack them closely to fill the bottom of the dish, leaving no gaps. Roll the pastry to a little more than a 9-in. circle. Lift it on to the apples and tuck in around the edges of the dish. Bake in the centre of the oven at 400°F, 200°C (mark 6) for about 30–35 minutes and turn out, apple side uppermost, on to a serving dish.

Golden apple Charlotte

When economy is needed, here's a quick, in-expensive hot pudding.

1 lb. cooking apples
2 oz. golden syrup
2 oz. thick-cut marmalade
white bread
2 oz. margarine or butter
2 level tbsps. granulated sugar
top of milk or single cream (optional)

SERVES 4

Peel, quarter and core the apples and cut them into slices. Warm the syrup and marmalade in a saucepan, add the apples and stir. Cook gently over a medium heat until the apples are soft but not too broken up. Meanwhile, prepare $\frac{1}{2}$-in. slices of bread without crusts (about 4 oz.). Cut them into even cubes. Melt the fat in an easy-clean frying pan, add the cubes of bread and fry gently until evenly brown, turning the cubes occasionally. Stir in the sugar, turn the apple into 4 small individual dishes, warmed, and top with fried bread cubes. If you like, drizzle each dish with top of the milk or single cream. Alternatively the apple Charlotte can be served in one large dish with the single cream.

✳ Plum crumb bake

An easy dessert with a sharp tang. For canned plums, drain off the syrup, reduce to a glaze by fast boiling and pour over the plums in the pie dish instead of using golden syrup.

2 oz. margarine
4 oz. fresh white breadcrumbs
$\frac{1}{4}$ level tsp. powdered cinnamon
1 oz. Demerara sugar
1 lb. plums (2 1-lb. 3-oz. cans)
3 tbsps. golden syrup

SERVES 4

In a frying pan melt the margarine, add the crumbs in a shallow layer and cook, turning often until they begin to colour. Combine the cinnamon and sugar and stir into the crumbs. Meanwhile, halve the plums and place in a $1\frac{1}{2}$-pt. pie dish. Spoon over the syrup and cook un-covered in the oven at 375°F, 190°C (mark 5) for about 20 minutes (5 minutes if canned fruit is used). Spoon the crumbs over and continue to cook for a further 15 minutes. Serve warm with pouring custard or cream.

✳ Almond figgy pudding

4 oz. margarine
$2\frac{1}{2}$ oz. caster sugar
2 eggs, beaten
4 oz. self-raising flour, sifted
grated rind of 1 lemon
4 oz. ready made marzipan, diced
15-oz. can figs, drained and quartered

SERVES 6

Grease a 2-pt. capacity basin. Cream together the margarine and sugar until light and pale. Beat in the eggs a little at a time until well mixed. Fold in the sifted flour, then the lemon rind and marzipan. Alternately layer the figs and sponge mixture in the basin starting with the figs and ending with the sponge. Cover with greaseproof paper with a centre pleat. Secure with string. Steam for $1\frac{1}{2}$–$1\frac{3}{4}$ hours until firm. Turn out on to a warm plate and serve with a jug of pouring custard.
Note: Marzipan melts during cooking – don't mistake it for uncooked sponge.

✳ Baked fruit salad

Truly delicious; easy for a dinner party.

$\frac{1}{4}$ lb. dried apricots
$\frac{1}{4}$ pt. white wine
15-oz. can sliced yellow peaches
juice from 1 lemon
1 can frozen Florida orange concentrate
2 oz. caster sugar
butter
3–4 bananas
3 oz. seedless raisins

SERVES 4–6

Using scissors, snip the apricots in half. Soak them overnight in the white wine. Drain the juice from the peaches into a measuring jug, add lemon juice and make it up to $\frac{3}{4}$ pt. with water. In a small saucepan combine the peach syrup and all the undiluted orange concentrate with the apricots, wine and sugar. Simmer over a low heat to dissolve the sugar then bring to the boil and simmer, covered, for 20 minutes until the apricots are tender. Butter a large ovenproof dish. Peel the bananas, cut them across in half and then in half lengthwise; lay the flat surfaces on a wooden board and cut in half again length-wise into narrow finger-lengths. Place the peaches and banana in the dish, sprinkle raisins over and pour over warm apricots and syrup. Cover and

Aubergines with parsley (*see page 152*) and
Cauliflower niçoise (*see page 151*)

bake at 375°F, 190°C (mark 5) for about 30 minutes. Serve warm, not hot, with pouring cream.

Moscovite of prunes

Unusual, but enjoyed by many who would otherwise shun prunes – it's a happy marriage of lemon, Cointreau and almond cream.

1 lemon or lime jelly tablet
10 whole almonds
angelica
2 1-lb. cans whole prunes
3 tbsps. Cointreau
grated rind and juice of ½ lemon
1 oz. caster sugar
½ oz. powdered gelatine
¼ pt. double cream
1 oz. nibbed almonds, toasted

SERVES 6

Make up the jelly according to the directions on the packet. Measure off ¼ pt. jelly and pour into the base of a 7-in. wetted, non-stick cake tin. Allow to set until firm. Arrange the almonds and diamonds of angelica around the outer edge, dipped first in a little jelly. Allow these to set before covering with more jelly – about ¼ pt. Drain the prunes and make the syrup up to ½ pt. with water if necessary. Stone the fruit and combine the fruit and syrup. Purée in an electric blender or sieve. Combine the purée, Cointreau, lemon rind, juice and sugar. Add another ¼ pt. jelly. Dissolve the powdered gelatine with 2 tbsps. water in a basin over a pan of hot water. Combine a few spoonfuls of prune purée with the gelatine before adding it to the bulk, then pour it into the prepared tin. Leave to set. Whip the cream until firm but not stiff. Add the nuts and fold them through. Spread the cream over the filling and chill until firm. Unmould carefully when set. Decorate with any extra jelly, roughly chopped.

✳ Orange apple crumble

1 small lemon
1½ lb. cooking apples, peeled and sliced
6 level tbsps. caster sugar
3 tbsps. orange marmalade
7 oz. self-raising flour
2 oz. butter or margarine
pinch salt
1 oz. ground almonds

SERVES 4–6

Grate the rind and squeeze the juice from the lemon into a 3-pt. Pyrex casserole. Toss the apples in the lemon, sprinkle over 2 level tbsps. caster sugar and add the marmalade. Cover with a lid and bake at 325°F, 170°C (mark 3) for about ½ hour. Meanwhile put the flour into a bowl and add fat grated straight from the refrigerator. Rub it in lightly, add the remaining 4 level tbsps. sugar, salt and ground almonds. Remove the apples from the oven and raise the oven temperature to 425°F, 220°C (mark 7). Sprinkle the crumble mixture over the apples and bake for a further 20 minutes.

✳ Lemon soufflé

A foolproof recipe with a pleasant lemon flavour and light as air texture.

3 egg yolks
2 oz. caster sugar
grated rind and juice of 2 lemons (4 tbsps.)
½ pkt. lemon jelly (½ pt.)
2 tbsps. water
¼ pt. double cream, whipped
3 egg whites
strawberries for decoration

SERVES 4

Prepare a 5-in. soufflé dish with a collar of greaseproof paper. Whisk together the egg yolks, sugar, lemon rind and juice in a deep bowl over hot water until really thick. Dissolve the jelly in water in a small pan, do not boil. When it is lukewarm whisk it into the egg yolk mixture. When half set, fold in the whipped cream. Lastly fold it into the stiffly whisked egg whites and turn the soufflé into the prepared dish. Chill. Remove the paper and decorate with strawberries.

Rum truffles

3 oz. plain chocolate
1 egg yolk
½ oz. butter
1 tsp. rum
1 tsp. top of the milk
chocolate vermicelli and drinking chocolate

MAKES ABOUT 12

Melt the chocolate in a small bowl over a pan of hot, not boiling, water. Add the egg yolk, butter, rum and milk. Beat until thick, then chill until firm enough to handle. Form the mixture into balls and toss at once into chocolate vermicelli and drinking chocolate to coat them. Serve in individual paper sweet cases, with the after-dinner coffee.

Cherry cream trifle

1 jam Swiss roll, sliced
6 tbsps. orange juice (1 large orange)
4 tbsps. sweet sherry
15-oz. can black cherries, drained and stoned
3 large eggs
1 level tbsp. cornflour
3 level tbsps. caster sugar
$\frac{3}{4}$ pt. milk
$\frac{1}{2}$ pt. double cream
2 tbsps. milk
1 tbsp. redcurrant jelly

SERVES 6–8

Line the base of a 3-pt. glass dish with Swiss roll. Blend together the orange juice and sherry and moisten the Swiss roll. Spoon the stoned cherries over. Whisk together the eggs, cornflour and sugar. Bring $\frac{3}{4}$ pt. milk to the boil, pour it over the whisked ingredients, return to the pan and bring just to the boil, stirring all the time. Remove it from the heat, strain, cool a little then gently pour it over the fruit and cover. Leave until cold. Whisk together the cream and milk until of a soft peaking consistency and spoon two-thirds over the custard. Beat the redcurrant jelly until smooth, spoon it into a small greaseproof paper piping bag, nip off the tip and pipe in 1-in. lines over the surface of the cream. Draw a fine skewer at right angles through the piped jelly. Whisk the remaining cream a little stiffer, spoon it into a piping bag fitted with a star vegetable nozzle and pipe it around the edge of the trifle. Keep in a cool place.

Apricot liqueur croissants

4 croissants
2 oz. butter
1-lb. 13-oz. can apricot halves
6 tbsps. Cointreau
16 pistachio nuts, peeled and halved
whipped cream

SERVES 4–6

Halve the croissants horizontally. Melt 1 oz. butter in a small pan and brush over the cut

surface. Toast until golden on both sides. Keep warm, cut side uppermost, on individual plates. Drain the juice from the apricots into the butter pan. Add 4 tbsps. Cointreau and 1 oz. butter. Reduce to $\frac{1}{4}$ pt. syrup over the heat. Sprinkle 2 tbsps. Cointreau over the toasted croissants, lay the apricot halves on top, sliced if large. Spoon hot syrup over each half croissant and decorate with nuts. Serve warm with lightly whipped cream.

Grape brûlée

1 lb. white grapes
Curaçao
$\frac{1}{2}$ pt. double cream
1 tsp. finely grated orange rind
soft brown sugar

SERVES 4

Skin the grapes and remove the pips, keeping the grapes whole. Place them in an ovenproof dish. Sprinkle very lightly with Curaçao or other orange liqueur. Whisk the cream until light and fluffy, but not over firm. Fold in the orange rind and spread it over the grapes. Cover with a thick layer of soft brown sugar – $\frac{1}{2}$ in. deep. Leave in a refrigerator overnight. Just before required, place the dish under a hot grill to just melt the surface of the sugar. When bubbly, serve.

Strawberry cream trifle

1 oz. plain cake-covering chocolate
2 8-oz. strawberry jam sponges
6 oz. almond macaroons
2 1-lb. 3-oz. cans strawberries, drained
6 tbsps. brandy
2 pt. milk
few strips of thinly pared lemon rind
6 eggs
$3\frac{1}{2}$ oz. caster sugar
$\frac{3}{4}$ pt. double cream
2 tbsps. top of the milk
1 oz. caster sugar
3 oz. shelled walnuts, chopped
$\frac{1}{2}$ oz. pistachio nuts, skinned and chopped

SERVES 12

Melt the chocolate in a bowl placed in a pan of hot water. Fill a paper icing bag with chocolate, snip off the tip and pipe overlapping loops of chocolate on non-stick paper to cover a 7-in. circle. Pipe a line round the outer edge. Chill until set and store in a cool place. Line the base of a 5-pt. serving bowl with cubed sponge cakes. Place half the macaroons around the edge. Combine 4 tbsps. strawberry juice and 3 tbsps. brandy. Spoon this over the sponge. Layer the fruit and the rest of the sponge and finish with macaroons. Infuse the lemon rind in warm milk for 10 minutes then pour it on to the whisked eggs and sugar. Strain the custard into a double saucepan and cook until it thickens to coat the back of a spoon. Cool, then pour it over the macaroons. Chill until set. Whip the cream, milk, sugar and the remaining brandy to hold their shape. Spread this over the custard. Ease the chocolate from the paper and place on top of the cream. Decorate with nuts.

Pears Bristol

(*see picture opposite*)

A delicate flavour.

4 firm dessert pears
3 oz. sugar
water
2 oranges
2 oz. caster sugar

SERVES 4

Peel the pears, cut into quarters and remove the cores. Dissolve the sugar in 12 tbsps. water in a small saucepan, bring to the boil and boil for 5 minutes. Add the pear quarters and simmer, covered, until the fruit is tender. Leave until cold. Using a potato peeler, pare the rind from

Pouding à la royale (*see above right*)

½ orange and cut into very fine strips. Cook in a little water until tender – about 5 minutes. Rinse the rind in cold water. Peel the oranges free of pith and cut into segments. Dissolve the caster sugar in a pan, shaking occasionally – do not stir. Bubble until golden, then pour it on to an oiled tin. When brittle crack with a rolling pin. Turn the drained pears into a serving dish and top with orange segments. Add the orange strips to the pear juice and pour over the fruit. Scatter caramel over and chill.

Pouding à la royale

(*see picture below left*)

The simplest of warming desserts to make. Swiss roll, jam filled, lines the dish and the custard centre – rich with eggs – can be flavoured in any number of ways. Orange is our first choice, then vanilla, lemon, or even chocolate, omitting the liqueur.

1 Swiss roll
cooking oil
½ pt. milk
1½ oz. butter
3 oz. caster sugar
4 eggs, separated
1½ oz. plain flour
grated rind of 1 orange
2 tbsps. Cointreau

SERVES 6

Dip a knife into water and thinly slice the Swiss roll. Use it to line the bottom and sides of an oiled 7-in. soufflé dish or cake tin. Heat the milk and butter in a pan. Beat the sugar and egg yolks together, stir in the flour slowly and pour in the warmed milk, stirring. Return the mixture to the pan, bring to the boil, beating well until smooth and thickened (sieve if necessary or alternatively use an electric hand mixer while heating the sauce). Cool, then add the orange rind and Cointreau. Stiffly whisk the egg whites and fold them into the egg mixture. Turn into the prepared dish. Place in a water bath – a roasting tin is suitable – half-full of hot water. Bake at 350°F, 180°C (mark 4) for about 1½ hours. Cover during cooking if the surface becomes too brown. Leave to stand for a few minutes, then invert on to a serving dish. Brush with glaze or serve the glaze separately.
Glaze: In a pan, blend 2 level tsps. arrowroot with 2 tbsps. orange juice. Add ¼ pt. water and 2 tbsps. jelly marmalade, sieved. Bring to the boil and cook for 2–3 minutes, stirring.

Pears Bristol (*see opposite*)

Pineapple-banana crush

15-oz. can crushed pineapple
2 level tsps. cornflour
4 tbsps. top of the milk
2 large bananas, sliced
glacé cherries and walnuts for decoration

SERVES 4

Drain any juice from the pineapple into a bowl. Blend the cornflour with the milk and pour it into a small pan with the drained pineapple juice. Combine the pineapple and bananas and divide them between 4 sundae glasses. Bring the fruit juices to the boil, stirring, pour over the fruit and chill. Decorate with halved glacé cherries and walnuts.

Pineapple meringue

1 ripe pineapple (about 1¾ lb.)
2–3 tbsps. brandy
3 oz. meringues
½ pt. double cream

SERVES 6

Discard both ends of the pineapple and cut the rest in thick slices. With a small sharp knife cut away the skin and stamp out the hard core centre with a plain cutter. Shred the flesh and place it in a bowl together with the brandy. Roughly crush the meringues. Just before serving, drain off the juice from the pineapple and with a balloon whisk whip the cream, gradually adding the drained juice until the cream is stiff enough to hold its shape. Lightly fold in the meringue and pineapple. Serve in a glass bowl.

Banana sundae

Have some coffee ice cream handy in the freezer.

4 bananas
grated rind and juice of 1 large orange
butter
1½ oz. light soft brown sugar
4 scoops coffee ice cream
whipped cream (optional)

SERVES 4

Peel and slice the bananas and place them in a baking dish with the orange rind and juice. Dot lightly with butter and sprinkle with sugar. Bake uncovered at 350°F, 180°C (mark 4) for about 15–20 minutes. Spoon over portions of ice cream and decorate if wished with whipped cream.

Baked bananas

12 large bananas
6 oz. dark soft brown sugar
8 tbsps. rum
2 oz. long thread coconut, toasted

SERVES 12

Bake the bananas in their skins on a baking sheet at 400°F, 200°C (mark 6) for 15 minutes. Remove the bananas from their skins and arrange in individual dishes or in one large dish. Sprinkle sugar over the bananas and then spoon on rum and set it alight. When the flame dies, sprinkle with coconut.

✳ Choc au rhum

6 oz. chocolate dots
3 large eggs, separated
1 tbsp. rum
¼ pt. double cream
grated chocolate

SERVES 6

Melt the chocolate in a bowl over a pan of hot water. Beat the yolks into the melted chocolate with the rum. Whisk the egg whites until stiff and fold evenly into the chocolate mixture. Chill well in individual dishes or glasses. Serve topped with whipped cream and a little grated chocolate.

✳ Alaska express

1 large chocolate Swiss roll
11-oz. can mandarin oranges
5 egg whites
10 oz. caster sugar
34-fl. oz. block vanilla ice cream
chocolate polka dots
1 individual chocolate roll
cotton-wool

SERVES 12

Cut the Swiss roll into 10 slices. Arrange 6 slices on a flat oblong ovenproof dish to form a rectangle. Spoon over 2 tbsps. mandarin juice from the can. Whisk the egg whites until stiff, add half the sugar and whisk again until stiff. Fold in the remainder of the sugar. Spoon the meringue into a fabric piping bag fitted with a large star vegetable nozzle. Place the block of *really firm* ice cream on the Swiss roll slices and arrange all but 6 of the drained mandarins on top of the block. Quickly pipe the meringue over the ice cream to form an engine shape to completely enclose the roll. Pipe rosettes down the back and decorate with the reserved mandarins and polka dots. Bake in a preheated oven at 450°F, 230°C (mark 8) for about 4 minutes until golden. Place the extra 4 slices of Swiss roll for wheels and use the small chocolate roll as a funnel with a puff of cotton-wool for smoke. Serve at once.

Quick Christmas pudding

Bought mincemeat takes the place of traditional dried fruit and suet, giving that left-to-mature flavour without storing.

4 oz. plain flour
1 level tsp. ground cinnamon
½ level tsp. grated nutmeg
4 oz. fresh white breadcrumbs
2 oz. soft brown sugar
grated rind of 1 lemon
4 oz. glacé cherries
2 oz. nibbed almonds
3 lb. ready-made mincemeat
3 eggs, beaten

SERVES 6

Grease two 1-pt. pudding basins and place a circle of greaseproof paper in each base. Sift together the flour and spices into a large bowl. Add the breadcrumbs, sugar, lemon rind, cherries and almonds. Stir in the mincemeat and eggs. Mix with a wooden spoon and divide equally between the basins. Cover with greased greaseproof paper and foil, pleated down the centre, and secure with string. Place in a pan with water to come half-way up the basins. Bring to the boil, reduce the heat and simmer for about 4¾ hours. To reheat, boil gently for 2 hours.

HANDY HINT

The bowl and beater should be completely greasefree when whisking the eggs for meringues.

Toffee plum croûte

A top of the cooker pudding – plums with a toffee sauce.

2 oz. butter
8 oz. soft brown sugar
1 tbsp. lemon juice
4½-in. slices from a 2 lb. loaf
1 lb. red plums, stoned and quartered
¼ pt. double cream

SERVES 4

Melt the butter in a thick frying pan. Add the sugar, stir and heat slowly to dissolve the sugar. Add the lemon juice. Remove the crusts from the bread and cut the slices into ½-in. squares. Gently fold through the toffee mixture and, when evenly coated, add the plums. Cover the pan and cook until the plums are soft. Serve hot with whipped cream or pour into a dish, chill and spread with whipped cream.

Mousseline sauce

Serve with steamed or baked puddings.

1 egg
1 egg yolk
1½ oz. caster sugar
2 tbsps. sherry

Put all the ingredients in a large heatproof bowl and place it over a pan of simmering water. Whisk until the sauce is thick and frothy and serve immediately.

Brandy butter

This is often known as hard sauce.

3 oz. unsalted butter
1 oz. caster sugar
2 oz. icing sugar
2–3 tbsps. brandy

Cream the butter and beat in the sugars. When they are thoroughly blended add the brandy a teaspoonful at a time, beating continuously.
Note: For rum butter use 3 oz. soft brown sugar and 2–3 tbsps. rum.

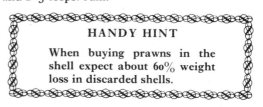

HANDY HINT

When buying prawns in the shell expect about 60% weight loss in discarded shells.

Winter cakes

✳ Grandmother's boiled fruit cake

Brown sugar, spice and tea go to make an old-time favourite – dark and moist with lots of plump fruit – you'll enjoy every crumb.

$\frac{1}{2}$ pt. tea
4 oz. margarine
5 oz. light soft brown sugar
6 oz. currants
6 oz. sultanas
3 level tsps. mixed spice
10 oz. plain flour
2 level tsps. bicarbonate of soda
1 large egg

Grease a 7-in. round cake tin. Put the tea, margarine, sugar, currants, sultanas and spice in a saucepan and bring to the boil, reduce the heat and simmer for 20 minutes. Cool. Lightly beat in the sifted flour and bicarbonate of soda with the egg. Turn the mixture into the tin and bake just below the centre of the oven for about 1 hour at 350°F, 180°C (mark 4). When the cake is beginning to brown, cover with a piece of damp greaseproof paper. Turn out and cool on a wire rack.

✳ Petticoat tails

These biscuits originate from Scotland; to serve, place the centre round in the middle of a flat plate and overlap the tails to look like a 'skirt'.

2 oz. caster sugar
4 oz. butter, softened
6 oz. plain flour

MAKES 12

Cream together the sugar and butter. Gradually add the flour and work together. Knead lightly. On a floured surface, roll out the dough to about $\frac{1}{8}$-in. thick. Cut a large circle using an inverted dinner plate $9\frac{1}{2}$ in. across. Lift carefully (using a large palette knife) on to a baking sheet lined with non-stick paper. Use a small plain 3-in. diameter cutter to cut a smaller circle in the centre. Leave this in position then with a knife cut 10 tails through as far as the centre round. Prick both discs and bake at 350°F, 180°C (mark 4) for about 15 minutes, until pale golden brown. Cool the Petticoat Tails on a wire rack.

✳ Mincemeat cinnamon meltaways

8 oz. plain flour
2 level tsps, cream of tartar
1 level tsp. bicarbonate of soda
$\frac{1}{2}$ level tsp. powdered cinnamon
pinch of salt
4 oz. butter or margarine
4 oz. caster sugar
1 egg, beaten
$\frac{1}{2}$ lb. mincemeat
flaked almonds

MAKES ABOUT 16

Sift together the flour, cream of tartar, bicarbonate of soda, cinnamon and salt. Rub in the fat, add the sugar and mix to a soft dough with the egg. Knead lightly and roll out to about $\frac{1}{8}$-in. thickness on a well floured surface or between sheets of waxed or non-stick paper; handle with care. Stamp out bases and lids with a plain cutter to line about 16 $2\frac{1}{2}$-in. diameter (top measurement) patty tins. Place the bases in the pans and add about 1 tsp. mincemeat to each. Top with the lids – which seal themselves during cooking; scatter nuts over. Bake in the oven at 400°F, 200°C (mark 6) for about 15 minutes. Leave the meltaways to cool for a short time then slip them out on to a wire rack to cool further.

✳ Plum cake with brandied orange butter

Caught on the hop without a rich fruit cake in the tin maturing? Don't worry. Light, albeit well fruited, this recipe is ready in one day.

6 oz. soft tub margarine
6 oz. light soft brown sugar
3 large eggs
2 tsps. golden syrup
3 tbsps. black currant jam
12 oz. raisins
6 oz. currants
2 oz. chopped mixed peel
2 pieces crystallised ginger, chopped
2 oz. shelled walnuts, chopped
2 oz. ground almonds
2 tbsps. rum
8 oz. self-raising flour
1 level tsp. baking powder
1 level tsp. mixed spice

In a large deep bowl place the margarine, sugar, eggs, syrup, jam, raisins, currants, peel, ginger, walnuts, ground almonds and rum. Sift in the flour, baking powder and spice. Beat well with a wooden spoon for about 3 minutes until all the ingredients are well combined. Turn the mixture into a greased and floured 3-pt. ring mould suitable for baking. Bake in the centre of the oven at 400°F, 200°C (mark 6) for 15 minutes then reduce to 300°F, 150°C (mark 1–2) for a further 2½–2¾ hours. Allow to cool slightly before removing the cake from the tin. Leave a day before serving in slices spread with orange butter.

Orange butter: In a deep bowl, cream together 4 oz. soft tub margarine, 12 oz. sifted icing sugar, 1½ tbsps. brandy, 1 tbsp. orange juice and ½ level tsp. powdered cinnamon.

⋇ Chocolate cup cake

piece of vanilla pod
4 tbsps. milk
8 oz. cooking chocolate
4 oz. plain flour
2 oz. ground rice
1 level tsp. baking powder
8 oz. butter
6 oz. caster sugar
4 large eggs, separated
grated chocolate for decoration

For chocolate glacé icing
4 oz. cooking chocolate
4 tbsps. water
2 tsps. glycerine
7 oz. icing sugar, approx.

Grease and line an 8-in. round cake tin. Infuse the vanilla pod in the milk for ½ hour then remove the pod. Melt the chocolate with the flavoured milk; do not overheat. Sift together the flour, ground rice and baking powder. Beat the butter until light and soft, add the sugar and cream until light and fluffy. Beat the egg yolks, one at a time, into the creamed mixture, followed by the cooled but still soft chocolate. Beat in the flour. Whisk the egg whites and lightly fold into the cake mixture. Turn into the prepared tin. Bake in the centre of the oven at 350°F, 180°C (mark 4) for about 1¼ hours. Turn the cake out and cool it on a wire rack. When cold, place a collar of greaseproof paper firmly round the cake and to come about 1 in. above the top. Pour icing (see below) in a thick layer over the cake top. Sprinkle grated chocolate round the edge. Leave until set before easing the paper away.
Chocolate glacé icing: Melt the chocolate with the water over a low heat. Add the glycerine and stir in enough icing sugar to give a thick coating consistency. Use quickly.

⋇ Viennese whirls

Decorative and delicious.

8 oz. butter or margarine
few drops vanilla essence
2 oz. icing sugar, sifted
6 oz. plain flour
2 oz. cornflour
glacé cherries, halved
angelica
icing sugar

MAKES 20

In a bowl, cream together the fat, essence and sugar until light and soft. Fold in the sifted flour and cornflour. Use this mixture to pipe out 2-in. diameter rings with a medium-sized star vegetable nozzle on greased baking sheets. Keep the rings apart. Decorate with glacé cherries and angelica leaves and chill them until firm. Bake in the centre of the oven at 375°F, 190°C (mark 5) for 10 minutes until pale golden brown. Cool them a little before lifting carefully from the baking sheet. Store carefully as these cookies are fragile. Dust with icing sugar to serve.

⋇ Date fingers

Quick for tea. If you prefer, substitute 3 oz. glacé cherries and 2 oz. chopped walnuts for the dates.

½ lb. plain flour
2 level tsps. baking powder
6 oz. block margarine
4 oz. soft light brown sugar
6 oz. stoned dates

Sift together the flour and baking powder (or use 5 oz. self-raising flour and 3 oz. plain flour). Rub in the margarine (or use 3 oz. margarine and 3 oz. butter) to resemble fine breadcrumbs – do this lightly to prevent the mixture getting sticky. Add the sugar and scissor-snipped dates. Combine well together and turn into an 8-in. shallow square tin. Press down lightly. Bake in the oven at 350°F, 180°C (mark 4) for about 30 minutes. Cool for a short time in the tin, mark into fingers; dust with icing sugar.

* Shortbread rounds

Shortbread can be stored for up to a week in an airtight container or kitchen foil.

5 oz. plain flour
1 oz. rice flour
4 oz. butter or margarine

Sift the flour and rice flour into a bowl, rub in the butter and then work with the fingertips until well blended to a dough. Liberally flour two ¼-pt. fancy wooden shortbread moulds or a 7-in. sandwich tin (with the latter, the mixture remains in the tin). Press the mixture into the moulds then remove by knocking the sides of the mould on a folded cloth. Turn the shortbread on to an ungreased baking sheet (or press the mixture smoothly into the tin). Prick the shortbread with a fork and mark portions with a knife; chill for 1 hour then bake for about 1 hour at 300°F, 150°C (mark 2) until pale straw colour.

* Petits fours

5 oz. ground almonds
3 oz. caster sugar
3 egg whites
few drops almond essence
1 tbsp. milk
1 level tbsp. caster sugar
1 oz. ground hazelnuts
4 oz. icing sugar, sifted
halved almonds, quartered glacé cherries, angelica, walnut pieces and extra icing sugar for decoration

MAKES ABOUT 30 EACH OF TWO VARIETIES

Sift together 4 oz. ground almonds and 3 oz. caster sugar into a bowl. Stiffly whisk 2 egg whites. Fold in the sugar mixture and essence, using a metal spoon. Place the mixture in a forcing bag with a plain or star shape ½-in. vegetable nozzle and pipe in small discs or scrolls on to a baking sheet lined with non-stick paper. Top each with almonds, cherries, angelica or walnut pieces. Bake at 350°F, 180°C (mark 4) for 15–20 minutes until golden. While hot, brush the petits fours with 1 tbsp. milk and 1 level tbsp. caster sugar blended together. In a deep bowl pound 1 oz. ground almonds and 1 oz. ground hazelnuts – this can be done with the end of a plain wooden rolling pin. Lightly whisk 1 egg white and gradually add 4 oz. icing sugar, beating after each addition until quite thick. Stir in the

nuts. Roll into about 30 small balls, roll each in icing sugar and place in tiny paper cases on a baking sheet. Bake at 325°F, 170°C (mark 3) for about 15 minutes until puffed and slightly tinged with colour.

Collettes

Keep these rich after dinner delicacies in a cool place but do not refrigerate. Eat fresh – there won't be any to keep!

10 oz. chocolate dots
4 tbsps. strong coffee
2 oz. butter, softened
2 egg yolks
rum

Melt 5 oz. chocolate dots in a small basin over hot, not boiling, water and use to coat 22 small paper sweet cases. Invert the cases and stand them to set on non-stick paper. Peel away the paper cases. Melt 5 oz. chocolate dots and add the coffee. When cool but not cold, beat in the butter and egg yolks. Add rum to taste. Allow the mixture to stiffen and then pipe into the chocolate cases, using a star icing nozzle.

* Date rockies

Don't let the unbaked mixture become too soft or these small cakes will loose their rough appearance.

½ lb. plain flour
1 level tsp. baking powder
½ level tsp. bicarbonate of soda
pinch of salt
4 oz. block margarine
4 oz. soft light brown sugar
3 oz. chopped dates
2 oz. chopped walnuts
1 large egg, beaten
milk

MAKES 12

Into a bowl sift the flour, baking powder, bicarbonate of soda and salt. Rub in the margarine, using the fingertips, until the mixture resembles fine breadcrumbs. Stir in the sugar, dates and walnuts. Add the egg and only just enough milk to knit the mixture together. A fork is good for the mixing. Grease 2 baking sheets and, using 2 forks, arrange 12 rough piles of mixture in rocky bun shapes, well apart. Bake at or just above oven centre at 425°F, 220°C (mark 7) for about 15 minutes. Lift them off carefully with a palette knife and cool on a wire rack.

* Orange chip cookies

In an airtight container these cookies stay beautifully crisp.

4 oz. butter or block margarine
3 oz. caster sugar
1 small egg, beaten
grated rind of 1 orange
2 oz. chocolate dots
4 oz. self-raising flour

MAKES 24–30

Cream together the fat and sugar until light and fluffy. Beat in the egg, then stir in the orange rind, chocolate and self-raising flour. Roll the soft dough into 24–30 balls about the size of a shelled walnut and place apart on an ungreased baking sheet. Make criss-cross patterns on top of each with a fork pressed into each ball. Bake in the centre of the oven at 350°F, 180°C (mark 4) for about 25 minutes. Cool on a rack.

< Roundabout cake

This cake for a children's party can be made several days ahead, providing the decoration is left until the day.

For cake
8 oz. butter
8 oz. caster sugar
4 eggs, beaten
8 oz. self-raising flour
juice of ½ lemon

For filling
8 oz. butter
12 oz. icing sugar, sifted
juice of ½ lemon

For decoration
½ lb. jellied orange and lemon slices
1 stick lemon rock
8 coloured ribbons ¾ yd. by ¼ in.

Cream the butter and sugar until light and fluffy. Add the eggs a little at a time, beating well after each addition. Fold in half the flour using a metal spoon, then fold in the second half. Lastly mix in the lemon juice. Divide the mixture between two greased 8-in. sandwich tins. Bake in the oven at 375°F, 190°C (mark 5) for about 25 minutes. Cool on a wire rack. Make up butter icing by creaming the butter till fluffy then gradually add icing sugar and lemon juice. Beat well. Sandwich the cakes together with a little icing then spread the remainder over the top and sides. Place the cake on a silver board and draw a serrated scraper round the sides. Cut the orange and lemon slices into little boys and girls, using scissors or a sharp knife. Arrange these round the sides of the cake. Fix the ribbons on to the stick of rock with icing then press the rock into the cake. Arrange the ribbons so that each person holds one.

* Lollipop cookies

When baked these cookies store well in an airtight container for up to one week.

4 oz. butter or margarine
4 oz. caster sugar
2 egg yolks
grated rind and juice of ½ lemon
8 oz. plain flour
18 lolly sticks

For icing
2 egg whites
1¼ lb. icing sugar, sifted
food colouring

MAKES 18

Cream together the butter and sugar until light and fluffy. Beat in the egg yolks and gradually work in the lemon rind, juice and flour. Knead lightly on a floured surface and roll the dough out to about ¼-in. thickness. Using a 2-in. fluted cutter stamp out 18 rounds, re-kneading and re-rolling as necessary. Place these apart on lightly greased baking sheets. Carefully press a lolly stick into the side of the cookie dough, one to each. Ensure that the stick is surrounded by the dough. Bake in the oven at 350°F, 180°C (mark 4) for about 20 minutes. Cool the cookies on a wire rack. To decorate, lightly whisk the egg whites, then gradually beat in the icing sugar. Divide into 4 parts and tint three parts: one green, one deep pink and one orange. Using an icing nozzle and paper forcing bag, pipe names and decorative borders on to each lollipop.

CHAPTER FIVE

KEEP IT FOR ANOTHER DAY

Refrigeration and more recently the accelerated acquisition of food freezers in the home mean that just nothing in the food line should be wasted. It is not really practical to give a host of hard and fast recipes for using leftovers, as no two cooks end up with the same amount or selection of bits and pieces. But with a little guidance and ingenuity these can be creatively turned into a very tasty dish. Remember however that all leftovers should be treated with care, not left around in a warm kitchen but stowed away quickly in the refrigerator, closely covered. It is wise to remove moist stuffings before refrigerating poultry. All cooked meat should be reheated slowly but thoroughly in stock, gravy or sauce, brought up to boiling point and simmered for at least 15 minutes. Don't try and stretch leftovers too far, diluting the flavours, and remember that careful seasoning is even more important the second time round.

Non-stick surfaces on frying pans are excellent for, say, cooking the ever-popular bubble and squeak mixtures, with only the minimum of dripping the crust is made beautifully crisp and golden. To a base of mashed potato can be added cooked cabbage, carrots, parsnips, leeks or for a main dish include scraps of cooked bacon joint, cubes of cheese, corned beef – and serve with poached eggs on top. Make concentrated stock from a chicken, turkey or duck carcass or giblets, treat roast joint bones in the same fashion; a little home-made stock is invaluable for second day sessions. Nobbly pieces of cheese not elegant enough for the cheese board are handy when grated ready for action and pastry scraps keep for a day or two wrapped in foil; breadcrumbs have a hundred and one uses.

Meat and poultry leftovers

A generous sized roast usually makes for the best eating but then there are always leftovers. Slightly rare beef is far juicier than meat with no pinky tinge when it comes to rechauffée dishes. One plain cold cut serving is usually accepted by the family with chutneys and jacket spuds as an accompaniment. As a change, any cold meat, sliced in cubes or strips, will also take happily to a marinade – well seasoned mustardy French dressing with parsley, capers or a little creamed horseradish; use enough just to moisten. Such a dressing will also help to revive over-cooked cold meat. Hot dishes such as Miroton de boeuf can be full flavoured if ingredients are carefully blended. Here the choice is cold boiled or braised beef, cut into slivers, put into a dish surrounded by piped potato and covered with browned onions; sprinkle with flour, tomato purée, a spoonful or so of stock, a dash of vinegar and heat together; then brown the whole dish in the oven and garnish with chopped parsley.

Never waste the drippings from any cooking sessions as these are so full of flavour; the jelly juices that collect under the bowl of dripping are also valuable for enriching savoury sauces. All cold meats and poultry curry well, especially lamb, chicken or turkey. Try lightly frying a small onion, adding the meat for two people, dredging with a little flour and about 1 level tablespoonful curry powder, then fry a little longer, stirring. Pour in the contents of a small can of tomatoes, add a tablespoonful or two of meat juices if you have any or half a stock cube, crumbled, also a spoonful of fruity chutney or cranberry sauce. Bring to the boil, stirring, and simmer on top of the cooker for about 30 minutes or in the oven, both ways covered. A piquant sweet-sour or devil sauce is the best answer for pork. End bits of bacon joint, which cut badly, can be chopped into omelettes or mixed with chicken remainders in a white sauce for a leftovers 'suprême' or you may care to mix them up with peas or put into vol-au-vent cases or oven-crisp hollowed-out rolls. Large deep red tomatoes, aubergines, marrows, courgettes and cabbage leaves all take kindly to a well seasoned stuffing of a little meat, ham or cold bacon, rice or breadcrumbs, herbs, onion, cheese and top of the milk or egg.

Because poultry is so good cold, alone or as part of a salad, chicken and turkey doesn't present quite the same problems but it can become monotonous. Open sandwich treatment presents odd scraps of cold poultry in a cheerful fashion. When reheating, remove the skin as this is not pleasant cooked a second time. Chop flesh finely with a sharp knife rather than mince; like over-cooked meat, poultry tends to break down into a paste when pressed through a narrow aperture. Collect a selection of small oven or flameproof dishes or even natural scallop shells for serving golden brown gratinés – spooned from one large dish sauce mixtures don't look nearly so appetising. Cheese sauce is a good foil for cold poultry, with a squeeze of lemon juice or a suspicion of mustard, perhaps Dijon, and a little sauté mushroom or tomato added.

Enclose a devilled chicken mixture in frozen puff pastry to make pasties or mask in a light creamy sauce to serve on freshly made buttered toast. Similarly, deep fried pastry, previously filled with a mixture of liver pâté, chicken, garlic and parsley butter makes an interesting appetiser. Make well filled sandwiches with bits of chicken and a mature hard cheese grated together with some chutney; shallow fried and served with coleslaw they make a handsome tray lunch.

Desserts from yesterday's fruit or pudding

When you open a tin of pineapples or peaches to add to a dish you can use any extra fruit or juice for jellies, trifles or to start off a fresh fruit salad. A little stiff apple purée used as the base for a French apple flan can be finished with wafer-thin slices of eating apple, or use it for a light fluffy apple snow or apple brûlée – topped with soured cream and a thick layer of brown sugar, then grilled. A leftover portion of steamed or baked sponge pudding is best reheated in a foil parcel. Fry slices of Christmas pudding and serve with whipped cream spliced with cooking sherry and stale ginger cake admirably replaces breadcrumbs to make a moist gooey syrup tart. Stale sponge cake, soaked with orange juice and rum and topped with a little fruit can be baked and topped with custard or meringue.

CHAPTER SIX

FREEZER NOTES

10 freezer points

1. Always start with good quality foods and freeze them at peak freshness. Food can only come out of the freezer as good as when you put it in.

2. Keep handling to a minimum and make sure everything is scrupulously clean.

3. Pay special attention to packaging and sealing. Exposure to air and moisture can damage frozen foods.

4. Cool food rapidly if it's been cooked or blanched; never put anything hot – or even warm – into your freezer.

5. Freeze food as quickly as possible and in small quantities.

6. When preparing a dish for the freezer, go easy on seasoning.

7. Always use shallow dishes for quick thawing.

8. Frozen foods that you want to serve hot should be heated as rapidly as possible as this preserves the flavour and texture. Whenever practical, heat from frozen. The advantage of freezing in smallish packages is obvious when it comes to heating.

9. If you are in a real hurry, a mixture that includes some sauce or liquid can be put into a saucepan and placed directly over a low heat, but watch it and beware of it sticking to the pan.

10. A sauce, once thawed, should be vigorously whisked to restore its smoothness, unless its ingredients would spoil if they were broken down.

Packaging

1. Always expel as much air as possible. Use crumpled non-stick, waxed or freezer paper to fill vacant space in the top of a rigid container. Always keep a selection of different sized containers.

2. Always leave $\frac{1}{2}$–1 in. headspace when packing liquids. This allows for expansion on freezing.

3. Anything with solids and liquids, e.g. stews, casseroles, fruit in syrup should have the solids covered by liquid. Again $\frac{1}{2}$ in. headspace is necessary.

4. When using polythene bags for liquids, fit the bag into a regular shaped rigid container (a pre-former) before filling. When the liquid is solid the pre-former can then be slipped off and the package is easy to store in the freezer.

5. Anything wrapped in foil should be overwrapped with polythene in case of puncturing the foil.

6. To enable casserole dishes to be free for use in the kitchen, line them with foil

before pouring in the mixture. The foil wrapped mixture can then be removed from the dish when solid, overwrapped with polythene, sealed, labelled and stored in the freezer – this is known as a preformed pack.

7. Freeze food in meal sized portions whenever possible. Individual foods like chops or steaks should be interleaved with waxed or non-stick paper. Do not freeze more than 2 pt. in one pack.

8. Small, shallow packs of soups, stews, casseroles etc. will reheat quicker than large, deep packs.

SPRING

Kipper pâté (page 12) – freeze in serving dishes. To use, thaw in the refrigerator, covered, for about 6 hours then leave at room temperature for about 1 hour.

Chicken liver pâté (page 13) – as kipper pâté; freeze without butter topping.

Taramasalata (page 13) – freeze in a $\frac{3}{4}$–1 pt. dish. Thaw covered in the refrigerator for about 8 hours.

Potted smoked salmon (page 14) – as for kipper pâté; freeze without butter topping.

Tunafish creams (page 13) – make up but do not garnish. Freeze in the ramekin dishes, cover with foil, overwrap in a polythene bag. To serve, thaw in the refrigerator for about 8 hours before garnishing.

Crème vichyssoise (page 10) – freeze without addition of egg yolk, cream and chives. To use, unwrap and reheat gently in a saucepan without boiling, stir in the egg yolk blended with the cream, chill. Garnish with snipped chives.

Country soup (page 10) – freeze completed recipe. To use, reheat unwrapped frozen soup slowly in a covered saucepan, stirring occasionally.

Casseroled heart (page 31) – freeze without orange shreds and walnuts. Reheat from frozen at 375°F, 190°C (mark 5) for about 2 hours, add blanched orange shreds and walnuts 15 minutes before end of reheating time.

Ragout of oxtail (page 29) – skim off fat as stated in method but omit reheating stage. To use, unwrap, cover with foil or a lid and reheat from frozen in the oven at 400°F, 200°C (mark 6) for about 2 hours.

Pigeons in cream (page 31) – freeze before pan juices are reduced. To use, reheat from frozen in a covered saucepan, over a low heat. When really hot reduce juices as in recipe.

Filet de porc chasseur (page 20) – freeze without chopped parsley and croûtons. To use, unwrap and reheat in the oven, covered, at 375°F, 190°C (mark 5) for about 1½ hours. Garnish.

Aberdeen sausage (page 22) – freeze the completed roll, wrap in foil. To use, reheat from frozen in foil in the oven at 400°F, 200°C (mark 6) for about 1 hour.

Curried beef balls (page 24) – freeze completed dish. To use, unwrap and reheat from frozen, covered, in the oven at 350°F, 180°C (mark 4) for about 1½ hours.

Swiss steak (page 22) – freeze completed dish. To use, reheat covered in the oven from frozen at 400°F, 200°C (mark 6) for about 1 hour, then reduce to 350°F, 180°C (mark 4) and continue until steak is really hot.

Beef goulash (page 22) – omit the potatoes and green pepper for freezing and cook for just 1½ hours. To use, cook from frozen, covered, in the oven at 375°F, 190°C (mark 5) for about 1¼ hours. Add the diced potato and green pepper for the last ½ hour of reheating time.

Beef double-crust pie (page 22) – make on a rigid foil plate. Freeze unbaked. To use, cook from frozen as in recipe, adding a little extra cooking time.

Beef olives (page 25) – freeze with unthickened beef juices. To use, place in a covered dish in the oven and reheat from frozen at 400°F, 200°C (mark 6) for about 1 hour. Thicken juices.

Battalian beef bake (page 24) – prepare the bake up to the potato peeling stage in shallow dishes of not more than 2 pt. each. Pack and freeze. When required, leave to thaw in the refrigerator for 24 hours. Add the freshly prepared potatoes and the sauce. Place the beef bake, uncovered, in the oven at 425°F, 220°C (mark 7) with freshly grated Parmesan added.

Fried salami chicken (page 27) – drumsticks can be prepared and frozen only if they are from fresh chickens. Make up to and including the breadcrumb stage. Freeze unwrapped until firm on a flat tray, then wrap. To cook, thaw in the refrigerator for 8 hours then proceed as in the recipe.

Latticed tuna flan (page 18) – freeze completed recipe.

Lemon cheesecake pie (page 42) – freeze completed dish. To use, thaw at room temperature for about 6 hours.

Streusel pear flan (page 43) – freeze the completed dish. To use, thaw at room temperature for 2 hours. Reheat at 350°F, 180°C (mark 4), covered with foil, for about 30 minutes.

Lemon fluff (page 35) – freeze in suitable serving dishes. To use, thaw in the refrigerator for about 6 hours, or 3 hours at room temperature.

Bakewell tart (page 35) – freeze completed recipe. To use, thaw covered at room temperature for about 2 hours. Reheat in a moderate oven if preferred.

Oranges in caramel syrup (page 36) – freeze completed recipe; slice the oranges and pack into syrup. To use, leave to thaw in covered container overnight in the refrigerator.

Peach and apple soufflé (page 36) – make soufflé in the dish for serving, freeze undecorated with the collar of greaseproof paper in position. When frozen, over-wrap. Thaw overnight in the refrigerator before removing the collar and decorating.

Chocolate fudge cake (page 46) – open freeze until frosting is firm then pack carefully. To use, unwrap and thaw at room temperature for 4 hours.

Lemon loaf cake (page 46) – freeze completed cake. To use, thaw in wrap at room temperature for about 3 hours.

Easter biscuits (page 46) – freeze when baked. To use, unwrap, place on a baking sheet frozen and refresh in the oven at 400°F, 200°C (mark 6) for about 10 minutes. Cool on a rack.

Hot cross buns (page 47) – freeze when baked but not glazed. To use, unwrap and place on a baking sheet, cover loosely with foil and refresh from frozen at 400°F, 200°C (mark 6) for 20–25 minutes. Meanwhile, combine 2 tbsps. milk, 2 tbsps. water and 1½ oz. caster sugar; warm, do not boil until sugar has dissolved. Brush glaze over buns straight from the oven. Cool on a wire rack.

SUMMER

Smoked trout pâté (page 52) – freeze in ramekin dishes, omit aspic glaze. Thaw overnight in the refrigerator, add aspic on thawing.

Peter's pâté (page 56) – turn out pâté, wrap closely in foil, overwrap in polythene bag and freeze. Thaw in the refrigerator for about 6 hours.

Chilled watercress soup (page 54) – omit cream and garnish, freeze in 1 pt. quantities. Thaw for about 24 hours in refrigerator. Stir in cream and add garnish.

Cream of cucumber soup (page 54) – omit egg yolks, milk and garnish. Pack in half amounts for quicker reheating. To use, place blocks of soup in a saucepan and heat slowly to thaw. Cream yolks and milk, add and bring to serving temperature.

Gazpacho (page 54) – omit garlic and garnish. Thaw in the refrigerator for 48 hours. Add crushed garlic and garnish.

Cold cheese soufflé (page 57) – keep greaseproof paper collar in position. Open freeze, then wrap. Thaw at room temperature with 'collar' in place.

Bumper sausage roll (page 67) – freeze uncooked without egg glaze. Thaw for 8 hours in refrigerator, glaze and bake as recipe.

Kulebyaka (page 70) – do not slash pastry, omit egg glaze, open-freeze before cooking until firm, then wrap. To use, unwrap, place on a baking sheet and cook from frozen at 400°F, 200°C (mark 6) for 1½ hours. After ½ hour slash pastry, brush with egg. Garnish to serve.

Salmon and cheese flan (page 70) – freeze after baking, omit garnish. Thaw at room temperature for about 2 hours, refresh in oven at 350°F, 180°C (mark 4) for about ½ hour. Serve warm or cold, garnish.

Picnic pies (page 66) – freeze baked, pack carefully. Thaw in the refrigerator for about 8 hours. Refresh in a hot oven for 7–10 minutes if wished.

Pork chops in orange-pepper sauce (page 64) – freeze completed dish but omit green pepper and garnish. Cook for 40 minutes only. To use, remove wrap, return to a frying pan with 1–2 tbsps. stock or water, add green pepper and reheat covered for about 45 minutes. Garnish.

Summer lamb casserole (page 63) – freeze after 1½ hours cooking. To use, thaw from frozen in the oven or on top of cooker then proceed as in recipe.

Osso buco (page 66) – do not garnish. To freeze, use the pre-former casserole method or a rigid foil container. To thaw, return to casserole after removing foil (or reheat in foil container), place covered in the oven at 350°F, 180°C (mark 4) for about 2 hours until bubbling. Garnish.

Chicken and banana curry (page 59) – pack in a large rigid foil container. To thaw, cook from frozen in the oven, covered, at 375°F, 190°C (mark 5) for 2 hours until bubbling.

Bobotie (page 60) – cook and when cold wrap pie dish in polythene bag. To use, unwrap and reheat from frozen in the oven at 350°F, 180°C (mark 4) for about 1 hour.

Iced zabaione (page 77) – freeze in dishes, overwrapped. To use, remove wrappings and serve.

Frosted gooseberry plate pie (page 84) – make on a foil plate, when cold over-wrap. To use, leave at room temperature for about 4 hours; reheat in oven if required hot.

Raspberry cream ring (page 82) – freeze only the sponge base, wrap in polythene bag. To thaw, leave in wrap at room temperature for about 3 hours.

Raspberry mousse (page 80) – freeze undecorated in suitable dish. Unwrap and thaw at room temperature for about 5 hours.

Strawberry split cake (page 87) – omit dredged sugar. Pack in polythene bag. To thaw, leave in open bag for about 4 hours. Finish with icing sugar.

Fruit and almond slice (page 88) – pack before slicing. To thaw, leave in wrap for about 2 hours.

Date and raisin teabread (page 88) – wrap in polythene film. To thaw, remove film and thaw at room temperature for about 2 hours.

Coffee whirls (page 88) – pack these fragile cookies in a rigid container. To thaw, leave unwrapped on a wire rack for ½ hour.

Buttermilk cherry loaf cake (page 89) – wrap in polythene film. To thaw, leave in wrap at room temperature for about 4 hours.

Peach and lime mousse (page 78) – freeze in a serving container such as a soufflé dish without decoration. To use, thaw at room temperature for about 5 hours.

AUTUMN

Three-fish pâté (page 93) – open freeze, then pack in polythene bags. To use, thaw in the refrigerator for 6–8 hours then leave at room temperature for 1 hour.

Bacon and liver pâté (page 93) – cook filling, cool and place in pastry but do not bake. Pack. To use, leave the lightly wrapped pâté in refrigerator for at least 5 hours. Brush pastry with water, bake in the oven at 400°F, 200°C (mark 6) for about 30 minutes; glaze with egg after 15 minutes.

Potage St Germain (page 93) – freeze in suitable amounts. Thaw at room temperature for about 2 hours, turn into a saucepan and reheat to serving temperature, add extra stock if needed.

Pumpkin and leek soup (page 93) – omit garnish, freeze in half quantities for quicker thawing. To use, reheat from frozen with a spoonful or two of stock or water in the pan over a low heat; when thawed bring to serving temperature.

Tuna-stuffed pancakes (page 98) – make and fill pancakes, omit margarine glaze. Place in a rigid container, wrap, seal and freeze. To use, unwrap, reheat covered from frozen for about 30 minutes. Remove cover, brush with melted margarine and continue heating at 325°F, 170°C (mark 3) for 20–30 minutes.

Sardine quiche (page 95) – pack when cold in polythene bag. To use, thaw at room temperature for 2 hours, reheat at 350°F, 180°C (mark 4) covered with foil, for 20–25 minutes.

Liver and bacon pudding (page 100) – make in a foil-lined pudding basin, do not bake. Open-freeze, remove from basin and over-wrap. Return to freezer. To use, remove wrap and foil, return to basin and thaw in refrigerator for 12 hours then cook as in recipe. Storage time 6 weeks.

Rich casserole of hearts (page 101) – prepare and freeze in pre-formed casserole, pack uncooked stuffing balls separately. To use, unwrap casserole, return to dish and reheat, covered, from frozen at 375°F, 190°C (mark 5) for about 2 hours. Thirty minutes before end of cooking time add frozen stuffing balls.

Paupiettes of pork (page 104) – pack in rigid container. To use, unwrap and reheat from frozen, covered, at 375°F, 190°C (mark 5) for 1½–1¾ hours. Garnish with chopped parsley.

Pork with peas (page 103) – prepare as far as the stage at which peas would be added. Cool quickly and freeze. To use, thaw by heating very slowly in a covered saucepan, continue as for recipe.

Sweet-sour pork balls (page 103) – pack fried pork balls and sauce separately. To use, thaw sauce in a pan over a low heat, add pork balls and simmer, covered, for 20 minutes, stir occasionally.

Barbecued spare ribs (page 102) – cool and skim off fat. Pack in a suitable container. To use, turn into a shallow pan, cover and thaw in the oven at 300°F, 150°C (mark 2) for 20 minutes. Uncover, separate ribs and cook a further 30 minutes; baste occasionally.

Steak and wine pie (page 106) – place cooked filling in pie dish with funnel, cover when cold with pastry lid, do not glaze or make slits. Pack in polythene bag to freeze. To use, brush with egg to which a pinch of salt is added. Bake in oven at 425°F, 220°C (mark 7) for about 55 minutes or until golden and bubbling. After first 15 minutes make slit in pastry.

Chilli beef beanpot (page 105) – pack without beans. Reheat from frozen at 350°F, 180°C (mark 4) in a covered casserole for about 2 hours. Add beans during last 15 minutes.

Beef and chestnut casserole (page 104) – freeze without chestnuts in pre-formed casserole. To use, unwrap and return to casserole, reheat from frozen, covered, in the oven at 350°F, 180°C (mark 4) for about 1½ hours. As the beef thaws, fork gently. Add chestnut garnish before serving.

Boeuf bourguignonne (page 104) – freeze in preformer. To use, thaw for about 12 hours in the refrigerator and then reheat in a heavy saucepan for about ½ hour. Or reheat from frozen in covered dish in the oven at 325°F, 170°C (mark 3) for 2 hours.

Moussaka (page 107) – make up to baking stage; omit egg topping. Freeze pre-formed in a casserole type dish. To use, return to casserole, cover and thaw at 375°F, 190°C (mark 5) for about 30 minutes. Pour topping over and continue as recipe.

Haricot lamb (page 106)- freeze completed dish. To use, reheat in a covered casserole from frozen at 375°F, 190°C (mark 5) for about 1½ hours.

Chicken cacciatore (page 108) – pack in a shallow container, omit garnish. To use, thaw in a heavy-based pan, covered, over a low heat for about 30 minutes; stir occasionally until really hot through.

Apple and blackberry compote (page 114) – prepare and pack in shallow containers. To use, thaw overnight in the refrigerator.

Caramel bavarois (page 116) – prepare and freeze in mould, pack sauce separately. To use, thaw at room temperature for about 5 hours before unmoulding.

Chocolate soufflé de luxe (page 116) – complete soufflé, leave collar in place, omit decoration. Open freeze; overwrap. To use, remove wrap, leave collar in position. Thaw in refrigerator for about 12 hours. Remove collar and decorate.

Spiced apple tart (page 111) – complete pie, do not bake or make a slit in pastry. Open-freeze, then wrap. To use, thaw overnight in the refrigerator then bake uncovered at 400°F, 200°C (mark 6) for 40–45 minutes. Decorate.

Almond loaf cake (page 119) – complete cake. To use, thaw at room temperature in wrap for 2–3 hours. Unwrap to serve.

Dark chocolate cake (page 119) – complete cake, omit dusting of icing sugar. To use, thaw wrapped at room temperature for 4 hours. Unwrap and dredge with sugar.

Honey butter sandwich (page 119) – see Dark chocolate cake.

Parkin (page 119) – complete recipe, leave for a week in a tin to mature before freezing. To thaw, leave wrapped for 3 hours.

Walnut cookies (page 120) – complete recipe. To use, thaw wrapped at room temperature for about 1 hour.

Ginger snaps (page 121) – complete recipe. To use, leave in wrap at room temperature for about $\frac{1}{2}$ hour.

WINTER

Farmhouse pâté (page 126) – freeze completed dish. To use, thaw in the refrigerator for about 12 hours.

Sild pâté (page 127) – freeze completed dish, omit butter topping. To use, thaw in the refrigerator for about 8 hours. Glaze with melted butter. Leave to set.

Vegetable broth (page 128) – freeze completed dish unthickened with milk and cornflour. To use, reheat gently in a saucepan from frozen; when thawed thicken with milk blended with cornflour, bring to boil.

Cream of artichoke soup (page 128) – prepare to purée stage, freeze. To use, place frozen in a saucepan with 2 tbsps. milk, heat slowly, stir in lemon juice, parsley and cream, bring to serving temperature.

Celery and carrot soup (page 127) – freeze completed soup in 2 packs, omit garnish. To use, heat slowly in a large saucepan with a spoonful or two of stock.

Chicken puffs (page 130) – freeze completed dish. To use, place frozen puffs on a baking sheet and reheat at 400°F, 200°C (mark 6) for about 30 minutes.

Chicken curry (page 130) – freeze completed dish. To use, reheat covered from frozen at 375°F, 190°C (mark 5) for about 2 hours.

Beef pies (page 137) – freeze completed dishes. To use, unwrap and reheat from frozen at 375°F, 190°C (mark 5) for 40–60 minutes, cover pastry if necessary to stop overbrowning.

Beef and carrot pudding (page 134) – freeze in basin uncooked. To use, cook from frozen in a saucepan with gently boiling water half-way up the basin for about 3 hours.

Chilli con carne (page 135) – cook meat for stated time but do not add beans or garnish. To use, place frozen meat in a saucepan with a spoonful or two of stock, heat slowly to thaw, add beans and heat to serving temperature. Garnish.

Les carbonades flamandes (page 135) – freeze completed dish without bread topping. To use, reheat covered in the oven at 375°F, 190°C (mark 5) for about 2 hours. Finish as in recipe.

West African beef curry (page 135) – freeze completed dish, pack in half amounts. To use, place frozen curry in 1 large or 2 smaller pans with a little stock and heat slowly; bring to serving temperature.

Buffet patties (page 137) – freeze baked patties. To use, reheat from frozen in the oven at 375°F, 190°C (mark 5) for about 30 minutes, cover loosely with foil.

Lamb and mushroom pudding (page 133) – freeze prepared pudding in basin, uncooked. To use, thaw in refrigerator for 24 hours, follow cooking directions.

Lamb Italian style (page 132) – freeze completed dish, omit garnish. To use, reheat from frozen in a covered dish at 375°F, 190°C (mark 5) for about 2 hours. Garnish.

Casserole of rabbit with juniper berries (page 143) – freeze completed dish, omit bacon rolls and garnish. To use, reheat from frozen at 350°F, 180°C (mark 4) for about 2 hours. After 1½ hours add bacon rolls.

Casserole of venison (page 142) – freeze completed dish. To use, reheat from frozen, covered, at 375°F, 190°C (mark 5) for about 1½ hours.

Queue de boeuf aux olives noires (page 138) – freeze completed dish. To use, reheat in a covered casserole from frozen at 400°F, 200°C (mark 6) for about 1½ hours.

Cranberry and bacon balls (page 149) – freeze dry mix without egg for 4 weeks or shape and cook balls then freeze. To use, prepare dry mix as for recipe, reheat balls from frozen at 400°F, 200°C (mark 6) for 20–30 minutes.

Ratatouille (page 151) – freeze completed dish. To use, reheat covered in the oven at 350°F, 180°C (mark 4) for about 1 hour.

Red sails (page 147) – freeze the scone bases only. To use, refresh from frozen on a baking sheet at 350°F, 180°C (mark 4) for about 15 minutes. Cool to use.

Lollipop cookies (page 167) – freeze completed recipe. To use, place on a wire rack for about 30 minutes.

Alaska express (page 162) – complete except for wheels and cotton-wool smoke. Protect in a rigid container to freeze. To use, remove from freezer 1 hour before slicing, decorate as suggested.

Roundabout cake (page 167) – freeze iced but undecorated cake. To use, unwrap, thaw at room temperature for about 6 hours then decorate.

Petits fours (page 166) – freeze completed recipe. To use, place on a wire rack, leave at room temperature for $\frac{1}{2}$ hour.

Date rockies (page 166) – freeze baked buns. To use, thaw covered for about 1 hour at room temperature.

Orange chip cookies (page 167) – freeze baked cookies. To use, leave on a wire rack for $\frac{1}{2}$ hour at room temperature.

Shortbread rounds (page 166) – freeze baked. To use, thaw on a wire rack at room temperature for about 1 hour.

Viennese whirls (page 165) – freeze baked, pack carefully. To use, thaw on a wire rack at room temperature for about $\frac{1}{2}$ hour.

Date fingers (page 165) – freeze baked, uncut, without icing sugar. To use, thaw, wrapped at room temperature for about 1 hour.

Grandmother's boiled fruit cake (page 164) – freeze baked. To use, thaw wrapped at room temperature for about 3 hours.

Petticoat tails (page 164) – freeze baked. To use, thaw on a wire rack at room temperature for about 1 hour.

Chocolate cup cake (page 165) – open freeze completed cake. To use, unwrap and thaw at room temperature for about 5 hours.

Plum cake with brandied orange butter (page 164) – freeze completed cake with orange butter in a rigid container. To use, leave cake wrapped to mature for a day at room temperature, leave butter in refrigerator for the same time.

Mincemeat cinnamon meltaways (page 164) – freeze baked, pack carefully. To use, thaw unwrapped at room temperature for 1–2 hours.

Plum crumb bake (page 156) – freeze completed dish. To use, reheat from frozen lightly covered with foil at 400°F, 200°C (mark 6) for about 20 minutes.

Almond figgy pudding (page 156) – freeze uncooked in basin. To use, cook from frozen in a saucepan with gently boiling water half-way up basin for about 2 hours.

Baked fruit salad (page 156) – freeze without bananas and raisins. To use, remove wrap and place frozen salad in a buttered ovenproof dish, cook covered from frozen at 375°F, 190°C (mark 5) for 30 minutes. Add bananas and raisins and bake for a further 30–40 minutes.

Orange apple crumble (page 158) – freeze completed dish made in an ovenproof container but omit final cooking stage. To use, remove wrapping and bake from frozen at 400°F, 200°C (mark 6) for about $\frac{3}{4}$ hour.

Lemon soufflé (page 158) – freeze completed dish without decoration. Leave collar in position. Freeze until firm then wrap. To use, thaw in the refrigerator overnight or at room temperature for 4 hours.

Choc au rhum (page 162) – freeze completed dish without decoration in freezer-proof serving dishes. To use, unwrap and thaw in the refrigerator for about 3 hours.

General guide to storage time in a freezer

MEAT, RAW	months
Beef	8
Lamb	6
Veal	6
Pork	6
Freshly minced	3
Offal	3
Cured and smoked meat	1–2
Sausages	3

MEAT, COOKED	
Casseroles, stews, etc.	2
Roast	1
Pâtés, loaves	1

POULTRY AND GAME	
Chicken	12
Duck	4–6
Goose	4–6
Turkey	6
Giblets	3
Game birds	6–8
Venison	12

FISH, RAW	
Salmon	4
Shellfish	3
White fish	6

FISH, COOKED	months
Pies, cakes, croquettes, kedgeree, mousse	2

SAUCES, SOUPS, STOCKS	2–3

PIZZA	
unbaked	3
baked	2

PASTRY	
Unbaked	3–4
Baked	
cases	6
meat pies	2–3
fruit pies	6

PANCAKES	
Unfilled	2
Filled	1

SPONGE PUDDINGS	
Uncooked	2
Cooked	3

MOUSSES, CREAMS	2–3

ICE CREAM	3
(commercial)	3

CREAM	4

CAKES, BAKED	
Plain, incl. scones and teabreads	6
Gateau type	2

CROISSANTS AND DANISH PASTRIES, BAKED	1

	months
BISCUITS	6

BREAD	1
(crusty)	1 week

SANDWICHES	1–2

BUTTER	
salted	3
unsalted	6

CHAPTER SEVEN

BASIC COOKERY METHODS

Chicken stock

1 chicken carcass
giblets
$\frac{1}{2}$ level tbsp. salt
cold water to cover
1 onion, skinned and sliced
1 carrot, peeled and sliced
outside sticks of celery, scrubbed and sliced
a bouquet garni

Place all the ingredients in a large pan, bring to the boil, skim, cover and simmer for 3–4 hours. Strain and when cold remove all trace of fat. Store in a cool place, preferably in a refrigerator; boil up daily.

Fried croûtons

Cut bread into $\frac{1}{4}$–$\frac{1}{2}$-in. cubes. Fry quickly in lard or oil until crisp and golden. Drain on absorbent kitchen paper.

Mayonnaise

2 egg yolks
1 level tsp. Dijon mustard
$\frac{1}{4}$ level tsp. salt
$\frac{1}{2}$ level tsp. sugar
shake of white pepper
$\frac{1}{2}$ pt. salad oil
1 tbsp. each white wine and tarragon vinegar
1 tsp. lemon juice

When making mayonnaise use fresh eggs at room temperature, stale ones will not form a stable emulsion. Although egg yolks are the usual choice, whole eggs give a lighter consistency and are well suited to blender mayonnaise. A little salt is necessary for flavour but too much may break down the emulsion. A wooden spoon and an average size deep basin are the basic implements but a ballon or rotary whisk are equally satisfactory. The rotary whisk gives a lighter coloured mayonnaise with a firmer texture.

By hand. Start by beating or whisking the egg yolks with the seasonings in the basin – have a damp cloth under the basin to hold it still – do this really thoroughly as it helps to make the job of adding the oil easier later.

The oil before starting should be at warm room temperature. Put the oil in a jug with a distinctive lip, add very slowly at the beginning, beating or whisking continuously at first until the sauce forms an emulsion and thickens. The rate of addition depends very much on a consistent beating action. Once the sauce is well amalgamated, the oil addition can be speeded up to a thin stream. Incorporate vinegar/lemon juice two-thirds the way through in teaspoonfuls.

By machine. A hand held electric mixer or an electric blender cuts the time to about 5 minutes. Machine made mayonnaise is thicker, with a less creamy texture. With some goblets it is best to bulk up the mixture by adding 1 tbsp. warm water or start with 2 whole eggs and no water.

Add oil slowly at first with the blender switched on, then as the emulsion amalgamates, increase the rate at which oil is added, switching off between additions to scrape down the sides of the goblet.

Gravy

A rich brown gravy is served with all roast joints – thin with roast beef and thick with other meats. If the gravy is properly made in the baking tin, there should be no need to use extra colouring. Remove the joint from the tin and keep it hot while making the gravy.

Thin gravy

Pour the fat very slowly from the tin, draining it off carefully from one corner and leaving the sediment behind. Season well with salt and pepper and add ½ pt. hot vegetable water or stock (which can be made from a bouillon cube – if this is used season *after* the addition). Stir thoroughly with a wooden spoon until all the sediment is scraped from the tin and the gravy is a rich brown. Return the tin to the heat and boil for 2–3 minutes. Serve very hot.

This is the 'correct' way of making thin gravy but some people prefer to make a version of the thick gravy below, using half the amount of flour.

Thick gravy

Leave 2 tbsps. of the fat in the tin; add 1 level tbsp. flour (preferably shaking it from a flour dredger which gives a smoother result), blend well and cook over the heat until it turns brown, stirring continuously. Carefully mix in ½ pt. hot vegetable water or stock and boil for 2–3 minutes. Season well, strain and serve very hot.

NOTES
1. If the gravy is greasy (due to not draining off enough fat) or thin (due to adding too much liquid) it can be corrected by adding more flour, although this weakens the flavour.

2. When gravy is very pale a little gravy browning may be added.

3. Meat extracts are sometimes added to give extra taste, however, they do tend to overpower the characteristic meat flavour. A sliced carrot and onion cooked with the meat in the gravy will give extra 'body' to the taste without impairing it. A tbsp. of cider or wine added at the last moment does wonders.

To flambé (or flame)

Warm the brandy, whisky, liqueur, etc. and pour it over the food just before serving. Ignite with a match and serve as soon as the flames have died down.

If food is being cooked over a gas ring or spirit stove the dish can be pulled off the flame and tilted slightly so that it ignites the spirit instead of igniting with a match.

Rich shortcrust pastry

8 oz. plain flour
pinch salt
5 oz. butter or margarine, or mixture of both
1–2 egg yolks
4–6 tsps. water
2 level tsps. caster sugar

Sift together the flour and salt and rub the fat into the flour, as for shortcrust pastry, until the mixture resembles fine breadcrumbs. Mix in the sugar. Mix the egg yolk(s) with water and add to the mixture, stirring until it begins to stick together. Lightly draw together into one piece with the fingertips. Leave to rest for 15 minutes. Use as required. The usual oven temperature is 400°F, 200°C (mark 6).

Pâte sucrée

6 oz. plain flour
pinch salt
1½ oz. caster sugar
3 oz. butter at room temperature
2 tbsps. beaten egg

Sift the flour and salt on to a pastry board, or better still a marble slab. Make a well in the centre and into it put the sugar, butter and egg. Using the fingertips of one hand pinch and work the sugar, butter and egg together until blended. Gradually work in all the flour and knead lightly until smooth. Put the paste in a cool place for at least 1 hour then return it to room temperature until easy to roll out.

Sugar boiling stages

To measure the temperature really accurately you need a sugar boiling thermometer, but for simple sweets you can use the homely tests described below:

Smooth (215°F–222°F, 110°C) For crystallising purposes. The mixture begins to look syrupy. To test, dip the fingers in water, and then very quickly in the syrup. The thumb will slide smoothly over the fingers, but the sugar clings to the finger.

Soft ball (235°F–245°F, 125°C) For fondants and fudges. When a drop of the syrup is put into very cold water it forms a soft ball. At 235°F the soft ball flattens on being removed from the water, but the higher the temperature the firmer the ball, till it reaches the next Firm Ball stage.

Firm or hard ball (245°F–265°F, 130°C) For caramels, marshmallows and nougat. When dropped into cold water the syrup forms a ball which is hard enough to hold its shape, but is still plastic.

Soft crack (270°F–290°F, 140°C–145°C) For toffees. When dropped into cold water the syrup separates into threads which are hard but not brittle.

Hard crack (300°F–310°F, 150°C) For hard toffees and rock. When a drop of the syrup is put into cold water it separated into threads which are hard and brittle.

Caramel (310°F, 160°C) For praline. Shown by the syrup becoming golden brown.

Cooking in a water bath

This has two uses:
1. A flat open vessel is half-filled with water and kept at a temperature just below boiling point. Sauces, soups, etc. are stood in pans in the water bath to keep them hot without further cooking.
2. Baked custards, pâtés, etc. are stood in their dishes in a baking tin half-filled with water during cooking. This prevents overheating and a hard crust forming around the outside.

Shortcrust pastry

4 oz. plain flour
pinch of salt
1 oz. lard or blended white vegetable fat
1 oz. block margarine or butter
cold water

Keep hands, utensils, working surface and ingredients cool. A special pastry blender with wooden handle and wire loops is good for those with warm hands. Self-raising flour can be used, but gives pastry a more 'cakey' texture. For a richer pastry increase fats to 1½ oz. each. Soft tub margarines are best used only in specially evolved, all-in-one pastry making methods. Put flour and salt into a bowl, add firm, not hard, fat cut into small pieces; with finger tips rub in until it is of a fine breadcrumb texture. Shake the bowl from time to time so that any larger crumbs can be seen. The hands should be lifted well up over the bowl so that air is incorporated in the mixture. Now add the water – allow about 1 tsp. water for each ounce of flour – too much liquid gives a difficult-to-handle sticky dough which results in tough pastry. Sprinkle the liquid over the surface all at once. Gradual addition gives an uneven texture and this tends to cause blisters when the pastry is cooked. Once the water is added, use a round-bladed knife to distribute water as evenly as possible and draw crumbs together. When large lumps are formed, finish knitting dough together with fingertips into a ball.

Bouquet garni

A bunch of fresh or dried herbs including parsley, thyme, marjoram, bay, etc. tied in a faggot with string. A sliver of orange or lemon rind is sometimes included. A ready made mixture of powdered dried herbs in a muslin bag makes an alternative. For easy extraction from a pan leave a long free end of cotton or fine string after tying the bouquet garni to attach to the pan handle.

Rubbing in

Blending flour and fat to a crumb-like consistency, using the tips of the fingers. Do not handle more than is necessary or the fat will become oily.

Creaming

Cut up the fat and place in a bowl large enough to allow the fat and sugar to be beaten well without flying out. With the back of a wooden spoon beat the fat against the sides of the bowl until soft, add the sugar and beat or cream the mixture until fluffy and pale. After 7–10 minutes the volume should be increased and the mixture drops from the spoon. With an electric mixer cut the time by about half and use a deep rather than an open bowl.

Folding in

The method used to incorporate sifted flour into cake mixtures, whisked egg whites or cream into soufflé mixtures, etc. The aim is to cut the mixture rather than beat so as to retain all the air already incorporated. Use a metal spoon or plastic spatula in a figure of eight movement.

Baking blind

Cooking a pastry shell without the filling. Line the pastry-lined dish or flan ring/tin with foil or greased greaseproof paper. Cut it to fit and come up the sides and weight down with dried beans (the stored beans can be used again and again). Bake the case in the oven at 400°F, 200°C (mark 6) for 15 minutes. Remove the beans, paper or foil and bake for a further 5–10 minutes or until the pastry is dry and a little coloured. For individual tartlet cases or when using a rich pastry like pâte sucrée, pricking the base well with a fork is usually enough but as an extra precaution line with foil.

Apricot glaze

½ lb. apricot jam
2 tbsps. water

Place the jam and water in a saucepan over low heat and stir until the jam softens. Sieve. Return the jam to the pan and bring to the boil, boiling gently until the glaze is of a coating consistency.

Vanilla sugar

This gives a better result in some cakes and sweet dishes than is obtained by adding synthetic vanilla essence. To prepare the sugar, place a vanilla pod in a jar with caster sugar and keep covered. Use as required.

French dressing

A good dressing is essential to a good salad. It may be a classic French dressing or one of many variants on this theme; or mayonnaise or cream dressing. There is ample scope for the cook in blending dressings, just as there is in concocting salads. A French dressing consists of oil, vinegar and seasonings whisked or shaken together. Olive oil is often the gourmet's choice for French dressing, but its distinctive flavour and rather rich consistency is not to everyone's taste. Vegetable oils pressed from corn, cotton seed or soya beans are less expensive, lighter and, blended with other ingredients, make delicious dressings. Wine vinegar – red or white – is usually top choice for French dressings. But do try, too, flavour variations with tarragon, cider, thyme and mint vinegars. Distilled vinegar is rather sharp and flavourless; malt vinegar tends to over-ride other flavours in delicate dressings. The proportion of oil to vinegar is variable. One part of vinegar to two of oil is generally acceptable; some people prefer one of vinegar to three of oil; for a sharp dressing try equal quantities, but let personal preference guide you. Increase the amount of sugar for a milder dressing.

Our favourite recipe has a tang of garlic to add to the interest.

1 clove garlic, skinned and crushed
freshly ground black pepper
pinch of salt
½ level tsp. caster sugar
½ level tsp. continental mustard
1 tbsp. tarragon vinegar
2 tbsps. salad oil

In a small basin or lidded jar, blend together the garlic, a good turn of the pepper from the mill, salt, sugar, mustard and vinegar. Add the oil and whisk or shake until thoroughly blended.

Note: The garlic in this recipe is optional, and may be replaced by very finely chopped onion or chives.

To make ½ pt. of dressing use 5 tbsps. vinegar, 10 tbsps. oil and other ingredients in proportion.

VARIATIONS
Cheese dressing: Add a little crumbled blue cheese.

Russe dressing: Add 2 tsps. thin cream, replace the vinegar by lemon juice and blend well.

Herb dressing: When in season use fresh chopped mint, parsley, chervil, rosemary, etc., with wine vinegar. In winter dried herbs are useful. Leave them to marinade in the vinegar for an hour or so before required, then blend in the oil just before use.

Pepper dressing: Add a mere touch of chilli or cayenne pepper. Alternatively, add a few drops of chilli sauce.

Crunchy seed dressing: Sprinkle in a few celery, poppy or caraway seeds.

The roast

Turkey If you're buying a fresh bird order early and remember that these are sold plucked weight – without feathers but undrawn. A 13–14 lb. bird is therefore equivalent to about a 10-lb. oven-ready; the price is based on weight before drawing.

Provided adequate time is allowed for thawing, frozen birds are fine. Allow 2–3 days in a cool larder; leave in polythene bag. If you have to cope with a frozen turkey in a real emergency, immerse it in warm water.

Don't order a monster bird unless your cooker has a big oven. Allow about ¾ lb. oven-ready weight per person; it cuts more economically when cold. As a rough practical guide, a good fleshy 10–12 lb. oven-ready bird would give 6–8 hot helpings with accompaniments, 8 cold cut helpings with some over for make-up dishes and the carcass for broth. A hen bird up to 18 lb. undressed weight is a good choice; a cock is best if over 20 lb.

Cooking times
On the day, wipe the bird, remove neck and giblets (in a frozen bird they're tucked into the cavity). Note oven-ready weight. Stuff bird, not too tightly, then truss. Brush skin well with softened butter, margarine or white fat and, if you like, cover breast with overlapping slices of fat bacon.

If you're roasting in foil, either wrap the bird loosely with the join on top and put into a roasting tin, or first put the bird in the tin, then make a foil tent, folding edges around tin. For clear roasting bags, do as makers say.

Approximate cooking times for quick oven method with foil – 450°F, 230°C (mark 8):

6–8 lb.	$2\frac{1}{4}$–$2\frac{1}{2}$ hours
8 10 lb.	$2\frac{1}{2}$–$2\frac{3}{4}$ hours
10–12 lb.	$2\frac{3}{4}$–2 hours 50 minutes
12–14 lb.	2 hours 50 minutes–3 hours
14–16 lb.	3–$3\frac{1}{4}$ hours
16–18 lb.	$3\frac{1}{4}$–$3\frac{1}{2}$ hours

Approximate cooking times for slow oven method – 325°F, 170°C (mark 3):

6 8 lb.	3–$3\frac{1}{2}$ hours
8 10 lb.	$3\frac{1}{2}$–$3\frac{3}{4}$ hours
10–12 lb.	$3\frac{3}{4}$–4 hours
12–14 lb.	4–$4\frac{1}{4}$ hours
14–16 lb.	$4\frac{1}{4}$–$4\frac{1}{2}$ hours
16–18 lb.	$4\frac{1}{4}$–4 hours 50 minutes

Foil is not necessary with the slow method, though if the bird almost fills the oven it may be wise to protect legs and breast. You *can* wrap the whole bird in foil, but if you do you should remove it a good 30 minutes before the end of cooking time, baste well and raise oven temperature to 425°F, 220°C (mark 7) to brown and crisp the skin. To test for done-ness, pierce the deepest part of the thigh with a skewer. When the juices are almost colourless, the bird is ready; if pink, cook a little longer.

Chicken/Capon A 5–7 lb. oven-ready capon will serve 6–8; a 4 lb. oven-ready chicken serves 4–5. Prepare as for turkey. Cook without foil at 375°F, 190°C (mark 5) for 20 minutes per lb. plus 20 minutes over. Vary times slightly depending on ratio of bone and tightness of trussing.

Beef Cook top-quality joints at 425°F, 220°C (mark 7) for 15–20 minutes per lb. plus 15–20 minutes over, depending on rareness. For less good quality joints cook at 375°F, 190°C (mark 5) for 25 minutes per lb. (boned and rolled 30 minutes). Cheap roasting cuts are best cooked at 325°F–350°F, 170°C–180°C (mark 3–4) for 40 minutes per lb.

Lamb Cook joints with bone at 350°F, 180°C (mark 4) for 27 minutes per lb plus 27 minutes over.

Pork Cook at 375°F, 190°C (mark 5) for 30 minutes per lb. plus 30 minutes over.

Veal Cook at 425°F, 220°C (mark 7) for 25 minutes per lb. plus 25 minutes over. Baste or cover with bacon.

To prepare a soufflé dish

For a cold soufflé, place the dish on a baking sheet and wrap around the outside of the dish a doubled sheet of greaseproof paper the depth of the dish plus about another 2 inches above the rim, and long enough to overlap a bit. Fix it with Sellotape, making sure the collar is upright and circular at the top edge, its folded edge around the base of the dish resting on the baking sheet. When the soufflé mixture is set, insert a palette knife between the two leaves of paper and lightly press against the soufflé; with the other hand, gradually ease paper away from 'risen' edge.

INDEX